RETHINKING PUBLIC ACCOUNTING

RETHINKING PUBLIC ACCOUNTING

Policy and Practice of Accrual Accounting in Government

S.K. DAS

OXFORD
UNIVERSITY PRESS

OXFORD
UNIVERSITY PRESS

YMCA Library Building, Jai Singh Road, New Delhi 110 001

Oxford University Press is a department of the University of Oxford. It furthers the
University's objective of excellence in research, scholarship, and education
by publishing worldwide in

Oxford   New York

Auckland   Cape Town   Dar es Salaam   Hong Kong   Karachi   Kuala Lumpur
Madrid   Melbourne   Mexico City   Nairobi   New Delhi   Shanghai   Taipei   Toronto

With offices in

Argentina   Austria   Brazil   Chile   Czech Republic   France   Greece   Guatemala
Hungary   Italy   Japan   Poland   Portugal   Singapore   South Korea   Switzerland
Thailand   Turkey   Ukraine   Vietnam

Oxford is a registered trademark of Oxford University Press
in the UK and in certain other countries

Published in India
by Oxford University Press, New Delhi

ISBN-13: 978-019-569833-6
ISBN-10: 019-569833-9

Typeset in Agaramond 10/12
by Sai Graphic Design, New Delhi 110 055
Printed in India by Sai Printopack Pvt Ltd, New Delhi 110 020
Published by Oxford University Press
YMCA Library Building, Jai Singh Road, New Delhi 110 001

Contents

Tables

Acknowledgements

I am indebted to Sudha Krishnan for taking the trouble of going through the draft and suggesting very creative changes. If there is any clarity about what I have to say, I owe it to Sudha.

It gives me great pleasure to acknowledge the support of Oxford University Press. They have been nice to me in countless ways, and this despite the fact that it must be particularly trying to put up with a civil servant, and that too writing a book on accounting.

My most profound thanks is to my wonderful family—my wife Malati and my sons Rohit and Siddharth. Malati was the epitome of patience and my sons were very supportive while I was writing the book.

Introduction

In countries across the world fairly fundamental changes are taking place in government financial systems. The changes are in response to the demand that governments should be fully accountable to the community for the resources entrusted to their care. There is also the realization that governments should not live on credit; this has led to the demand that governments need to fulfil their responsibilities without leaving a huge burden on the future generations. Faced with such demands, governments are looking for accounting systems that can provide information on how to improve their use of public resources.

That is why government accounting assumes an important role in providing information on how public resources need to be managed. In the last two decades, a number of countries have implemented reforms seeking to improve their accounting processes so that they can have information on how their total economic resources—both cash and non-cash—are allocated and managed. They have also required their accounting systems to generate information on how to enhance decision-making, reflect accountability, and ensure control over the long-term consequences of government policies. These requirements have called for the use of accrual accounting in the core, budget-dependent departments of the government.

This book brings together the experiences of four countries—New Zealand, Australia, the United Kingdom, and Sweden—in introducing accrual accounting in their government departments and suggests possible directions in which India can implement the system. For example, the government in New Zealand now operates on an accrual basis using essentially the same accounting policies, rules, and procedures as used in the private sector. Government accounts in New Zealand are more actuarially sound now: future expenses and income, which create liabilities or assets and are caused by decisions in the current period, are estimated and recorded in the accounts. The government now generates aggregate financial information including an estimate of the overall net worth of the government as a whole, which makes it possible to assess how the entire government is managed.

Australia's budget for 1999–2000 completed the transition from cash to accruals. In the new accrual output budgeting (AOB), which has been adopted right across Australia, accrual accounting is combined with output costing to measure the full cost of governmental activities. Information generated by AOB has been a powerful tool in driving efficiency improvement. With the adoption of accrual accounting, government departments in Australia are now seen as business entities with their own operating statements.

In the United Kingdom, resource accounting and budgeting (RAB) became operational in April 2001. Accrual accounting now provides the management information based on which government departments cost the resources they consume and match them with the outputs they deliver. Adoption of accrual accounting has made it possible for the government to make more informed decisions on the balance between current and capital expenditure, by taking into account the opportunity cost of capital and its consumption over time. Accrual accounting now provides the government, Parliament, and members of the public with better information on whether objectives of the government are being fully achieved by the use of public resources.

Since July 1993, the Government of Sweden has been using accruals as the basis of its accounting. The government departments now provide information on cost per unit, quality, and measurable effects in respect of all their activities. The information is collected by management accounting of the departments: where internal economic events show the distribution of cost and revenue between various activities, and the development of costs per branch of operations is accounted for and commented upon. The government now prepares its annual accounts on an accrual basis, which consist of: an operational statement, a balance sheet, and a statement of the application of funds.

The adoption of accrual accounting in each of these countries was not an isolated event. It was a part of comprehensive public-management reforms, which corresponds to the reform agenda called 'new public management'.[1] The point to be noted is that, while adoption of accrual accounting does not necessarily lead to the implementation of ideas associated with new public management, the fact remains that a wider reform agenda would have been difficult to realize without the adoption of accrual accounting.

What are these ideas associated with the new public management? They are overlapping but a distinctive set of ideas, derived from Public Choice Theory, and the frontier areas of economics such as New Institutional Economics.[2] The main idea comes from the public choice theory, which uses the perspective of self-interest to document and explain: how those in the government pursue their self-interest rather than the common good, why government spending and employment are overextended, and how government policies and programmes create opportunities for corruption. As Anne Krueger says, 'competition for entry into government service is, in part, a competition for rents.'[3]

The ideas of new institutional economics, which have also shaped new public management, trace their intellectual roots to a 1937 article 'The Nature of the Firm', by Ronald Coase, which sought to explain different forms of business organizations. Coase's article was grounded on a very old idea: people act in their self-interest. This article extended the study of self-interested behaviour beyond market transactions, to situations where other values— such as loyalty, duty, contacts, and other obligations—come into play. Building on the point made by Coase, new institutional economics argues that members of a firm are bound together by self-interest as are parties to a contract but the very self-interest that motivates parties to enter into a contract means that contracts are rarely self-enforcing. One or both parties may seek to implement the bargain in ways that put the other party to disadvantage; which is to say that they may behave opportunistically.

Opportunism flourishes because rationality is bounded and the cost of getting sufficient information is high: as a result principals and parties to a contract do not have all the information they need to ensure that the bargain is being honoured. It so happens that the agents know more about their performance than their principals do; the possession of essential information is often asymmetrical. This asymmetry exposes principals to the risk of capture: agents give principals the information that impels them to act in the interest of those who serve them. On the whole, because of the failure of principals to monitor agents' behaviour and enforce performance standards, agents behave opportunistically. In such cases, the agent complies with the goals of the organization only to the extent whereby, by doing so, it can also promote its own interest.[4]

Such opportunistic behaviour abounds in the government. Because the principals in a government—namely, the people, or the legislature, or the ministers—fail to monitor civil service behaviour and enforce performance standards, the civil servants behave opportunistically. Civil servants who work for the government tend to pursue their own goals and are indifferent to how public resources are used. They promote collective interest only in cases where they can also promote their own interests.

One particular form of opportunism that is rampant in government is the capture of government's policy-making apparatus by service providers. Such a capture takes place because civil servants have better information about how government services are actually delivered, than their principals. Such asymmetry in information facilitates opportunism by civil servants that ranges from shirking and budget maximization to following generally inefficient policies for the community as a whole.

So the question arises: How does one align the behaviour of agents in a government with the interest of the principals? The solutions provided by public choice theory and new institutional economics are to:

- have clear objectives, which inform civil servants about what is expected of them and enables their performance to be monitored
- bring transparency in explicating these objectives and the means by which they are to be pursued
- minimize the scope for capture of policy by service providers
- give civil servants incentives to achieve government's goals rather than their own
- have incentives and information that enhance accountability of agents to principals
- promote contestability of both policy advice and service delivery.[5]
- ensure efficient use of information

Consistent with the solutions suggested by public choice theory and new institutional economics, new public management advocates:

- Privatization
- Deregulation
- Encouraging competition
- Taxpayers and ministers as principals
- Performance measurement through which outcomes can be measured.

Adoption of new public management by the government requires organizational changes that would provide for:

- alternatives for government provision of services such as public–private partnerships
- separation of purchasers of services from providers: decentralization of organizational structures with the creation of autonomous agencies for service delivery
- competition between different service provider organizations
- generation of revenues through user fees
- defining users of public services as customers rather than citizens
- systematic evaluation of programmes through performance indicators
- significant delegation of responsibility, including budgeting

- shifting of emphasis from inputs towards outputs and outcomes
- use of performance contracts to hold staff accountable for realizing these outcomes.[6]

Without the adoption of accrual accounting, the changes required to implement the new public management reform agenda would be difficult to realize.

What about the Indian government? One would have thought that with the liberalization of 1991, which led to a number of significant initiatives emphasizing cost effectiveness of government activities and calling for better management of public resources, reform measures on the lines of new public management would have been undertaken—but this is not the case. There has been no systematic evaluation of government activities through performance indicators, neither is there any attempt to hold government employees accountable for what they are expected to do. There is no significant delegation of responsibility to the line departments. Cash continues to be the basis of government accounting, although it does not serve the needs of the government, either from the perspective of the information needed for decision-making or for reflecting accountability.

This book finds that the four countries which implemented public management reforms have reaped rich dividends. They have achieved favourable fiscal outcomes by way of budgetary surpluses. They have also achieved economy, efficiency, and effectiveness in the provision of public services. There is now much more information generated by the accounting system, which has enhanced decision-making, reflected accountability, and ensured control over the long-term financial consequences of government policy. That being the case, the book recommends that there is a compelling case for the Indian government to introduce accounting reforms without losing much time.

The book makes a final caveat. As a result of globalization, there is now a great deal of competition amongst countries. These countries, whose experiences with accounting reforms we study in the book, realized that if their governments were to survive in this competitive environment they needed to make a transition to the more disciplined and rigorous model of accrual accounting. It so happened that these countries felt the pressures of globalization earlier than India did and they responded by adopting reforms. In this era of increasing globalization, the same forces of globalization will, sooner or later, persuade the Indian government to embark upon accounting reforms. So, why not take them up now?

NOTES

1. Hepworth (2002), p. 5.
2. Scott (1994), p. 172.
3. Krueger (1974).
4. Das (1998), p. 11.
5. New Zealand Treasury (1987).
6. Hepworth (2002), p. 6.

1

Government Accounting

Most government accounts are on a cash basis. It means that money is brought to account when they are paid or received. Such an accounting regime is consistent with the arrangements whereby the legislature votes the government's request for funds. Single entry has traditionally been the recording procedure used for the reporting model; wherein the elements reported consist of cash and near-cash items. These items could be cash receipts plus short-term receivables, cash disbursements plus short-term payables, and cash and near-cash balances.

Compliance with the budget is particularly important in a cash-accounting system. The annual budget presented to a legislature seeks approval for the government's expenditure proposals for the year ahead. A legislature's consideration of expenditure proposals generally follows several stages.

- The government requests for certain funds.
- Information is provided about what these funds will be spent on.
- Legislature considers these requests, scrutinizes them, and debates some of them.
- If the legislature votes in favour of the proposals, an act is passed to make the funds available to the government.
- After expenditures are incurred, they are audited by an independent audit that reports to the legislature.

Expenditure limits voted by the legislature provide the means of control over a government's expenditure. The ministry of finance profiles, monitors, forecasts, and analyses expenditure against the funds voted by the legislature.

HOW GOOD IS THE SYSTEM?

To answer the question, it is necessary to lay down a benchmark. The Public Sector Committee (PSC) of the International Federation of Accountants describes the purpose of accounting and financial reporting in government in these words.

Financial reporting should demonstrate the accountability of a government—or a unit for the financial affairs—and resources entrusted to it, and provide information useful to assess:

- *Compliance and stewardship:* whether resources were obtained and used in accordance with legal constraints and contractual requirements, and whether stewardship over the custody and maintenance of resources (both financial and physical) was observed
- *State of finances:* sources and types of revenues; allocation and use of resources including the split between operating and capital costs; the extent to which revenues cover costs of operations including non-cash costs; the timing and volume of cash flows; the ability to meet financial obligations both short- and long-term; and to assess overall financial condition
- *Performance:* the economy and efficiency of operations and whether goals and objectives of the operation have been met
- *Economic impact:* economic impact of the government on an economy; and to enable evaluation of government's spending options and priorities.[1]

Such a benchmark, however, misses out on an important feature of how most governments function. Typically, governments tend to represent a financial position or performance in a manner that the position looks better than it really is. So, to test the efficacy of a government accounting system, the question that should also be asked is: does the system ensure reliability of reported information?

COMPLIANCE AND STEWARDSHIP

Compliance

The function of compliance consists of ensuring that an executive uses resources only as voted by the legislature. If a budget is cash-based, financial reports generated by a cash accounting system are in a position to demonstrate compliance with the budget. This is done by including a column in the financial statements to allow direct comparisons between the budgeted amount and actual expenditure incurred by departments.

Stewardship

The function of stewardship consists of the management of public resources, both financial and physical. To help the government exercise it, an accounting system should generate information on the assets owned by departments and on how they are managed. Asset management is particularly important in the context of a government because most of its physical assets have a very long life. Ideally, the level of inventory in any government department should be maintained at a level that is consistent with operational requirements. A high level of inventory together with a low rate of use can be costly in terms of holding costs and obsolescence.[2]

However, a cash accounting system does not help in asset management. The problem stems from how capital expenditure is reported in the system. Capital expenditure—on something that is used over many years—is recorded only in the year when an expenditure is incurred. This system does not distribute the cost of capital over an asset's useful life. There is no framework in a cash accounting system to account for assets. Once an asset is acquired, it effectively disappears from the accounts. The accounting system takes no subsequent notice of how the asset is used or what are its returns to the government. The cash system provides no incentive to government departments to extract the best value from their capital.

The cash accounting system does not generate the sort of information on the basis of which a government can decide whether to use an existing infrastructure or take up new capital investments. In fact, the system does not even take notice of the costs involved in neglecting the maintenance of existing infrastructure.[3] This is why the decision makers in a government are unable to reach the desirable balance between capital and current expenditure. As a result, the capital–output ratios in government departments are usually very high.

STATE OF FINANCES

Sources and Types of Revenues

The cash budget presented to a legislature shows the sources and types of revenues to be generated. The budget indicates the cash required to finance the activities, and the allocation and use of cash resources.

Revenues Covering the Cost of Operations

A cash budget is in a position to indicate how the costs of an operation would be met—whether completely from revenues wholly or partially or from other sources—depending on whether it is a surplus or a deficit budget. However, the measurement of deficit or surplus in a cash budget can be manipulated by varying the timing of cash payments or receipts.

Cash Flows

The cash accounting systems record the inflows and outflows of cash whenever it is received or paid. The system, in fact, provides a useful tool to control cash flows.

Assessment of the Overall Financial Condition

Whether or not an accounting system is in a position to assess the overall financial condition of the government, depends a lot on the reporting framework it uses. The reporting framework defines what assets and liabilities are to be recognized in determining the financial position. There are three main frameworks for reporting on assets.

1. Current financial resources
2. Total financial resources
3. Economic resources[4]

Cash accounting recognizes revenues and expenditures only when cash is collected or paid. Financial results for a period indicate the difference between cash received and cash disbursed, and provide information on the cash balance at a reporting date. Typically, cash-based reports recognize expenditures rather than expenses. Therefore these reports are for short-term financial purposes and not for economic or equity-reporting purposes. Since the focus of measurement is on cash balances and changes therein, the reporting frameworks in cash accounting systems can only be categorized as 'current financial resources'. Total assets and equity amounts are not reported, and the system does not provide for costing of physical assets at current valuation. In the absence of these details, a statement of financial position cannot be prepared. And without a statement of financial position, it is not possible to evaluate the government's overall financial condition and the changes in it.

PERFORMANCE

For performance to be measured, information on the true cost of government's activities must be available. Such information needs to take into account all the relevant costs—including the use of assets, cost of capital, and non-cash costs—and relate them directly to the revenues generated by those activities. The cash accounting system does not generate such information, because it has no requirement for matching expenditure with revenues for the period to which the two relate. Also, capital expenditure is accounted for wholly in the year in which capital asset is acquired, without allocating the cost of capital over the useful life of that asset.

A cash accounting system does not generate information about the period of expenses and their matching revenues. Performance indicators such as total or segment revenues (expense balances), different expense, or revenue items per person and by year cannot be determined on the basis of information generated by the cash system.[5] In the absence of such indicators, it is not possible to evaluate the performance of government departments in terms of economy and efficiency. Information about cost of services, however, is a necessary tool for performance evaluation and control. In fact, if cash is the basis for reporting, accounting data plays a very limited role in the decision-making process as it does not enable a realistic estimation of whether the government can afford to continue a service it currently delivers and whether it can afford to have new services. On the whole, the cash accounting system provides no basis for judgement of performance in terms of economy and efficiency, or for that matter, on achievement of goals or objectives.

ECONOMIC IMPACT

The cash accounting system does ensure compliance with expenditure limits. The system is useful in tracking expenditure in a financial year and in identifying short-term effects of current policy. However, it is not in a position to provide information on the longer-term economic impact and sustainability of current policies because it fails to account for the future expenditure implications of decisions. Assessing the long-term economic impact of current policies is important because future revenues have to pay for past debts as well as future services.[6]

RELIABILITY OF REPORTED INFORMATION

A government is often tempted to show a financial position and performance that is better than what it really is. For example, the government may like to present a healthy picture of its current financial position for political reasons. A cash accounting system allows the government to present its financial position different from what it really is.[7]

There are a number of ways in which governments do this when they keep accounts on a cash basis. First, they do not report their full liabilities. For example, future liabilities by way of pension payment are not reported because these are not taken into account while determining the total amount of government's liabilities.

Second, when governments grant subsidies or loans, their accounts do not reflect the value of the subsidies or the subsidy value of the loans, nor do the accounts contain an estimate of the losses, which could reasonably occur over the lifetime of loans and subsidies. When governments give subsidies or loans at lower than market rates, there is a cost to the government. Though purely from a cash consideration, there is very limited immediate impact when subsidies or loans are given, but over time the costs accumulate. This has serious financial implications because future revenues of the government get committed to meeting the difference between what the government pays to borrow money from the market and the rate at which the subsidies or loans are given.[8]

Third, when a government gives guarantees for repayment of loans, the cash accounting system does not reflect the long-term costs involved in these guarantees. Neither does it provide borrower's characteristics such as financial solvency of the parties involved, nor does it generate information about the future economic conditions which are likely to affect the repayment of loans guaranteed by the government. It does not provide any estimate of how many of the loans guaranteed are expected to default and what would be the likely losses to the government.

Fourth, government departments routinely manipulate deficit or surplus by varying the timing of payments or receipts. When it comes to cash payments, the departments often postpone the payments due in the current financial year to the next one. Sometimes they incur expenditure in the current financial year by making payments which are not due, only to spend the budgeted outlay. In respect of receipts, the departments collect advance tax in the last quarter of a financial year, which is refunded during the first quarter of the next financial year. In either case, cash accounting system enables the departments to present the fiscal reality differently from what it is.

Fifth, liberties are often taken with how expenditure is entered in the books. For example, departments often transfer moneys—which are left unspent by the end of a financial year— to public sector undertakings (PSUs). Since PSUs keep accounts on accrual basis, money transferred to them will not lapse to the consolidated fund, if left unspent. The advantage of this scheme is, the government accounts show expenditure that has not really taken place.[9]

On the whole, a cash accounting system offers ample scope for fiscal trickery: it provides opportunities to the government to massage financial information in order to disguise the fiscal reality. In other words, the financial information provided by a cash accounting system is not altogether reliable.

AN ASSESSMENT

It is now possible to comment on how good the cash basis is as an accounting system. On the positive side, the system:

- generates information to assess compliance with legislative requirements
- provides information to assess the short-term economic impact of current policy.

On the negative side, the system:

- does not help in asset management
- does not provide information to assess the long-term economic impact and sustainability of current policies
- does not provide information to assess performance of the government departments in terms of economy, efficiency, and achievement of goals and objectives
- provides opportunities for fiscal trickery.

Clearly, the cash accounting system does not meet the requirements of a government. It does not provide the information needed for effective decision-making or accountability. Obviously a change is needed, but what are the alternatives? There are three alternatives, as set out below.

Modified Cash System of Accounting

A modified cash system of accounting is similar to the cash accounting system in that it recognizes transactions and events when cash is received or paid. The only difference being that under the modified cash system the books are held open for a specified period after the end of the financial year—generally for about a month. Receipts and disbursements, which occur during the specified period but which originated in the previous reporting period, are recognized as receipts and disbursements of the previous fiscal year. Its financial reports recognize revenues and expenditures only when cash is collected or paid, and when related receivables and payables have a short term to maturity. The financial reports in modified cash system continue to be, as in the cash system, for short-term financial purposes and not for economic and equity reporting purposes, and they recognize expenditures rather than expenses in the budgetary reports.

Modified Accrual System of Accounting

A modified accrual system recognizes transactions and events when they occur rather than when cash is paid or received except that physical assets are not carried forward to the next fiscal. All financial assets and liabilities—including borrowing and debt—are accounted for. Physical assets of the government, meant for direct public use, are recognized as capital investments during construction period and written off when completed. As a result, no depreciation expense is recognized for these capital assets. Since depreciation for physical assets—especially for infrastructure assets—is not recognized, it becomes difficult to determine the true cost of services, the operating result and the impact on equity.

Accrual System of Accounting

An accrual system of accounting recognizes transactions and events when they occur rather than when cash is paid or received. The key elements in an accrual system are: assets, liabilities, net worth, revenues, and expenses. An accrual system provides users with information about the resources of an entity: its revenues, the cost of its services, and any other information needed to assess its financial position and changes to it, and the means to assess the performance of the entity in terms of economy and efficiency. In other words, the measurement focus in an accrual accounting system is on economic resources and changes therein. In an accrual system the financial reports consist of three primary statements:

1. operating statement
2. balance sheet
3. cash flow statement.

The question arises: what information do these statements provide which the cash reports do not? To answer that, we need to describe what information the system can provide if the government keeps accounts on an accrual basis.

To begin with, the operating statement will provide information on total costs of government's activities undertaken today, whether they involve payment and disbursal of cash or not. It will show whether taxes and other revenues of today are sufficient to cover today's costs. If today's revenues are less than today's costs, the balance sheet will reflect the deficit as a reduction in net worth; if today's revenues are greater than today's costs, there would be an improvement in net worth. Changes in net worth will be effected by

- an increase in liabilities either by borrowing to fund the deficit or obligations to make payments in the future
- an increase in assets, which would provide future economic benefits to the concerned department.

The balance sheet will, thus, be a list of assets and liabilities of a department with the difference between assets and liabilities being its net worth. The balance sheet will provide a link between operations of the government from one reporting period to the next. A time-series of balance sheets will give an indication of the financial health of the department. The statement of cash flow will provide information on how the liquid resources are used by a department for its current operations as well as the impact of these resources on future activities—through changes in assets and liabilities.

Accrual accounting is a mechanism that condenses a large mass of data into a single set of useful information. Since an accrual system records transactions as they occur, irrespective of cash movements, it is in a position to distinguish expenditures that provide economic benefits in the short term (current consumption) from those that will benefit the government and the community well into the future (capital expenditure).[10] The key features of an accrual accounting system in the government departments would be:[11]

- an accounting framework meeting requirements ranging from low-level management information to high-level financial reports
- a technique for providing more accurate measurement of resources consumed
- a reporting structure to match resources to the objectives of the government, and linking the objectives to quantified measures of performance
- accounting for the consumption of capital in terms of resources consumed
- provision of essential cash-accounting information
- a system of reporting the accounting information to legislature and members of the public
- auditability of the financial statements generated by accrual reporting.

WHAT ARE THE BENEFITS?

The government will benefit from the use of accrual accounting in several ways. First, accrual data will provide information on total costs of the government activities undertaken today, showing whether the taxes and other revenues are sufficient to cover today's costs. It will provide useful information on the government's financial performance and future economic viability. It will generate accurate information on capital consumption: this will lead to improvements in the use of existing assets and future investment decisions, and the information will also help the government to evaluate its ability in meeting future obligations.

Second, accrual accounting will provide segment-wise information on the operations of government departments. Accrual data will make available performance indicators such as total or segment revenues/expenses balances, and different expense or revenue items by per person and by per year. As a result, it will be possible to get information on the true cost of services that a government provides. Armed with information about the true cost of services, the government will be in a position to make informed decisions on the allocation of resources consistent with its overall priorities. For example:

- the government can decide whether to provide a particular service itself or through an external contractor, because the cost of various options can be compared
- the government will have enough information to monitor performance against objectives
- with access to better information on working capital, the government can control cash flows more effectively
- the government will be in a position to introduce a system of user charges.[12]

Third, accrual accounting will improve transparency in the government because there will be externally imposed rules and standards on how government activities should be accounted for. To that extent, opportunities for manipulation inherent in a cash accounting system will be reduced and the government will be kept from showing a better financial position than what it actually is. As a result, there will be improvement in the reliability of reported information, credibility of the government will be enhanced, and members of the public will have greater confidence in the government's capability for financial management—particularly when they recognize that information provided by the government is in conformity with externally imposed rules and standards.

Fourth, accrual accounting will help in addressing intergenerational equity issues, whose basic principle is that taxpayers in each time period (current and future) should—as a group—contribute to public expenditures from which they derive benefits, in accordance with their share of the benefits generated by those expenditures. It implies that, while future taxpayers should pay for the benefits generated for them, costs should not be transferred from the current tax payers when there is an increase in current expenditure. In other words, intergenerational equity is concerned with the appropriate balance between taxes, user charges, and borrowings to finance today's current expenses and capital expenditures.

Pension liability is an example of the costs of the current taxpayers being transferred to the future taxpayers. Accrual accounting will record the accruing pension costs, and this will show the extent to which the costs are being transferred from the current taxpayers to future taxpayers, particularly when there is an increase in the level of pension liabilities.[13] Only when the pension costs are recorded, can the government of the day make plans to fund these liabilities, possibly by renegotiating the terms with its employees.

Capital expenditure is another example. Accrual accounting will make a structural distinction between current and capital expenditure—it will record capital use (depreciation) in the operating statement instead of capital expenditure. The distinction between current and capital expenditure, and changes in the balance sheet, will throw light on the impact of government's fiscal policies on the current and future taxpayers.

Accrual accounting will provide a government with the information needed to assess fiscal sustainability of its policies over a period of time. By generating information on the future expenditure implications of the current decisions, in the period in which the decisions were made, accrual accounting will provide information about the long-term sustainability of government policies. Accrual accounting will make it possible to treat transactions creating future liabilities on a similar basis as cash transactions, and in the process, it will prevent the transfer of costs to future generations.[14]

ACCRUAL BUDGETING

Accrual accounting is only a means to an end; accounting is but one element of the whole management function: it provides the reporting structure for financial management that has as its objective a more efficient and accountable government. Accrual accounting by itself would not bring about the changes required to achieve efficiency and accountability: that would require changes to be made in the budgetary process.

As we noted, accrual reports provide a useful database that contains the basic information to enable financial analysis in budgeting, either at the whole-of-government level or at the level of individual departments. The introduction of accrual budgeting will mean that the

- process of planning expenditure would be for the government as a whole and for individual departments based on better information,
- pressure for spending the full budgeted outlay at the end of a financial year would be reduced,
- control of expenditure would be on a sounder basis because civil servants will have more relevant, information,
- procedures for deciding on the level of capital would improve,
- system would provide informed choices between the spending options.

At the level of individual departments, accrual budgeting will

- encourage departments to focus on services that they deliver rather than on the inputs that they consume,

- allow departments to plan internally and be controlled externally on the same parameters.

For the econom·· as a whole, it will

- provide information for formulating economic policies and deciding on the value and use of fixed assets and capital consumption in the government,
- reduce the government's demand on funds by promoting better use of public resources.[15]

A caveat is in order. Accrual accounting in a department does not necessarily imply accrual budgeting. It is possible for accounting to be on an accrual basis while the budgeting is on a cash basis. The problem with such an approach is two-fold. First, it will result in dual, potentially conflicting, performance objectives: accrual performance against accrual expectations while compliance with cash transactions. Second, cash accounting will not give a legislature effective control over utilization of resources by the departments: cash-based information is too limited for a legislature to scrutinize and approve expenditure for activities of the departments in a meaningful manner.

PROBLEMS

It is clear that introduction of accrual accounting in government departments will yield tangible benefits but there are other arguments too that consider the use of accrual accounting in a government setting to be inappropriate. How valid are these arguments?

ACCRUAL ACCOUNTING AND POLITICS

It is argued that the idea of introducing accrual accounting in a government does not quite recognize the essential nature of how a government functions. The government exists to achieve its political purposes therefore an accounting system in the government should essentially serve the needs of the ruling politicians. Political horizons are short-term: a politician's time-frame is, at best, limited to winning the next election, while the use of accrual accounting would mean taking a longer-term view. Moreover, political decisions are geared to winning votes and appeasing voters; and politicians, while making their decisions, would not like to be constrained by the hard fiscal realities that accrual accounting offers.[16]

However, if politicians can be persuaded to look beyond their short-term political horizons—to the comprehensive information that accrual accounting offers—they will realize that they stand to benefit immensely from the use of accruals. It will give them better information to make decisions about priorities, and assist them in allocating resources in accordance with these priorities. From a political point of view, voters will have better information to assess the performance of politicians, and this should help politicians—who have done good work—to get elected.

WEAKENED CONTROL OVER PUBLIC SPENDING

Introduction of accrual accounting, it is argued, will weaken control of government expenditure by the ministry of finance. The ministry's attention is likely to be diverted from (a) manageable concerns with cash inputs and (b) from the money spent in a particular year—both of which can be measured with precision—to concerns about accrued costs and liabilities; concerns over which the ministry would have no control. More importantly, these concerns are difficult to measure with as much precision as cash inputs and cash balances.[17]

In response to this argument, it is to be pointed out that accrual accounting does not weaken the finance ministry's ability to control public expenditure. On the contrary, because accrual systems provide a more comprehensive database to assist in the development of policies and assessment of their sustainability in the longer term, adoption of accrual accounting would strengthen the ministry's ability to control public expenditure. In fact, armed with such a database, the ministry can also undertake comprehensive analyses with a longer-term, financial planning perspective.

WEAKENING THE PROCESS OF AUDIT

It is argued that accrual accounting may erode the process of audit, by turning away attention from the traditional auditing concerns such as compliance with expenditure limits as well as regularity and propriety in government expenditure. In response, it has to be pointed out that even with the adoption of accrual accounting, cash-based information would still be available, therefore audit bodies can still carry on their audit with reference to concerns of regularity, propriety, and compliance with expenditure limits. In addition, with information from the accrual system, audit bodies will be in a better position to assess whether resources are obtained and used in accordance with limits set by the legislature, legal constraints, and rule requirements.

HIGH COST

It is also said that the cost of developing information systems for accrual accounting can be high. While it is true that new processes have to be set up throughout the government and the systems are expensive, things have changed of late. The standard commercial accounting systems can now be used to set up accrual processes, and their cost can be effectively lowered by ordering them in bulk. Since the commercial systems are standardized, there is practically no risk in operationalizing these systems. In addition, since the systems will be common between the government departments and private sector companies, skilled accounting personnel can freely move from private sector to government departments, thereby ensuring an uninterrupted flow of staff and skills.[18]

COMPARABILITY

It is also argued that since most governments account on a cash basis, cash reports can be used to compare fiscal settings across governments and through time. Since only a few governments have adopted accrual accounting, there would be a loss of comparability. But as we have pointed out, adoption of accrual accounting does not preclude preparation of traditional cash-based accounts therefore comparability is not necessarily lost.

GOVERNMENT AND PRIVATE SECTOR ACTIVITIES

Above all else, the debate on cash versus accruals hinges on the intrinsic differences between the nature of the activities performed by governments and the private sector. In order to have a better understanding of this debate, differences between the accounting requirements of these two sectors need to be put in perspective.

Private sector companies adopted accrual accounting in response to two historical developments.[19] First was the separation of their owners from their day-to-day managers, and the establishment of financial markets to lend money to these companies. The owners and financial markets needed critical financial information to make important decisions. For example, when there was accumulation of long-term liabilities or when equipment became obsolete, the owners and lenders wanted to have such information immediately. They were not interested when the liabilities had to be eventually discharged or when the equipment was to be scrapped. Accrual accounting was designed to give such critical information to owners and lenders. In other words, adoption of accrual accounting was prompted by the need for critical financial information on how well the entities were managed.

Second, the process of growing competition in the private sector required high-quality management information to determine and set prices. In the absence of management information to set prices, the entity could be rendered uncompetitive. Only an accrual accounting system was capable of providing the kind of high-quality financial and management information required for taking such strategic decisions.

There were no comparable developments in the government sector. Accounting systems in the government started on a cash basis and have continued to remain on that basis. Several explanations have been offered why this is so. One explanation is that the government functions in an environment that is different from the private sector; an environment that is essentially legal; therefore the government is highly legalistic in nature. Consistent with its legal environment, the government needs an accounting system that is capable of satisfying its legal requirements, and the cash system is in a position to do this. In essence, the legal environment—in which a government resides—determines the nature of government accounting.

The other explanation is less charitable. It argues that government is a monopoly and, like all monopolies, it is inefficient: it overcharges and underproduces. All the systems in a government, including its accounting, are designed to protect and reinforce its monopolistic nature. In other words, they are designed to help a government reduce the disclosures of its inefficiency. A cash system is suitable for governments because it reduces disclosure of government's inefficiencies, while an accrual model would typically require a fuller disclosure. Since a government is not interested in full disclosure, its accounting system continues to remain on cash basis.[20]

A more charitable explanation is that the accounting system in government has remained on a cash basis because no change in the system was called for. The cash system has worked rather well in controlling expenditure. Those charged with running the government have found no need to question the adequacy of this accounting system so long as it demonstrates compliance with expenditure limits. In fact, demonstrating compliance with expenditure limits, as voted by the legislature, has so far been accepted as the paramount objective of an accounting system—this being the basis on which governments budget and upon which the executive is held accountable.

In the last two decades, however, the nature of this accountability has changed from a focus on compliance with expenditure limits to one on accountability for performance. This has led to demands for better information on the basis of which effectiveness of programmes can be assessed and resources can be allocated and managed more efficiently. More comprehensive information on revenues and expenses, and assets and liabilities is a subset of such information. It also means taking into account a number of non-cash resources—depreciation, cost of capital, debtors, creditors, stock balances, rents, and pension—which are considered relevant for achieving the result-oriented goals set for government departments. A cash accounting system cannot meet these requirements; alone, it provides neither the basis for judging performance in terms of economy and efficiency, nor the achievement of goals and objectives.

In the next chapter we look at the cash accounting system in the Indian government to see how it has worked, and in particular, how it has responded to the challenge of change in the nature of accountability. In the subsequent chapters, we analyse the experience of governments in New Zealand, Australia, the United Kingdom, and Sweden in converting to accrual accounting. We then discuss the gains these countries have achieved in the process and the issues involved. We also take a look at the experience of a few municipal bodies in India, which have converted to accrual accounting. Based on an assessment of the experience of these countries and municipal bodies, we delineate a roadmap for the introduction of accrual accounting in the core departments of the Indian government.

NOTES

1. IFAC-PSC (1991), paragraph 63.
2. Mellor (1997), pp. 52-3.
3. HMSO (1994a), p. 4.
4. Montesinos and Bargues (1997), pp. 19–20.
5. Ibid., p. 21.
6. Hillier (1997), p. 12.
7. Ibid., p. 13.
8. Redburn (1997), p. 40.
9. Hillier (1997), p. 16.
10. Mellor (1997), p. 52.
11. HMSO (1994), p. 6.
12. HMSO (1994a), p. 7.
13. Mellor (1997), p. 54.
14. Ibid.
15. HMSO (1994a), viii.
16. Jones (1997), p. 34.
17. Ibid., p. 35.
18. Ball, Dale, Eggers, and Sacco (2000), p. 10.
19. Ibid., p. 8.
20. This view comes from public choice literature.

2

Government Accounting in India

The Indian government accounts on a cash basis. The system was established in colonial India: it started with the Regulation Act of 1773, which provided for a system of unified financial control over the whole country. An accountant general was appointed and by the Accounting Act of 1779 and Indian accounts were required to be consolidated and rendered to the British Parliament. By 1858, departments of accounts had been established in all the provinces with accountant generals located in the presidencies of Bombay, Madras, and Bengal. A system of annual budgeting was introduced from 1861–2, and by the year 1865 a system of monthly consolidation of accounts had been brought into force in place of annual consolidation. In 1884, a comptroller and auditor general was appointed, charged with the twin responsibilities of conducting appropriation audit and supervising government accounting. When India became independent, the office of Comptroller and Auditor General (CAG) was continued and the CAG was allowed to retain the accounting and audit functions.

THE SETTING

The main problem with the accounting system in independent India was poor maintenance of accounting records[1]. Civil servants themselves suffered as a result of this: the final accounts of their general provident fund and house building advances could only be generated after a great deal of delay because of missing credits. As a result, the retiring government servants had to wait well beyond their superannuation to get their pension benefits. In addition, comprehensive accounting data was hard to obtain and decision makers in the government did not have access to accounting data. Compilation of accounting data at the national level was a slow process and more often than not, by the time the data could be compiled for the government as a whole, it was outdated and had lost its utility.

There was also a problem with how the financial administration functioned: it was characterized by day-to-day, itemized control exercised by the finance ministry. There was virtually no delegation of financial powers to the administrative ministries and departments: every government scheme or programme with financial implications had to be approved by the finance ministry. As a result of the system whereby controls were exercised centrally, there were considerable delays in approval and implementation of schemes and programmes.

FINANCIAL MANAGEMENT REFORMS

The functioning of the financial management system—poor maintenance of accounting records and centralized control by the finance ministry—came in for considerable criticism. The Public Accounts Committee and the Estimates Committee in their various reports between 1951 and 1954 commented on it. In 1954 C.D. Deshmukh, the then finance minister, stated in the Parliament, 'Authority administering a grant is responsible for watching the progress of expenditure in public services under its control and for keeping the expenditure within its grant. This is the responsibility of the administrative ministry and not of the finance ministry.'[2]

In March 1973, a committee was set up under the chairmanship of M.R. Yardi to suggest improvements in the area of financial administration.[3] Yardi Committee recommended that the responsibility for internal financial management should be entirely on administrative ministries, and there should be adequate delegation of financial powers to match their responsibilities. The committee also recommended performance budgeting and increased delegation of powers to administrative ministries. Recommendations of the committee were accepted in 1974 and as a result, several financial reforms were introduced in the government.

SEPARATION OF AUDIT AND ACCOUNTS

The scheme of separating accounts from audit was implemented in a phased manner from: 1 April 1976, 1 July 1976, and 1 October 1976. On 1 April 1977, the CAG was relieved of the responsibility of compiling accounts of the revenue receipts of central government. Article 150 of the Constitution was suitably amended through the Forty-fourth Amendment Act of 1978 to reflect the fact that the CAG had ceased to be the principal central accounting authority. From the financial year 1977–8, the CAG was also relieved of the responsibility of preparing finance accounts of the Union government.

CREATION OF A CENTRAL ACCOUNTING AUTHORITY

The organization of the Controller General of Accounts (CGA) was created as the centralized coordinating accounting authority. The CGA was made responsible for:

- laying down the general principles of government accounting relating to the Union and state governments and the form of accounts, and to frame or revise rules and manuals
- overseeing the maintenance of adequate standards of accounting by the central civil accounts offices
- reconciliation of cash balances of the Union government with the Reserve Bank of India (RBI) in general and, in particular, of reserve deposits pertaining to civil ministries or departments
- consolidation of monthly accounts, preparation of review trends of revenue realization and significant features of expenditure, and preparation of annual accounts showing annual receipts and disbursements for the purpose of the Union government under the respective heads
- administration of the central treasury rules
- coordination and assistance in the introduction of management accounting system in the ministries.[4]

In other words, CGA became the principal accounting authority of the Indian government and, in that capacity, became responsible for establishing and maintaining a sound and efficient accounting and financial reporting system.

DEPARTMENTALIZED ACCOUNTS

In 1976, the scheme of departmentalization of accounts was introduced. Under this scheme, the functions relating to receipts and payments were taken away from the treasuries and entrusted to a network of departmentalized pay and accounts offices (PAO). Secretary of a ministry was designated the chief accounting authority and he was made responsible for discharging accounting functions with help from the integrated financial adviser. A principal accounts office was set up in each ministry or department headed by a chief controller of accounts under whom a number of PAOs were positioned to look after the payment and accounting functions of the ministry including those of its subordinate and field formations.

INTEGRATED FINANCE

In 1975, the system of integrated financial advice (IFA) was introduced. Under the IFA system, a financial adviser (FA) is appointed for every ministry and made responsible for the scrutiny of proposals and tendering advice to the ministry. The FA controls disbursement of funds allotted to the ministry by allocating them to various attached and subordinate offices, establishes letters of credit on behalf of these offices, assigns drawing limits to them, and enforces exchequer control against voted grants and appropriations as passed by the Parliament. The FA is in charge of budget formulation, scrutiny of projects and programmes, post-budget vigilance, preparation of performance budget of the ministry, and monitoring of progress of schemes against the budget.

The idea behind establishing a system of integrated finance was to empower administrative ministries for exercising enhanced financial powers. Has that happened? The answer, unhappily, is in the negative: for the simple reason that the financial powers delegated to them are not quite enough. In that sense, the devolution of financial powers to the administrative ministries is incomplete: in most important matters, approval of the finance ministry is still a requirement. In fact, insufficient devolution of financial powers has had important consequences for developing accountability in the administrative ministries.

PERFORMANCE BUDGETING

A scheme of performance budgeting was introduced in the Indian government from the budget year 1975–6. Under this scheme, along with the detailed demands for grants, a performance budget document is presented to the Parliament. The performance budget is intended to present a meaningful relationship between inputs and outputs, and indicate the correlation between planned programmes and their performance in financial and physical terms. Broadly, the performance budget has four parts, indicating:

- broad objectives, programmes and projects or activities to achieve them, the organizations and agencies charged with the responsibility to implement them, the highlights of performance during the previous financial year, progress during the current year, and the programme for next year.
- linkages between the Five Year plans, the achievements so far, and the tasks ahead.
- financial statements showing the outlays required for the programmes,

projects or activities and the provisions in the current and next financial year (a link between the provisions and source of finance is also indicated).

- details of the scope, plan of action, achievements, programme, and performance during the current year and future programmes, along with outlays in respect of each activity in the various broad programmes of the department.

Although the scheme of performance budgeting was introduced as early as 1975–6, it has not achieved its objective. The performance budget is not even an integral part of the budgetary process: the performance budget documents are separately tabled in the Parliament. Worse still, the Parliament, while approving the expenditure for a department, does not even take into account the performance of a department.[5] Performance budgeting in India has been reduced to being just a ritualistic exercise.

ZERO-BASED BUDGETING

In the mid-1980s, the scheme of zero-based budgeting was introduced in the government departments. The objective of the scheme was to

- involve civil servants at all levels in the budgetary process,
- justify the resource requirements for existing activities as well as new activities,
- focus justification on the evaluation of discrete programmes or activities of each unit of the administration,
- establish objectives against which accomplishments could be identified and measured, and assess alternative methods of accomplishing objectives,
- analyse the probable effects of different budgetary provisions or performance levels on the achievement of objectives, and
- Provide a credible rationale for reallocating resources, especially from old activities to new activities.[6]

The scheme was a failure and it has now been, more or less, abandoned in spite of occasional efforts by the ministry of finance or the Planning Commission to revive it.

THE ACCOUNTING SYSTEM

Elements of the accounting system as it operates in the Indian government, after the introduction of financial reforms, are described below.

CASH BASIS OF ACCOUNTS

Accounts in the Government of India are maintained on a cash basis. As a general rule, transactions are recorded in the government accounts representing actual cash receipts and disbursements during a financial year.

PRINCIPLE OF LAPSE

The financial year commences on 1 April and ends on 31 March of the next calendar year. While revenue arrears payable to the government are taken into account, the budgetary provisions that are not spent by the end of the financial year are not carried forward to the next financial year; in other words, the accounting system follows the principle of lapse.[7] The cash transactions that take place after 31 March are not included in the accounts of the previous year. But, even after 31 March, the accounts are kept open to include some adjusting account entries like crediting the 'fund and deposit accounts' with interest for the financial year by contra debit to the interest head.[8]

THE STRUCTURE OF GOVERNMENT ACCOUNTS

Accounts in the Indian government are prepared in three parts: consolidated fund, contingency fund, and public account. A common bank account is maintained for all the three parts.

Consolidated Fund of India

All the revenues and receipts of the Government of India are credited to the consolidated fund. So are the proceeds from the loans floated by issue of public notifications and treasury bills; loans secured from foreign governments and international financial institutions; as well as all money received from recovery of loans and interest thereon. The expenditure incurred for the conduct of government's business, including repayment of internal and external debt and release of loans to the state and union territory governments, is debited to the consolidated fund. In other words, consolidated fund reflects the government's fiscal operations.

Expenditures from the consolidated fund are subject to legislative approval. Article 114 of the Constitution provides that no money shall be withdrawn from the Consolidated Fund of India except under the appropriations made by laws passed in accordance with Articles 114, 115, and 116 by way of expenditure grants on the basis of demands for grants presented to Parliament, supplementary grants, additional or excess grants, advance grants, credit grants and exceptional grants. The appropriation act, authorizing withdrawals from the consolidated fund during a particular financial year, specifies the amount under revenue and capital (separately indicated for expenditure charged and voted) for specific services and purposes represented by a demand.

Contingency Fund of India

The fund records transactions connected with the contingency fund set up by the Government of India under Article 267 of the Constitution. Money from the contingency fund is primarily used for providing immediate relief to victims of natural calamities; it is also used for implementing new policy decisions of the government, pending their approval by Parliament. Money taken out of the fund are recouped from the consolidated fund. In other words, the contingency fund is a revolving corpus of funds to meet unforeseen expenses. No estimates of expenditure from the contingency fund are made as it is in the nature of an imprest and any advance from it has to be reimbursed.

Public Account of India

All public money received by the government, other than those intended for being deposited in the consolidated fund, are accounted for in the public account. It records transactions relating to small savings, provident fund, reserve funds, debt, deposits, advances, suspense, and remittances. In essence, money deposited in the public account are held in trust on behalf of the public and are to be returned in due course. Explicit approval of the Parliament is not required to incur expenditure from the public account. To that extent, the principle of lapse does not apply to funds held in the public account.

CLASSIFICATION OF EXPENDITURE

There are three broad classifications of expenditure: charged and voted, revenue and capital, and plan and non-plan.

Charged and Voted

The Union Budget shows separately the money required to meet the expenditure, which is to be *charged* on the Consolidated Fund of India, and other expenditures that are a part of the *voted* grant. The expenditures to be charged on the Consolidated Fund of India are defined in Article 112(3) of the Constitution. These include emoluments and allowances of the President of India; salaries, allowances, and pensions payable to judges of the Supreme

Court, the speaker and the deputy speaker of the Lok Sabha, the chairman and the deputy chairman of Rajya Sabha; the salaries, allowances, and pension payable to the CAG; and the expenditure incurred on the repayment of debt including interest. There can be discussion on charged expenditure in Parliament but no voting. Any demand for charged expenditure is shown separately as *charged* under the relevant subheads.

Revenue and Capital

Expenditure of a capital nature is broadly defined as expenditure incurred with the object of increasing the concrete assets of a material and permanent character.[9] Capital expenditure is generally met from the receipt of: a capital debt; deposit of banking character as distinguished from ordinary revenues derived from taxes, duties, fees, fines; and similar items of current income including extraordinary receipts.[10] Revenue expenditure is the expenditure for normal running of government departments and various services, interest charges on debt, subsidies, etc. Broadly speaking, expenditure that does not result in the creation of assets is treated as revenue expenditure. Expenditure of a capital nature is distinguished from revenue expenditure in the budget estimates.

Plan and Non-plan

Broadly, non-plan expenditure during a plan period represents the continuation of activities committed at the end of the previous plans. The following principles are adopted in the bifurcation of expenditure between non-plan and plan.

- All capital outlay is treated as plan.
- All capital and revenue expenditure on projects and activities not completed by the end of the previous plan period are treated as plan.
- All capital and revenue expenditure on new projects taken up during the current plan are treated as plan.
- Revenue expenditure on research and development schemes and continuing services is bifurcated between non-plan and plan.

The estimates of receipts and disbursements in the annual financial statement are shown in the same classification as in the departmental accounts. The idea of a common classification is to enable Parliament to make sense of the expenditure incurred by the departments and monitor their performance.

SECTORAL CLASSIFICATION

Chart of Accounts

The chart of accounts in the Indian government is made up of

- budget lines and their appropriations,
- expenses incurred against the budget lines,
- tax and non-tax revenues collected for financing government activities,
- grants and other capital receipts, and
- financing activities of the government.

Structure of the chart of accounts is based on a decimal classification, with hierarchically categorized levels such as the coded digital positions. The coding scheme allots four digits to a major head, each digit indicating the characteristics of the transaction as in the following.

0 or 1	revenue receipt
2 or 3	revenue expenditure
4 or 5	capital expenditure
6 or 7	public debt, loans, and advances
8	public accounts

There are major heads such as, 4000 for capital receipts and 8000 for the contingency fund. Generally, by deducting 2000 from the revenue expenditure major head, the corresponding revenue receipt major head can be obtained. Similarly, addition of 2000 to the code number major head of revenue expenditure would give the code number for the corresponding capital expenditure major head. Addition of 4000 to the revenue expenditure major head gives the code number for the corresponding loans and advances major heads. As a general rule, the second, third, and fourth digits are almost the same for the corresponding major heads in all the sections.

ACCOUNTING CLASSIFICATION

Till 1974, the accounting classification was with reference to the department in which the receipts and expenditure occurred, rather than to the functions, programmes, and activities to which they related. With effect from April 1974, the classification of transaction is made on a function-cum-programme basis. The system was further modified in April 1987, providing for listing plan programmes at the minor head level, and allotting four digits to major heads so as to provide room for accommodating new functions, as and when required. The classification of government accounts in India now follows a six-tier pattern.

First Tier: Sector Classification

This tier represents sectors and subsectors in terms of their broad economic category.

A. Consolidated Fund:
   - general services
   - social and community services
   - economic services
   - grants-in-aid and contributions
   - public debt, loans, and advances
   - inter-state settlements, transfer to contingency fund, etc.
B. Public Account:
   - small savings, provident fund
   - reserve funds
   - deposits and advances
   - suspense and miscellaneous
   - remittances
   - cash balance

Second Tier: Major Heads

Within the sectors there are subdivisions called major heads, corresponding to the various functions of government within the sectors. If several major heads have a common broad base within the sector this is indicated by subsector nomenclature such as general economic services, agriculture and allied services, industry and minerals, etc., in the sector economic services. Since most functions of the government also entail receipts, expenditure on revenue account and expenditure on capital account—major heads with the same or similar nomenclature often appear in the receipts section, revenue expenditure section, and capital expenditure section. Major head is a four-digit code. Sometimes, a sub-major head with a two-digit code representing a sub-function is also opened when a major head is subdivided, depending upon functions and needs.

Third Tier: Minor Heads

These form the next subdivision under major heads and relate generally to the various plan and non-plan programmes under a particular function represented by a major head. The expenditure on a programme is classified under the minor head relevant to the programme, below the concerned functional major head independent of the department that incurs the expenditure. In other words, the accounting classification is relevant to the purpose for which the expenditure is incurred, regardless of which organization incurs the expenditure. This is a three-digit code.

Fourth Tier: Subheads

Representing the next tier of classification, subheads show the activities, schemes, services and organizations under various programmes—and to that extent—the subheads reflect and identify the schemes undertaken in pursuance of a programme. In respect of non-developmental expenditure or expenditure of an administrative nature as distinguished from the schemes themselves, a subhead reflects the components of a particular programme, represented by the minor head. Subhead is a two-digit code.

Fifth Tier: Detailed Heads

These represent subschemes or organizations at the various subordinate administrative levels. Detailed head is a two-digit code.

Sixth Tier: Object Heads

These heads are primarily meant for itemized control over expenditure and indicate the object or nature of expenditure on a scheme or activity or organization in terms of inputs such as salaries, travel expenses, investment, and loans; otherwise known as objects of expenditure. They correspond to units of appropriation.[11]

Suspense Heads of Accounts

Transactions in government departments are carried out by issue or receipt of cheques or bank drafts by the concerned PAO. There is no system for exchanging accounts with other accounting authorities: settlement is made by issue of cheques. Accounting for the cheques issued is initially in the suspense section of the public account. The initial booking under a suspense head is cleared by a responding or contra-entry, that is, withdrawal of debit by minus debit and withdrawal of credit by minus credit. There is a system called review of balances, by which the precise liabilities in respect of outstanding balances in the public account are assessed. All accounts officers in the government are required to review and verify the balances and ascertain the correctness of the balances. The purpose of conducting this review is to ascertain the quality of maintenance of various books of accounts and reconciled figures in the public account.

COMPILING ACCOUNTS

The Rule 14 of Delegation of Financial Power Rules, 1978 authorizes a department to declare any gazetted officer as head of office. General Financial Rules permit the declaration of the head of office, or any other gazetted officer, as the drawing and disbursing officer (DDO). The DDO is responsible for examining the claims presented to ensure that a budget provision exists for payment of that claim, and then submitting the bill to his accredited PAO. The DDO is also responsible for (a) the amount drawn on a bill signed by him until he has paid it to the correct claimant and has obtained a legally valid acquittance and (b) the correct maintenance and timely rendition of accounts in respect of government funds handled by him. The payments are made only after precheck of the claims by the PAO but sometimes cheque drawing powers have also been delegated to some cheque drawing and disbursing officers (CDDO) who are located in places far away from the PAO but whose transactions are somewhat urgent and immediate.

Precheck Payment by the PAO

The most important function performed by a PAO is to verify the position regarding provision of funds. Before authorizing any expenditure from the consolidated fund, it is the responsibility of the accounts officer to ensure that: budget provision under the relevant head of account is available to meet the expenditure, the expenditure to be incurred conforms to the relevant provisions of the act, and the expenditure is covered by a sanction issued by the competent authority. To exercise exchequer control, the PAO maintains an appropriate audit register.

Banking Arrangements

The Reserve Bank of India (RBI) is the banker of the Government of India. As the RBI has branches only at a few places, all public sector banks have been designated as accredited banks for the ministries or departments to transact government business. A designated branch—the dealing branch— of the accredited bank handles the banking transactions of a PAO or CDDO of the ministry or department.

Payment Scroll and Receipt Scroll

A dealing branch honours the cheques issued by the PAO or the CDDO, enters all the cheques paid by it daily in a scroll in the form prescribed by the RBI. The dealing branch also renders daily, a payment scroll to a focal point branch of the accredited bank, and a copy of the scroll is also sent to the Cheque Drawing DDO (CDDO).

Transfer Entry

Transfer entry is a formal mechanism for making corrections in accounts and also for incorporating certain transactions in the accounts. In a transfer entry, the debit (or minus credit) appears on top from/(or to) which credit or minus debit flows to/(or from) the head of account indicated below. Amount transferred from one head to another is identifiable from the transfer entry. Typically, transfer entries are prepared to rectify misclassification in accounts, release grant in aid, and carry out periodic adjustments that do not involve cash outflow or inflow.

On the whole, there are three sources from which accounts are compiled, namely (1) bills that are passed for payment (vouchers) and delivered to the party concerned, (2) transfer entries, and (3) bank scrolls. The data for government accounts are generated at the PAOs. Except in the public works department, where the accounts are fed from adjustment and stock accounts also, accounts generated at the PAOs are cash transactions—money received and paid. When receipts are more than the payments, the difference is shown as payment to the Reserve Bank of India (debit to deposits with RBI); and when payments are more than the receipts, the difference is shown as withdrawal from the RBI(credits to deposits with RBI), and the accounts squared.

PERIODICITY OF COMPILING ACCOUNTS

Closing of Daily Transactions

At the end of each day, the cheques drawn are tallied with the entries in the cheque book and the 'register of cheques drawn'. Entries in the 'register of cheques delivered' are totalled at the end of each day and tallied with the total of the paid bills that are sent for compilation.

Compilation of Receipts

The receipt scrolls are linked to the challans enclosed and the totals are checked. Receipts are compiled in the compilation sheet under the concerned major heads. Debit side of the compilation sheet has a column for suspense and minus debit entries under the expenditure major heads, wherever necessary. At the end of each month, a grand total of credits in the compilation sheet—based on the postings of the receipted challans—is prepared and tallied with the grand total of the receipt scrolls.

Compilation of Expenditure

The paid vouchers are compiled daily. Correctness of the posting of each voucher is ensured by tallying the total of the debit of each voucher with the total of the credit noted for that voucher plus the net amount of the voucher, which represents the value of the PAO cheque or departmental cheque delivered.

Preparation of Departmental Classified Abstracts

This is prepared in two parts. Part one records the receipts under revenue, capital, debt, deposit, remittance, and suspense heads. These are arranged in the ascending order of major heads along with minor-, sub-, and object-heads.

Part two records the details for expenditure heads as well as advances in the public accounts section. These heads also show entries as being under the consolidated fund, contingency fund, and public account. Entries are posted for bills passed by the PAO and each DDO reporting to the PAO, as well as the transfer entries that have been made. The grand total in part one is tallied with the grand total in part two.

Departmental Consolidated Abstract

The consolidated abstract for a department is prepared in two parts. Part one for recording receipt transactions and part two for recording transactions for each year. Monthly totals are posted from the departmental classified abstract and progressive totals are struck for each month.

Proforma Corrections

Sometimes, after the accounts for a financial year are closed, there are cases in which corrections—to the figures already reflected in the previous financial years—are called for. In such cases, approval of the CGA is necessary for making these corrections. After obtaining his approval the corrections are reflected in the opening balances of the current year. In certain cases, proforma corrections are effected through an identifiable channel called Prior Period Adjustment Account (PPAA) after obtaining the approval of the CGA. Such a case could arise when the government changes the classification of financial transactions or loans given to the state governments as a result of implementing the recommendation of the Finance Commission, or with the takeover of institutions and conversion of the grant in aid given to the state governments into a loan.

While the accounts of the ministries and departments in the Government of India are compiled on a monthly basis, the appropriation accounts and finance accounts are prepared on an annual basis.

SINGLE-ENTRY SYSTEM

The government accounts are maintained on a single entry system, barring a few exceptions such as in the public works department, where entries are made for goods received on credit. The government accounts give the accounts of receipts and disbursements for the year, the accounts of the public debt, and the liabilities and assets as worked out from the balances recorded in the accounts. The revenue surplus or deficit is on cash basis therefore items receivable (arrears of tax where a demand is raised but accounts show the revenue only when realized) or payable (orders placed for purchases, liability incurred but accounted for only when the payment is actually made, or payment of interest on debts and loans and advances) or provision for depreciation of capital assets or valuation in stock do not figure in the accounts. When grants and loans (revenue expenditure) are used for capital formation, their classification in the accounts is not affected by the end use.

CASH ACCOUNTING IN PARLIAMENTARY SYSTEM

Cash accounting system is consistent with the legislative requirement for appropriating funds for the government. The finance ministry places before both the houses of Parliament in accordance with the provisions of Article 112(1) of the Constitution, an annual financial statement or the budget showing the estimated receipts and expenditure of the central government in respect of a financial year—before the commencement of that year. Under Article 151 of the Constitution, annual accounts of the Government of India along with the audit report of the Comptroller and Auditor General of India are to be placed before each house of Parliament. These accounts consist of appropriation accounts and finance accounts.

Appropriation Accounts

The appropriation accounts are statements of accounts indicating

- original budget estimates, supplementaries, surrenders, and reappropriations
- actual expenditure as a sum total of all the expenditures listed above
- excess or savings under the heads.

The appropriation accounts are prepared separately for revenue and capital sections and exhibit the charged and voted expenditures separately. In addition, all cases of variations exceeding one crore rupees—both savings and excess—are also explained in the appropriation accounts. The Comptroller and Auditor General of India certifies that the appropriation accounts have been examined under his direction and on the basis of information that his officers have obtained and that as a result of the test audit of the accounts, these accounts are correct.

Finance Accounts

The finance accounts are the nearest approximation of an auditor's presentation of the general accounts of the government to the Parliament. They present the classified and consolidated accounts of all transactions of the government under the consolidated fund, contingency fund, and public account. The finance accounts need to be certified by the CAG as, 'Correct statements of receipts and disbursements for the purpose of the Union, for a particular year, according to the best of his information as a result of test audit of the accounts.'[12]

The finance accounts are prepared in two parts, consisting of 12 statements. Part one includes:

1. statement of revenue receipts and expenditures
2. statement of debt position of the government
3. statement of the loans and advances given by the government
4. statement of the list of government guarantees provided
5. statement of the summary of balances as at the end of the financial year.

Part two provides:

1. statement of revenue receipts
2. statement of expenditure distributed between charged and voted in the consolidated fund
3. statement of revenue and capital receipts and expenditure by minor heads
4. statement of expenditure on the capital account
5. statement of investment in government corporations, companies, and cooperative societies
6. statement of receipts, disbursements, and balances relating to debt, deposits, and remittances in the contingency fund
7. statement of the debts and other interest-bearing obligations of the government

8. statement of the loans and advances given by the government
9. statement of the opening balance, the closing balance, and the interest received and credited to the government account.

The finance account, with its various statements, is a very important accounting document but the levels of disclosures in the statements are unacceptably low. The summary of balances— the statement number 5 in part one—is a case in point.

Summary of Balances

This is an important statement because it is more or less the trial balance of the Government of India. The following is a typical summary of positions as depicted in the finance accounts and presented to the Indian Parliament.

TABLE 2.1: SUMMARY OF BALANCES

Debit balances 1	Name of account 2	Credit balances 3	
	Consolidated Fund		
	(a) Government account		
	Public Debt		
	Loans and Advances		
	(a) Loans and advances	State	7601
	to state and union	UT	7602
	territory governments		
	(b) Other loans		7615
	Contingency Fund		
	(a) Contingency Fund		8000
	Public Account		
	(a) Small savings		8007
	(b) Provident Funds, etc.		8006
	Reserve Funds		
	(a) Reserve funds bearing interest		8116
	Gross balance		
	investment		
	(b) Reserve funds not		
	bearing interest		8228
	Deposits and Advances		
	(a) Deposits bearing interest		8336
	Gross balance		
	investment		

(b)	Deposits not bearing interest	8443
	Gross balance	
	investment	
(c)	Advances	8550
	Suspense and Miscellaneous	
(a)	Coinage accounts	8650
(b)	Suspense	8656
	Gross balance	
	investment	
(d)	Accounts with governments of	8679
	foreign countries	
	Remittances	
	Cash balance (closing)	8999

Source: The Budget Document.

Some headings in the summary of balances need explaining. The head titled government account in the consolidated fund receives certain debits and credits at the end of every financial year. Balances in heads 'inter-state settlement' and 'transfer to contingency fund' end up in the government account every year, and the balances in the two heads are transferred, at the end of the financial year, to the government account. The revenue account is also closed every year as the capital receipts and expenditure account (other than public debt and loans and advances accounts). The net deficit or surplus in these accounts, closed every financial year, is transferred to the government account. Under the system of bookkeeping followed in the Indian Government, the balances under government account represent the cumulative surplus and deficit of past years in the heads of accounts whose balances are not carried forward to next year's accounts. After adding to the government account, the balances under heads debt, loan, deposit, advances, suspense, and remittance and the contingency fund—the net amount is the closing cash balance at the end of the year and the balances thus worked out are proved.

The other headings in the summary hold balances for which the government has a liability to repay the money received or has a claim to recover the amount paid or they represent transactions pending for adjustment, as in the suspense or remittance heads. The balances are more or less the trial balance of the central government. But as we can see, this statement is not a complete record of the financial position of the Government of India because it does not account for the physical assets such as land and buildings owned by the government, nor does it give an indication of accrued dues or outstanding liabilities which are not brought into account.[13] Typically, neither the government accounts nor any other accounting document in the government provide a count of the total assets of the government and their value—either in terms of historical cost or the current market value.[14]

Some general observations about the budgetary process in Indian government need to be noted. First, a budget tells Parliament about the cash required to finance governmental activities, the cash to be raised to meet those requirements including the taxes received during a period, and the cash position of the government. It addresses the key question of affordability of government programmes and operations, and to that extent, it is also an accounting document.

Second, the budget estimates are made on a cash basis—they embody the cash outgo during a financial year, including the liabilities of the past years, to be paid during the current financial year or to be adjusted in the accounts of the current financial year before they are closed. The accounts of a financial year are kept open, for effecting adjustments, for about a month or two after the close of the year—provided that the adjustments in question relate to transactions completed in the concerned financial year.

Third, the estimates are not based on commitments. If an order is placed in a particular year and if the whole or part of the payment is to be effected during the next year, only the payment to be made in the particular year is included in estimates of that year and the balance is included in the estimates of the next year. Alternatively, if payment for an order placed in the previous year is made during the current financial year, the amounts needed for such payment are included in the estimates of the current year. Any unspent balance, out of the grants for a financial year, lapses and is not available for utilization in the following year.

Fourth, the estimates incorporate the requirements of government departments on a gross basis. Any recoveries from other departments or governments for joint projects or schemes or programmes are shown as deduct recoveries below the line at the end of the head Demand for Grant. The underlying principle is that Parliament gets the total picture of an expenditure at the point where it is incurred by withdrawal from the consolidated fund. If the partial recovery in question is from a public sector undertaking (PSU) or a non-government body, it is treated as the receipt of the government and no deduct recovery is made.

Fifth, estimates are based on the actual minimum requirements. Cushions for escalations which may arise in future or other additional requirements that may or may not arise on the basis of unexpected situations, are not provided. They are dealt with, if and when they arise.

On the whole, the budget in India is a compilation of highly detailed revenue mobilization and expenditure proposals that after their approval by the Parliament, are required to be scrupulously executed. So far as the accounting system in the Indian government is concerned, its sole purpose is to ensure that the departmental receipts and expenditure are in terms of the approval sanctioned by the legislature. It is as if the accounting system operates only to enable the legislature to discharge its appropriation function; in other words, to record and report whether the resources are obtained and used as voted by the legislature.

CONTROL OF EXPENDITURE AND CASH FLOW

Under the scheme of departmentalized accounting, monthly abstracts of expenditure and progressive total for each primary unit of appropriation are prescribed. The accounts officer concerned compiles an abstract of expenditure—by primary units—for each period, within three days of the close of the period. An abstract of liabilities is also prepared, primary unit-wise, within three days of the close of the period. The purchase section furnishes a statement to the accounts officer within three days of the close of the period. The accounts officer then submits to the head of the line department the statement of progress of expenditure during the remaining part of the year under each primary unit. The chief controller of accounts in the ministry makes an assessment of the likely expenditure during the remaining financial year and prepares a statement for the entire grant pertaining to each month, together with a note highlighting significant distortions and the likely savings and excesses in the grant as a whole.

The chief controllers of accounts in the ministries and the accounts officers in the line departments examine whether the excesses or savings foreseen are inevitable or whether they can be modified by corrective action such as enforcement of strict economy measures and pruning requirements (in the case of faster flow of expenditure) and quickening the pace of procurement and removing bottlenecks (in the case of slower flow of expenditure). If the decision is that the distortions cannot be removed and savings or excesses are inevitable, action to modify the sanctioned appropriation is taken by recourse to surrender, reappropriation, or sponsoring of supplementary grants.

HOW GOOD IS THE INDIAN ACCOUNTING SYSTEM?

In order to answer the question, we need to look at the functioning of the system with reference to the benchmark we had delineated in Chapter 1, namely compliance, stewardship, state of finances, performance, economic impact, and reliability of reported information.

Compliance

The function of compliance relates to the role of accounting system in demonstrating compliance with legislative approval. The cash accounting system in India is in a position to indicate whether the resources have been obtained and used in accordance with the budget. The inclusion of a column in the financial statements allows a direct comparison to be made between budgeted outlay and actual expenditure. The departments follow the scheme of departmentalized accounting, in terms of which statements of the progress in expenditure are prescribed (these provide abstracts of expenditure and progressive totals for each primary unit of appropriation on a periodic basis). With such information, it is possible to estimate savings from, and excesses over, the various grants and appropriations. On the whole, the system helps in demonstrating compliance with expenditure limits as voted by the Parliament.

Stewardship

An important objective of the accounting system is to generate information that is useful for exercising stewardship of public resources—both physical and financial. However, in this respect, accounting system in the Indian government starts with a handicap: it provides information on cash resources only. Consequently, the departments do not have a complete record of all the physical or financial assets they own, including the current value of these assets. Also the system does not fully record financial dues or outstanding liabilities that have accrued. The function of stewardship is also linked to how the departments use their resources, and the accounting system is not in a position to record how the resources have been used. This is primarily because expenditure on capital assets, which are used over many years is recorded only in the year when the expenditure is incurred and no subsequent account is taken of whether the assets created are still in use and what are the returns to the government from such use.

Added to this is the confusion created by the plan and non-plan distinction, which is essentially an adaptation of a pre-Independence mode of accounting. Plan expenditure is supposed to indicate developmental and capital formation activities, which increase the productive capacity of the economy, and the distinction between plan and non-plan expenditure is expected to accentuate the splitting of resources into capital and revenue (operating) costs. In practice, however, plan expenditures in the Indian government have always had a sizeable component of revenue expenditure, a subject which we discuss later in the chapter.

In the Indian government, all plan expenditure is regarded as developmental, and therefore 'good', while non-plan expenditure is regarded as wasteful, and therefore 'bad'. This being the case the size of the plan is considered politically very important, and that explains why there is always a tendency to inflate the size of plan expenditure. In order to have a bigger plan budget than the resources actually permit, the standard practice is to make over-optimistic revenue forecasts that ultimately do not materialize. Capital projects, even when unviable, are considered good proposals only because the expenditure is classified as plan. On the other hand, the plan and non-plan distinction has a clear bias against allocations for operating and maintenance expenditure, for the simple reason that such expenditures are classified as non-plan, and this has led to a situation where departments do not make adequate provision for operating and maintenance expenditure.

That brings us to the larger question of how financial resources are managed in the Indian government. The emphasis generally is on the control of inputs purchased rather than the outputs produced; in fact, even the most conscientious civil servant tends to concentrate on purchase of inputs, while paying very little attention to how these inputs are utilized to provide the promised output. For the less conscientious, procurement of inputs becomes the sole parameter of functioning. Typically the emphasis in a department is on how much money can be obtained, and not on how the best results can be achieved with an optimal use of resources. Every department looks for more land, larger buildings, and more equipment, with the result that success in procurement of inputs has become the synonym for achievement in government departments.

This also happens because the measured financial flows are in terms of expenditures incurred. Expenditures are not the same as expenses: expenses measure this year's costs of production whereas expenditures do not. Depreciation, for example, is an expense whereas capital expenditures are not. This is because capital expenditure during the current year create assets that are useful over a number of years into the future and cannot, therefore, be regarded as a cost of production for the current year only.

There is yet another serious flaw in how the accounting system encourages errant spending behaviour in government departments. Since the measured financial flows are in terms of expenditures for a financial year, there is a compulsion to spend the entire budgeted outlay by the end of it. In the accepted administrative vocabulary, if outlay is not spent it is considered a lapse; departments unable to incur expenditure for the entire budgeted outlay are taken to task and departments spending the entire outlay earn plaudits.

There is thus an incentive built into the accounting system encouraging the departments to spend their full budgeted outlay by the end of every financial year. The departments also have recourse to subterfuges such as parking the money in PSUs under their control, simply because money does not lapse in these undertakings as they account on an accrual basis.

This has other repercussions as well. The compulsion to spend the full budgeted outlay by the end of a financial year results in acquiring a level of inventory that far exceeds the requirements of the operations of the departments. For example, many departments (whose activities have a component of civil works) store up on cement and steel—carried forward in suspense accounts—ostensibly for works to be taken up in the future whereas, the entire exercise is undertaken to spend the annual budgeted outlay.

Ideally, the level of inventory in a department, and also for the government as a whole, should be set and maintained at the lowest possible level consistent with operational requirements. The high level of inventory results from an accounting system that enjoins the government departments to spend their full annual outlay through means fair or foul.

In respect of controlling expenditure and cash flows, elaborate procedures have been put in place to monitor departmental expenditure. In actual practice, however, departmental expenditure is never spaced evenly during the course of the financial year. The last quarter of the financial year invariably sees the most expenditure, and what is even worse, the last month of a financial year witnesses the highest expenditure behaviour. The result of such unevenly spaced expenditure is that the expenditure and receipts very rarely match in terms of time period.[15]

There are numerous cases of unreconciled suspense balances, extraordinary delays in remittance of government receipts by agency bankers, flagrant cases of excess reimbursement sought by the banks from the Reserve Bank of India, and underremittance of revenue to the government account.[16] What is worrisome is that they have serious implications for cash management and accountability to the legislature.

For example, the balances pending in suspense accounts relate to items that either have an expenditure impact or those which lead to an increase in the cash balance. This can hide functional expenditure by not reflecting them in the budget and in the accounts of the Consolidated Fund of India therefore it can be used as a subterfuge for incurring expenditure without proper parliamentary approval, and it can also lead to mismanagement of cash.[17]

A major critique of the cash accounting system in the UK government was that it allowed large sums of government moneys to be carried over as balances in suspense accounts, without being reconciled. Billions of pounds had been held in suspense accounts in the UK government by way of working capital. Elimination of suspense accounts altogether and a clearer accounting for capital in the UK government have brought about better management of cash.

STATE OF FINANCES

The accounting system records inflows and outflows of cash, whenever it is received or paid. On the basis of accounts generated at PAOs, cash flows are reported for budgetary revenues and expenditures as well as budgetary and non-budgetary receipts and payments. It is therefore possible to exercise control over the flows of money to the extent that they are not misappropriated or misused or diverted for purposes not officially intended. At the economy wide level, the annual financial statement shows the sources and types of revenues to be generated. It shows the cash required to finance the activities of the government, the cash raised to meet those requirements—including the taxes received during a period, and the cash position of the government.

The accounting system indicates how the expenditure is split into revenue (operating) and capital costs. But, as we noted, the distinction between operating and capital costs is not as sharp as it ought to be. This is for historical reasons. Ever since the adoption of a planned model of development, expenditure budgets are drawn up in two columns: plan and non-plan. Although the focus of planning is on capital formation, plan outlays have a complement of revenue expenditures as well. This did not matter in the early years because the revenue component of plan expenditure was tiny, and more importantly, there was enough revenue to take care of it.

Matters started taking a turn for the worse when surpluses evaporated from the non-plan revenue account, but revenue expenditures continued to be budgeted under the 'plan' head. Things were still manageable because of the regime of controls, which consisted of a high statutory liquidity ratio (SLR) mandate and administered interest rates. When liberalization came in in the early 1990s, the regime of controls was dismantled but the revenue component of plan outlays kept growing. In the absence of commensurate growth in resource mobilization efforts, this led to sizeable revenue deficits. In fact, the size of revenue deficit continues to grow at an alarming rate. For the Indian government, the revenue deficit increased from 4.2 per cent of

GDP in 1990–1 to 6.6 per cent in 2001–2.[18] The magnitude of revenue deficit is evident from the fact that it constituted 49.4 per cent of the fiscal deficit in 1990–1 and accounted for 70.2 per cent of the fiscal deficit in 2001–2.[19] The position in respect of the state governments is no better: the revenue deficit of the state governments has nearly trebled from 0.9 per cent in 1990–1 to 2.6 per cent of GDP in 2001–2.[20]

The quality of government expenditure has worsened over the years, because the rising revenue deficit makes it imperative that consumption expenditure takes precedence over public investment. This is clear from the fact that while the revenue deficit has mounted in the past several years as a percentage of GDP, public investment as a percentage of GDP has fallen steadily. From an average of 6.8 per cent of GDP in the latter half of the 1980s, capital expenditure of the central government has come down to 2.8 per cent today. The position obtaining in the states is no better. Capital expenditure of the state governments put together now stands at 2 per cent of GDP as against 3.2 per cent earlier. That being the case, it is clear that today's consumption expenditure is not being used to maintain the stock of assets. What is worse, it has squeezed the Indian government's capability to finance productive expenditure in the future.

Because of the growth in revenue deficits, the fiscal deficits have gone up. The consolidated fiscal deficit of the central and state governments, at 10 per cent of the GDP, is exceptionally high; in fact, the second highest in the world after Turkey.[21] As of now, over two-thirds of the consolidated fiscal deficit originates in the revenue budget and the bulk of the revenue receipts is spent on administrative expenditure, thereby making it imperative that large parts of other current expenditure are met out of borrowings. In fact, borrowings have come to finance bulk of the fiscal deficit; for example, net market borrowing financed 64.8 per cent of the gross fiscal deficit in 2001–2.[22] It is therefore not surprising that interest payments are the single largest item of expenditure on revenue account. In the budget for 2002–3, interest payments constituted 34.5 per cent of revenue expenditure and 47.9 per cent of net revenue receipts of the Centre.[23]

There is yet another disturbing trend. As we noted earlier, money deposited in the public account are mostly held in trust on behalf of the public and are to be returned in due course. But accruals in the public account are being used to finance the fiscal deficit. For example, in 2001–2, net accruals in the public account financed 27.19 per cent of the fiscal deficit,[24] and since the revenue deficit constituted 70.2 per cent of the fiscal deficit, a large part of the accruals in public account went to finance the revenue deficit.

What it means is that, liabilities in the public account have financed consumption expenditure; therefore, to return the money that is merely held in trust, fresh borrowings are necessary.

On the whole, the Indian government has reached a situation where it has to borrow or dip into trust money in order to meet administrative expenditure or service the debts. Clearly, the government is spending beyond its means; today's taxes and revenues are insufficient to cover today's costs. Reprehensibly, the cash accounting system is not in a position to indicate the appropriate balance between taxes and borrowing to finance the current expenses of the Indian government. Obviously, this is a clear case where the government is transferring costs from the taxpayers of the current generation to the taxpayers of future generations. It is a serious intergenerational equity issue, but the accounting system in the Indian government is unable to assess the degree to which the burdens being left to the future generations exceed those of the current generation.

PERFORMANCE

It is problematic to cost the activities of the departments in the Indian government because, with the information generated by the accounting system, it is not possible to determine the true cost of departmental activities. As we noted, costing of departmental activities fully is possible only when one takes into account all the relevant costs, including the non-cash costs, such as depreciation, cost of capital, debtors, creditors, stock balances, rents and pension, and then relate them more directly to the revenues generated by these activities. The biggest problem with the accounting system in the Indian government is that expenditure on a capital asset, which is used over many years, is recorded only in the year when the capital expenditure is incurred. In the absence of information on capitalization of assets, it is not possible to calculate depreciation and account for the assets in each period during which they were used. The other problem relates to pension costs— accounting system in the Indian government treats pension costs of government employees as an item of expenditure when the employees retire, instead of attributing the pension costs to the time period when they were working. On the whole, the accounting system has distorted the true costs of governmental activities.

As we discussed, information on the full costs of operations and costs of services is a powerful tool with which to drive efficiency improvement. In the absence of information on full costs, departmental activities cannot be appraised realistically. As a result, it is not possible to assess the economy and efficiency of operations of the departments or, for that matter, to judge whether the goals and objectives of a department have been fully met. In addition, in the absence of such information, the decision makers in the Indian government are not in a position to decide whether the government can afford to pay for the services it currently delivers and even more importantly, whether it can afford to pay for new services.

ECONOMIC IMPACT

The accounting system helps in monitoring progress of expenditure in a financial year. Since it recognizes only cash transactions, a liability is not recognized until cash is paid to discharge that liability. Two specific examples are government guarantees and pension payments.

Government Guarantees

Article 292 of the Constitution authorizes the Indian government to give guarantees for repayment of loans. Similar provisions exist authorizing the state governments to give guarantees. The Government of India provides many guarantees every year, and the worth of aggregate outstanding guarantees keeps growing from year to year. For example, the aggregate outstanding guarantees of the central government and 17 major state governments increased from Rs 90,734 crore to Rs 1,18,204 crore between March 1992 and March 1996.

The point to note is, when government provides guarantees, the long-term costs involved in these guarantees are not computed. For example, the system does not estimate how many loans guaranteed by the government would default and what would be the extent of losses to the government as a result of such default. Admittedly, when the government gives a guarantee—there is no immediate impact on expenditure—as there is no immediate cash paid to discharge the guarantee. That is why, the accounting system does not compute or reflect the extent of long-term costs hidden in the guarantees given by the Indian government. But the fact remains that liabilities on a large scale are being created and in case of their default, either fully or partially, the Indian government would be in serious financial difficulty.

Some of the recent developments are alarming. State governments are increasingly offering guarantees to finance state-sponsored entities in sectors such as power and irrigation. Very few of these projects are financially viable and the likelihood of default is very high. A study by CRISIL estimates that a sharp rise in debt service defaults is likely from 2003–4 onwards. Interestingly, the debt market has begun to price in a higher risk premium on state government guaranteed bonds.[25]

Pension Liabilities

It is difficult to make a proper estimation of the pension liability of the Indian government because the pension data generated by the accounting system is unreliable. This fact is evident from the slippages between budget estimates and the actual pension payments made by the departments, as the table below shows. In essence the slippages mean that the accounting is not capable of making an accurate estimate of the pension liability, even for one year.

TABLE 2.2: DIVERGENCE BETWEEN BUDGET ESTIMATES AND ACTUAL EXPENDITURE

Year	Defence		Civil		Railways	
	BE*	Actuals	BE*	Actuals	BE*	Actuals
1	2	3	4	5	6	7
						(Rs in crore)
1990–1	1500	1670	503	480	835	886
1991–2	1750	1840	552	583	963	1040
1992–3	1780	2313	602	701	1144	1251
1993–4	2379	2531	745	818	1516	1448
1994–5	2706	2704	910	934	1700	1686
1995–6	3082	3197	998	1103	1970	2117
1996–7	3300	3683	1220	1425	2350	2509
1997–8	3715	4947	1550	1948	2500	3509
1998–9	5923	7270	1432	2803	2300	4144
1999–2000	7349	11,024	2800	3286	3300	4018
2000–1	12,000	10,539	3865	4021	5314	5167

Source: Ministry of Finance (2001).
Note: *Budget estimates.

Pension Liability in the Medium and Long-Term

The Indian government had set up a working group in October 1999 to 'make a scientific and comprehensive assessment of the liability arising from payment to current and future retirees',[26] and the working group gave its report in June 2001. It projected, pension liability of the Indian government would rise to Rs 29,891 crore in the fiscal year 2009–10 given an inflation rate of 6 per cent. At an inflation rate of 10 per cent per annum, the liability would increase to Rs 33,558 crore. Interestingly, the working group took great pains to point out that its projections regarding the pension liability in the medium or long term might at best be unreliable. It said, 'the working group has serious reservations that the projections of pension outlays in this report are extremely unreliable.'[27]

On the whole, the accounting system is not in a position to estimate the costs involved in pension payments, neither for the present or in the medium and long term. The point to note is, medium- and long-term pension liabilities of the Indian government are liabilities that are created by the current generation for the future generations. But the exact amount of liability shifted to future generation is not recorded by the accounting system.

Our discussion of government guarantees and pension liabilities makes it clear that the accounting system in Indian government does not generate information to assess the longer-term economic impact and sustainability of the fiscal policies (by not bringing to account the future expenditure implications of decisions in the period in which these decisions were made). This is primarily because of the unacceptably low levels of disclosure that the accounting system permits. In fact, the advisory group on fiscal transparency set up by the Reserve Bank of India emphasized the need for greater transparency in government accounting; the group highlighted the essentiality of improved disclosure norms for government debt, subsidies, off-budget borrowings, contingent liabilities, and revenue exemptions granted by the Indian government.

RELIABILITY OF REPORTED INFORMATION

The media routinely reports a succeeding government (belonging to a different political party) accusing the previous government of having drained the official exchequer and leaving the finances in a dreadful mess. This happens all the time, but the question is—how could this possibly happen if the accounting system generated information that is reliable? The simple answer is, the accounting system allows the Indian government to massage financial information in order to present the fiscal reality differently from what it actually is. This is commonly done in respect of government subsidies and loans, the trick is to record the cash outlay at face value. This is to make the financial implications of the subsidies and loans look much smaller than they really are.

Another common trick in India is to defer or advance the cash payments or receipts. The idea is to manipulate the measurement of surplus or deficit by the simple expedient of varying the timing of the cash payments or receipts.

Yet another trick is to overestimate revenues and underestimate expenditure while presenting the budget. For example, the deficit of the Government of India for 2002–3 was presented in the budget at 5.3 per cent: it was stated that the tax revenue for the year would increase by 22.8 per cent over the previous year's actual receipts and total revenues would increase by 17.6 per cent. But the deficit went up to 5.9 per cent in the revised estimates, and the deficit went up even further by the time the actual numbers were available. Same is the case with revenue deficit; it was budgeted at 3.8 per cent of the GDP, it had gone up to 4.3 per cent in the revised estimates and in reality, the actual numbers were even higher.[28]

The departments routinely book expenditure when, in effect, no expenditure has been incurred. This may sound like a conjurer's trick, but all that the departments do is to park their unspent moneys in public sector undertakings. The practice is so widespread that even the CAG has stopped objecting to this. In any case, the overall result is that expenditure is shown while no expenditure has been incurred.

The whole idea is to show a financial position and performance that is better than it actually is. The provocations may vary; over-optimistic revenue forecasts so as to permit a bigger plan budget for political reasons, parking money in non-lapsing havens and showing more expenditure than is incurred. Whatever the provocation, the fact remains that the accounting system in the Indian government has offered excellent opportunities for fiscal trickery.

SHORTCOMINGS OF THE INDIAN SYSTEM OF ACCOUNTING

Our discussion throws up several shortcomings in the functioning of the accounting system in the Indian government. These are:

- it does not help in management of assets and cash
- it distorts the true cost of government
- it concentrates on control of inputs purchased rather than the outputs produced and outcomes achieved
- it does not address intergenerational equity issues
- it provides opportunities for fiscal trickery.

These are serious shortcomings and have important consequences for the Indian government as a whole. A number of countries have implemented accounting reforms in the last two decades, seeking to address these shortcomings. It is to a discussion of the experience of these countries with their accounting reforms that we return in the next few chapters.

NOTES

1. Pant (1998), p. 21.
2. Department of Expenditure (2003), p. 7.
3. Ramanathan (1999), p. 18.
4. Department of Expenditure (2003), p. 8.
5. Pant (1998), p. 121.
6. Ibid., p. 130–1.
7. Thapliyal and Pattanayak (2003), p. 5.
8. Ramanathan (1999), p. 87.
9. General Financial Rules, Rule 291(1).
10. General Financial Rules, Rule 291 (2) notes.
11. Thapliyal and Pattanayak (2003), pp. 7–9.
12. Ramanathan (1999), p. 240.
13. Ibid., pp. 243–4.
14. Pant (2003), p. 32.
15. Pant (1998), p. 127.
16. Ibid., p. 22.
17. Burman (2003), p. 67.
18. Economic Survey (2002–3), p. 40.
19. Ibid., p. 22.
20. Ibid., p. 38.
21. Aiyar (2003).
22. *The Economic Times*, 28 February (2003b), p. 3.
23. Economic Survey (2002–3), p. 30.
24. Burman (2003), p. 61.
25. Ganguly (2002), p. 3.
26. Ministry of Finance (2001), p. 1.
27. Ibid., p. 4.
28. Rao (2003).

3

Accrual Accounting in the New Zealand Government

Historically, the government in New Zealand has played an active role in regulating economy; at least from the late nineteenth century. Based on its experience of the Second World War, during which central planning was successfully used to direct the economy, a consensus developed among three major groups of New Zealand society—farmers, manufacturers, and workers—on the usefulness of an interventionist state to regulate the economy. The consensus, based broadly on the understanding that the government should act when matters needed attention and intervene when market failed to produce the desired outcomes, was sustained for almost two decades of full employment.

However, the period from the 1960s to 1980s was a bad time for the economy. In terms of GNP (gross national product) per capita, the country fell from fifth place in the world to the twentieth. During the period, New Zealand's economy suffered from two major shocks. The first shock was in the 1970s—New Zealand was deprived of its assured market when United Kingdom joined the European Community. The second shock came from the OPEC oil crisis. The first deprived New Zealand of its protected market for agricultural exports, the second drove up the cost of energy. Growth came to a virtual halt. Inflation soared as it did in other countries, but it persisted in double digits even after cost pressures had eased in other countries. Unemployment rose steadily. So did the fiscal deficit—it reached 9 per cent of the GDP in 1984. Interest rates spiralled, as did the budget deficit. Most ominous was a run on the New Zealand dollar, which lost more than half of its value against the US dollar during 1974–83.

A currency crisis developed in the first half of 1984; there was a substantial outflow of foreign exchange, and to add to the government's woes, the crisis coincided with its 1984 parliamentary elections. In the elections, the National Party lost its majority and was replaced by a Labour Party government. The foreign exchange market was shut down immediately after the election; when it reopened, the New Zealand dollar was devalued by 20 per cent.

The 1984 election was a watershed. It signalled a fundamental change in the attitudes of people in the New Zealand regarding the interventionist state and its role in the economy. There was now an acceptance that the interventionist state had not done much to relieve the economic stress. Clearly, the post-war consensus on the efficacy of an interventionist state had broken down. This was also the time when people talked of new economic and management concepts, which suggested novel ways of managing the State. The convergence of economic stress, a non-performing government, new political capacity, and new economic and management concepts made the adoption of radical public management reforms possible in New Zealand.

The results of 1984 election were seen as a mandate for change, and the newly elected Labour Party government of Prime Minister David Lange came out with its agenda of making sweeping changes in the public sector. The case for reforms was most forcefully argued by Roger Douglas, minister of finance in the new government, therefore the changes in economic policy brought about by the Labour Party governments (1984–90) were known collectively as Rogernomics—after Roger Douglas. The essence of Rogernomics was dismantling of the regime of regulation and subsidies and a conversion to the free play of market forces.[1]

PUBLIC SECTOR REFORMS

The period from 1984 to 1987 saw the introduction of some preliminary reforms in the area of decentralization of decision-making.[2] An exercise known as the Removal of Constraints was undertaken in mid-1986. The State Services Commission, after a detailed review, abolished a large number of controls that the government exercised over day-to-day management of the line departments. These central controls were largely in the areas of fixation of salary, job classification, appointment, dismissal, and other aspects of personnel management. As a result, some 95 per cent of the 2000 or so detailed instructions contained in the Public Service Manual—the code governing the conditions of employment—were withdrawn.

THE LEGAL FRAMEWORK

The more serious public sector reforms started with the enactment of three legislations: the State-Owned Enterprises Act 1986, the State Sector Act 1988, and the Public Finance Act 1989. These three legislative enactments provided the basis for public sector reforms in New Zealand.

The State-Owned Enterprises Act 1986

The State-Owned Enterprises Act provided the basis for corporatization of the old trading departments of the government. The legislation was enacted in 1986, changing the trading departments into state-owned enterprises (SOEs)— business organizations along private sector lines. The SOEs were set up with a capital structure, but expected to function like private sector companies. They were required to pay taxes and earn a competitive rate of return on equity. Many functions of the government were corporatized with the result that these organizations became much more efficient. The process of corporatization proved that, inefficient organizations could register strong efficiency gains with the introduction of modern commercial financial management systems and infusion of professional competence.[3]

RESTRUCTURING

It was the rewarding experience of corporatization efforts that encouraged the government to introduce similar measures in the core, budget-dependent departments. The results were impressive. From 53 departments with approximately 86,000 staff in mid-1984, the public service was reduced, by 31 December 1993, to 35 departments with 34,000 full time equivalent staff. A substantial number of core public service jobs were also eliminated through downsizing, reorganization and rationalization, and in some cases, by direct privatization of departments.

State Sector Act 1988

The State Sector Act of 1988 made major changes in the management, personnel, and labour practices of the government. Chief executives were now appointed to be in charge of line departments for a fixed term, under contract with the State Services Commission. They were given all the rights, duties, and powers of an employer in respect of their departments. They were also authorized appoint staff and remove them. In addition, labour relations in the government departments were no longer subject to legislative provisions and central control.

Public Finance Act 1989

The Public Finance Act of 1989 introduced financial management reforms, key elements of which are set out below.

CLARIFICATION OF THE NOTION OF PERFORMANCE

The Public Finance Act introduced the output and outcome system as the basis for accountability relationship between ministers and chief executives. Under the new system, a conceptual distinction was made between the two interests that a minister has in his department: a purchase interest and an ownership interest. When exercising the ownership interest, the minister seeks to get the best possible returns on the resources invested in the department. In respect of the purchase interest, the minister purchases the agreed outputs and the chief executive of a department supplies them. What this means is that the minister can purchase services from departments other than his own, or even from the private sector, if the outputs provided by his department do not compare favourably in terms of cost, quality, and timeliness.

PERFORMANCE AGREEMENT

The Public Finance Act provides for a performance agreement to be signed between the chief executive and the concerned minister every year. The performance agreement is in three parts. The first part describes key result areas that require personal attention of the chief executive. The expected results are expressed in verifiable terms, and include output-related tasks. The second part sets out detailed information about the outputs to be purchased. Since 1993–4, this output information has taken the form of purchase agreements. The purchase agreement is intended to provide the minister with information to assess the value of departmental outputs, and make comparison with similar outputs across the public and private sectors. The third part provides information on the stewardship of public assets. It describes the ways and means by which the medium and long-term commitments of the government are managed. In other words, this part is intended to reflect the appropriate levels of investment and, to that extent, ownership interest of the minister.

APPROPRIATIONS

In respect of appropriations, the Act replaced the previous line-item system. The system consisted of single departmental votes subdivided into programmes, and programmes into categories of inputs, with an accrual appropriation system based on outputs. The act calls for separate appropriations to be voted, authorizing resources for the purchase of outputs, capital, and transfer payments. Resources voted by Parliament follow the costing provided by the agencies themselves and are in terms of outputs as agreed in the performance agreements.

FREEDOM FROM TREASURY CONTROL

The act devolves financial management and control from the treasury to the line departments. The chief executives are made responsible for financial management, financial performance, accounting requirements, and asset and cash management in their agencies. In other words, the tight regimen of input control that the treasury exercised was dismantled and there was devolution of financial management to the line departments.

INCENTIVES

Combined with the devolution of financial management, three kinds of incentives were provided to the line departments.

1. *Levy of a capital charge:* A capital charge is a charge on the cost of capital tied up in the assets of a line department. The capital charge applies an interest rate to capital invested in the department, creating an actual cost for capital. The capital charge is paid into the central accounts of the treasury by the line departments.
2. *A cash management scheme:* Under the cash management scheme, while the government's aggregate cash position is centrally managed, the line departments are permitted to have their own bank accounts and are made responsible for managing their own working capital. There is now a system of rewards and penalties (in terms of interest) on the basis of how well the line departments manage their working capital, thereby providing the incentives to plan and forecast departmental cash requirements and align them with the planned levels and disincentives for default.
3. *The facility of retaining the proceeds from the sale of their assets:* This is a dispensation under which the line departments are allowed to retain the proceeds from the disposal of their surplus assets and, to that extent, the line departments are encouraged to improve their asset management.

ACCOUNTING SYSTEM REQUIREMENTS

These changes meant that the government's accounting system needed to reflect the new structure of accountabilities required by the public sector reforms. In designing the new accounting system, the way performance was defined became the determining factor. It was understood that various elements of the reforms should reinforce each other, with performance being the common referent. In order to reflect performance, the accounting system had to meet several requirements. It needed to generate information to enable comparisons of efficiency and effectiveness of government activities across public and private sectors. It also needed to generate information to produce statements of service performance. In addition, the accounting system had to generate aggregate financial information for the government as a whole.[4] The most critical element in defining performance was the distinction between the government's ownership interest and its interest as a purchaser. The distinction implied that the accounting system had to be in a position to capture both these perspectives.

An accrual system of accounting was in a position to meet all these requirements. It was a necessary prerequisite for the measurement of both the ownership and purchase interests of the government. In effect, the ownership interest implied using of the same financial reporting format as used in the private sector. This included distinguishing the capital and current expenditure, and use of full accrual accounting to monitor the performance of government's investment. The purchase interest implied using the same type of information as provided in the sales contracts in private sector, such as quantity, quality, time and place of delivery, and price. Decisions about output pricing and production required information about total resources used (costs) and not merely the cash outlay. In other words, adoption of accrual accounting was necessary to fully assess the ownership interest and to accurately cost the resource use in producing outputs.

In addition, the use of accrual accounting enabled assessment of performance in relation to output production, provision of information to the legislature about the effectiveness and efficiency of resource use, comparisons of efficiency and effectiveness across governmental activities and between the government and private sector, assessment of the performance of government departments and the achievement of the government's wider strategic goals, and production of aggregate financial information for the government as a whole.

ADOPTION OF GENERALLY ACCEPTED ACCOUNTING PRACTICE

The Public Finance Act made the adoption of accrual accounting a statutory requirement. The act also stipulated that the financial statements of the departments, and for the government as a whole, should conform to the generally accepted accounting practice (GAAP). This served three strategic purposes.

1. Given the fact that GAAP was oriented to private sector companies, private sector resources could be used in the process of implementing accrual accounting arrangements in the government departments, thereby avoiding the need for treasury to engage in policy-making activities.
2. The flow of financing skills and accounting staff between the government departments and private sector could be facilitated.
3. Use of the same reporting practices as in the private sector could facilitate the understanding of government financial information by the members of the public.

On the whole, while developing an accounting system in New Zealand, practices from the private sector and overseas were adopted. But in areas where neither private sector practice nor overseas experience was applicable, accounting policies specific to the item being reported were developed.

STANDARDS SETTERS

The Accounting Standards Review Board (ASRB), a statutory body, was established as the standards setter. It was stipulated that the Institute of Chartered Accountants of New Zealand (ICANZ) would submit financial reporting standards and the ASRB would review and approve the reporting standards. The Financial Reporting Standard Board (FRSB) of ICANZ is the primary developer of financial reporting standards. Approval by the ASRB means that the standards have legal backing as they apply to the Crown, government departments, Crown entities, local authorities, issuers of securities, and to all companies.[5] A significant feature of the standards setting arrangement in New Zealand is that a common set of standards is established both for the public and private sectors.

IMPLEMENTATION

An implementation strategy was also planned. There were three main stages in the process of implementation.[6]

- The first stage was to fulfil the statutory requirement of the Public Finance Act for all departments to conform to GAAP.
- The second stage involved establishing a relationship between the

departments adopting accrual accounting and accrual reporting for the whole-of-government.

- The third phase involved adoption of accrual accounting by other entities owned by the Crown. The act required these bodies to report to the New Zealand Parliament on their services and financial performance in the same format as the line departments were required to do.

The implementation strategy set out the responsibilities for the various levels of the government.

THE TREASURY

The treasury was made responsible for:

- ensuring that all participants involved in the process of implementation fully understood the nature of the changes to be introduced. The treasury did this with three tools: (a) a video which captured the key ideas, (b) a plain-language booklet which described the elements of the reforms and the nature of the new legislation, and (c) briefings for senior civil servants in the line departments
- developing accounting policy parameters, within which departmental accounting policies were to be grounded. As the standards used in the private sector—under GAAP—were adopted as the default standards for the government, policy making by the treasury was required only in exceptional cases where neither GAAP nor private sector experience was available
- establishing the central cash-management system and contracting out for the government's banking services. The work, in turn, was entrusted to Westpac Banking Corporation—a major trading bank in New Zealand— which provided state-of-the-art banking services with low transaction costs as well as centralized cash and debt management for the treasury
- exercising quality control over the reform implementation process and approving the readiness of departments to move on to the new system.

THE DEPARTMENTS

The responsibilities of each line department included:

- developing accrual accounting arrangements within a two-year time frame from 1 July 1989

- preparation of an opening balance sheet. A necessary prerequisite for preparing the balance sheet was to identify surplus properties which had to be sold off subsequently
- specifying in consultation with the treasury, its broad classes of outputs, which, then, became the basis for accrual based appropriation
- development of cost allocation systems to enable the allocation of all departmental costs to outputs. The costs to be allocated included overhead costs, depreciation, and a charge to be levied on the capital employed by the department
- development of a system of cash management including the opening of departmental bank accounts. Idle balances were to be deposited with the central treasury where they earned interest
- the chief executive taking full responsibility for financial management of the department including the integrity and reliability of the information which he provides to the treasury and the minister.
- six-monthly and annual requirements to report a full set of financial statements on an accrual basis as well as statements of service performance (delivery of outputs) and a statement of responsibility for the reliability of information in the statements and the internal control system operated by the department. These statements were required to be audited.

These departmental developments were completed by 1 January 1991.

ACCRUAL REPORTING FOR THE WHOLE-OF-GOVERNMENT

The first set of financial statements for the Government of New Zealand on an accrual basis were prepared for the six months ending 31 December 1991. For this set of statements and the following annual set, the reporting entity was limited to ministers, departments and offices of Parliament. The financial statements showed more clearly the economic impact of government activity and allowed the determination of government's net worth.

TIMELINE FOR IMPLEMENTATION

The transition to accrual accounting in New Zealand was achieved in a relatively short period of time. The Public Finance Act, requiring departments to develop accrual accounting arrangements, was passed in early 1989; it gave the departments two years to move from cash to accruals systems. However, all but three of the approximately 45 departments made the transition within one year. From the time the Public Finance Act was passed in 1989 to the time when the first Crown financial statements with full budget and actual comparisons were presented in 1994, it had taken only five years. The following table gives the time taken for implementation of accrual accounting.

TABLE 3.1: IMPLEMENTATION OF ACCRUAL ACCOUNTING

Year	Event
1989	Public Finance Act passed
	Departments begin the move to accrual accounting
1990	All departments on accrual accounting
1991	Capital charge introduced
	First Crown financial statements
1992	First annual Crown financial statements
	First consolidated Crown financial statements and Public Finance Amendment Act passed
1993	First annual consolidated Crown financial statements
	Purchase agreements and nondepartmental output specification
	Financial Reporting Act passed
1994	First accrual budget for Crown
	Fiscal Responsibility Act passed
	First Crown financial statements with full budget actual comparison

Source: Ball, Dale, Eggers, and Sacco (2000).

ELEMENTS OF THE ACCOUNTING SYSTEM

The principal elements of the accounting system are assets, liabilities, revenues, and expenses. The elements were defined as in the following.

ASSETS

Foreign Monetary Assets

Where foreign monetary assets are subject to forward exchange contracts, they are translated at the contract rate. Otherwise, foreign monetary assets are translated at the closing exchange rate.

Receivables and Advances

Receivables and advances are recorded at the amounts expected to be ultimately collected in cash.

Inventories

Inventories are valued at the lower of cost and net current value.

Investments

Marketable securities held for trading purposes are recorded at net current value.

Equity investments (other than those forming part of the reporting entity) are recorded at the lower of the cost and net current value.

Other investments, including marketable securities held for investment, are valued at lower of the cost and net current value.

Physical Assets

Land and buildings are recorded at net current value. In cases where valuations conducted in accordance with New Zealand Institute of Valuers' standards are not available, valuations conducted in accordance with the Valuation of Land Act 1951 are used.

Specialist military equipment is recorded at depreciated replacement cost. Valuations are done on the basis of specialist assessment by New Zealand Defence Force advisers.

Other plant and equipment, which includes motor vehicles and office equipment, is recorded at cost minus accumulated depreciation.

State highways are recorded at depreciated replacement cost based on the estimated present cost of constructing the existing asset. Land associated with the state highways is valued at net current value.

Commercial forests are recorded at estimated net current value. This takes into account age, quality of timber, market expectations, and the forest management plan.

Other physical assets, for which an objective estimate of market value is difficult to obtain (the national parks for example) are recorded at the best estimate of net current value. The valuation base and amount are disclosed in the notes to the financial statements.

Intangible assets that can be sold or have been acquired separately from other assets are recorded at the net current value if a foreseeable future benefit exists. Otherwise, intangible assets are not recognized.

LIABILITIES

Borrowings including swaps, are recorded at nominal value adjusted for the unamortized portion of the premium or discount on issue.

Foreign Monetary Liabilities

Where foreign monetary liabilities are subject to forward exchange contracts, these are translated at the contract rate. Otherwise, foreign monetary liabilities are translated at the closing exchange rate.

Exchange gains and losses are included in the operating statement of the period in which they arise.

Pension Liabilities

Pension liabilities, in respect of the contributory service of superannuation scheme members, are recorded at the latest actuarial value of the Crown's liability for pension payments, adjusted for any subsequent movements in value.

Currency Issued

Currency issued represents a liability in favour of the holder.

Currency issued for circulation, including demonetized currency, is recognized as a liability at face value. There is also a liability for the face value of collectors' currency. However, as it is most unlikely that the collectors' currency will be returned for redemption, its face value is classified as a contingent liability. Unissued currency stocks are reported as inventory and expensed when issued.

Compensated Absence

Liabilities for annual leave are recognized as they accrue to employees. Provision is also made for expected payments of long service and retiring-leave obligations to employees.

Leases

Finance leases transfer to the Crown (as lessee) substantially all risks and rewards incident on the ownership of a leased asset. The obligations under such leases are capitalized at the present value of the minimum lease payments. The capitalized values are amortized over the period in which the Crown expects to receive benefits from their use.

Operating leases, where the lessors substantially retain the risks and regards of ownership, are recognized in a systematic manner over the term of the lease.

The cost of leasehold improvements is capitalized and amortized over the unexpired period of the lease or the estimated useful life of the improvements, whichever is shorter.

Other Liabilities

All other liabilities are recorded at the estimated obligation to pay.

REVENUES

The revenue recognition points are as in the following.

Revenues	Recognition Points
Source deductions	When an individual earns income

Residents withholding interest tax	When an individual is paid dividends, subject to deduction at source
Fringe benefit tax	When benefits are provided that give rise to the fringe benefit tax
Provisional tax	Payment due date
Terminal tax	Assessment filed date
Goods and services tax	Payment due date
Excise duty	When goods are subject to duty
Road user charges	When payment for the charge is made
Motor vehicle fees	When payment for the fee is made
Stamp cheque and credit card duties	Assessment filed date
Other indirect taxes	When the debt to the Crown arises

Revenue Earned Through Operations

If revenue has been earned by the Crown in exchange of provision of outputs (products or services) to third parties, then the Crown receives its revenue through operations. Such revenue is recognized when it is earned.

Investment Income

Investment income is recognized in the period in which it is earned.

Premiums

Premiums arising on the issue of a debt instrument are treated as a reduction in the cost of borrowing.

Premiums are recognized on issue, and amortized over the period of the instrument on a yield-to-maturity basis.

Gains

Realized gains arising on sales of assets or on the early repurchase of liabilities are recognized in the operating statement of the period in which the transactions occur.

Unrealized foreign exchange gains, on monetary assets and liabilities and unrealized gains arising from change in the value of commercial forests and marketable securities held for trading purposes, are recognized at the balance sheet date in the operating statement.

Unrealized gains arising from changes in the value of physical assets (excluding commercial forests) are recognized at balance sheet date. To the extent that a gain reverses a loss previously charged to the operating statement, the gain is credited to the operating statement. Otherwise, gains are credited to an asset-revaluation reserve for that class of asset.

Unrealized gains (excluding foreign exchange gains) arising from changes in the value of investments and marketable securities held for investment are recognized at balance sheet date only to the extent that they reverse a loss previously charged to the operating statement. Gains effecting such reversal are credited to the operating statement.

Expenses

Expenses are recognized in the financial period to which they relate.

Welfare Benefits

Welfare benefits are recognized in the reporting period when an application for benefit has been accepted and the eligibility criteria met.

Grants and Subsidies

Where grants and subsidies are discretionary until payment, the expense is recognized when the payment is made. Otherwise, the expense is recognized when the specified criteria has been fulfilled and notice has been given to the Crown.

Discounts

Discounts arising on the issue of a debt instrument are treated as an increase in the cost of borrowing.

Discounts are recognized on issue and amortized over the period of the instrument on a yield-to-maturity basis.

Losses

Realized losses arising from sales of assets or the early purchase of liabilities are recognized in the operating statement in the period in which the transaction occurs. Unrealized foreign exchange losses on monetary assets and liabilities and unrealized losses arising from changes in the value of commercial forests and marketable securities held for trading purposes are recognized at balance sheet date in the operating statement.

Unrealized losses (excluding foreign exchange losses) arising from changes in the value of physical assets (excluding commercial forests), investments, and marketable securities held for investment are recognized at balance sheet date. Unrealized losses are first applied against the revaluation reserve for that class of asset. The balance, if any, is charged to the operating statement.

Foreign Currency Transactions

For short-term transactions covered by foreign exchange contracts, the forward rates specified in those contracts are used to convert the transactions to New Zealand dollars.

Otherwise, transactions in foreign currencies are converted into New Zealand dollars using the exchange rate on the date of the transaction. Exchange variations arising out of the transactions are recognized in the operating statement.

Outstanding foreign exchange contracts are translated at the closing exchange rate. Exchange gains and losses are included in the operating statement in the period in which they arise. The forward margin associated with forward exchange contracts is amortized over the period of the contract on a straight-line basis.

Depreciation

Depreciation is provided on a straight-line basis at rates calculated to allocate the cost or valuation of an asset, less any estimated residual value, over its estimated useful life. Typically, the estimated useful lives of different classes of assets are as follows:

Assets	Useful lives
Freehold buildings	25 to 60 years
Specialist military equipment	5 to 25 years
Other plant and equipment	3 to 25 years
State highways	
Pavements	25 years
Bridges	90 years

Research and Development Costs

Research costs are charged to the operating statement as incurred. Development costs are also charged to the operating statement as incurred, except where future benefits can be reasonably expected to exceed those costs. Where development costs are deferred, they are amortized over future periods on a basis related to expected future benefits.

REPORTING SYSTEM

As a subset of the accounting reforms, a comprehensive system of financial reporting was developed. The groundwork was laid with the passage of the Public Finance Act 1989, which required a full set of financial statements from the government. Each government department was required to generate the following:

- statement of financial information
- operating statement
- statement of cash flow
- statement of objectives
- statement of service performance
- statement of commitments
- statement of contingent liabilities
- statement of unappropriated expenditure
- statement of accounting policies
- comparative actual figures for the previous year.

The system of financial reporting is at different levels of aggregation for different principals. The most disaggregated information is reported to the minister associated with each chief executive. A recent innovation has been the concept of the purchase agreement, which is a fairly detailed account of the service delivery that is contracted for by the minister and is made available to the treasury, to other ministers, and to central agencies for preparing the annual budget and for considering longer-term financial planning.

At the next level of aggregation, information is made available to the cabinet for its consideration in preparing the budget. For parliamentary appropriation, outputs are aggregated to the output classes: homogeneous category of outputs are entered into the estimates document that accompanies the appropriation bill presented to the Parliament. This has produced far greater amount of information about the activities of the government departments than in the cash accounting system. The information is intelligible in terms of what is being delivered rather than how much has been spent on labour, capital, or equipment. For example, the New Zealand Defence Force now has about sixty pages in the estimates document, compared with about six in the cash-based format.

Parliament is also presented annually with a corporate plan for each department, which summarizes both the output and ownership plans that are scrutinized by parliamentary committees at the beginning of the financial year. During the financial year the treasury monitors, on a monthly basis, the expenditures on outputs and scrutinizes significant exceptions. At the end of the financial year, a full set of accounts and a statement of output delivery are prepared, which are scrutinized by the Parliament.

At the highest level of aggregation, a full set of accounts, consolidated for the entire government, is prepared. These documents form part of the information base to interpret the health of New Zealand's economy and the public sector, particularly with reference to indicators such as debt accumulation and the build-up of contingent liabilities. As a result, the government's financial assets and liabilities are managed in the total context of its overall balance sheet in a manner similar to a private company.[7]

ACCRUAL BUDGETING

As a part of the reforms, the budgetary process in New Zealand also made the transition from cash to accruals. The accrual appropriation process reflects two key features.

1. The need of the legislature to exercise effective control over the activities of government departments.

2. The requirement to reflect performance expectations arising from the government's purchase and ownership interest in the departments.

Appropriations under the accrual system are made for:

- purchase of outputs from departments, other agencies, and third parties;
- capital injections to increase the government's net asset holding in a department or agency; and
- other payments of benefits and grants.

Appropriations are made for costs to be incurred in producing the outputs. Full cost is measured on an accrual basis, including depreciation and capital charge. Capital injections are appropriated and paid in cash in the year appropriated. Benefits and grants are appropriated on a cash basis, although it is now considered that there may be merit in accrual appropriations, as situations arise where an obligation to pay a benefit or grant occurs near the year's end but the payment is not made until the following year.

HOW HAS IT WORKED?

The reforms in New Zealand were a response to

- concern at the size of the government sector
- a growing fiscal deficit
- desire for greater transparency and accountability in the provision of public services
- dissatisfaction within the public service with centralized input control, primarily through treasury instructions and the Public Service Manual
- dissatisfaction and frustration among the ministers that the existing system did not provide them with the information they needed for decision making
- concern about inefficiency in the public sector[8]

Have these concerns been addressed by the reforms?

SIZE OF THE GOVERNMENT

The impact of the reforms has been substantial: from 53 departments and agencies with approximately 86,000 staff in mid-1984, the public service was reduced, by 31 December 1993, to 35 departments and 34,000 full-time equivalent staff. As the State Services Commission observed in a paper in 1994, 'The reforms did bring an end to public sector careers for a very significant number of people.'[9]

FISCAL PERFORMANCE

Since 1989, fiscal performance of the New Zealand government has improved dramatically. It moved from deficit to surplus and net public debt fell from 52.5 per cent of GDP in 1991–2 to 26.4 per cent of GDP in 1996–7.[10] There is also evidence of an enhanced ability to control government expenditure. For the year ending 30 June 1992, cash flows declined by approximately NZ $1.5 billion on a base of NZ $31 billion.[11]

GREATER TRANSPARENCY AND ACCOUNTABILITY

Greater transparency and accountability have been achieved in government operations as a result of the reforms. For example, the legislative appropriation process now provides more comprehensive and intelligible information on the outcomes sought by the ministers and the outputs they seek (as funds) for realizing these outcomes. Ministerial accountability has been enhanced to the extent that the legislature and members of the public have better information. The legislative framework now demands a much greater degree of disclosure of financial and non-financial information in respect of actual performance, and it specifies the kind of information that the government has to provide.

Within the government, accountability is ensured by the contract that is entered into, between the ministers and chief executives. This contract specifies the performance expected of the chief executive and the outputs to be purchased by the department. This has led to greater clarity in responsibilities, and as a result, in accountabilities. Equally important is the fact that there is substantial delegation of authority to the chief executive. Given such delegation of authority, the chief executive has incentives to perform and deliver the promised outputs, and in turn, his performance becomes the sole criterion for deciding whether he gets a fresh tenure.[12]

CONTROLS OVER THE PUBLIC SERVICE

Traditionally, the State Services Commission had exercised strong central control. Its powers extended from management of office accommodation to review of efficiency and economy in each department, and being the ultimate authority in personnel matters. In an exercise known as Removal of Constraints, control of the commission over the day-to-day management of the departments—such as salary fixing, job classification, hiring and firing of staff, and other aspects of personnel management—was removed. This resulted in the deletion of some 95 per cent of the 2000 or so detailed instructions contained in the Public Service Manual, which was later abolished altogether.[13] Similarly, the system of tight centralized control by the treasury was dismantled, and the financial management control was devolved to the line departments. The departments were made responsible for financial management, financial performance, accounting requirements, and asset and cash management.

MINISTERS' SATISFACTION WITH INFORMATION

Prior to reforms, the ministers were dissatisfied that they did not get enough information for taking decisions. After the reforms, the ministers have much better information. In fact, the ministers have started demanding better specifications of departmental outputs, and they now use the information as a basis for decision-making.[14] The costing of outputs has enabled the ministers to make comparisons between alternative sources of supply across public and private sectors. The information has actually helped in the macromanagement of the economy. Faced with choices in respect of government spending, the ministers are now making decisions with a clearer understanding of their total impact because they have a better specification of exactly what services the departments will deliver, and this has provided a better basis for analysing the effect of departmental services on the government's strategic goals. On the basis of information provided, the ministers have also decided—in many cases—to discontinue services that were being earlier offered by the departments.[15]

EFFICIENCY GAINS

The State Services Commission had this to say in 1994, 'The now much smaller core public service is beginning to show clear improvements in operating efficiency and in responsiveness to clients. It costs the government less than it did ten years ago, and is no longer a regulatory impediment to ideas and productive energies in the wider economy and community.'[16] One reflection of efficiency is that in the period of three years after the introduction of the reforms, the departments showed no evidence of any decline in the volume or quality of output, even without adjustments to their budgets to reflect price increases.

There are observable improvements in the use of assets generally, and in working capital and cash in particular.[17] Government departments in need of new assets are not automatically given a capital injunction to finance the purchase of new assets. They are expected to examine whether the purchase of new assets can be financed from their existing budget. The discipline is reinforced by the capital charge that is levied on the government's investment in each department. This acts as a disincentive for a department to seek a capital injunction unless it is fully satisfied that the incremental amount of capital charge can be met from increased sales of outputs to other departments or third parties. In addition, the departments, by capitalizing the costs of capital assets and depreciating them during their useful lives, are now in a position to match their capital costs to revenue flows. This has enabled the full costs of output production to be ascertained each year and compared between years. The focus on outputs has made it necessary to recover costs for services that yield private benefits. This has made the departments ask questions such as

- To whom is this service being provided?
- Should the recipient or the taxpayer meet the cost of the service?

Full costing has provided a better basis for cost recovery calculations.

In addition, the budgetary process—with an output-price focus—has moved the departments away from a cost-plus mentality and has generated savings. For example, the departments now meet the cost of wage settlements out of their existing budgets. Output prices are not increased merely because there is a change in the price of an input. Line departments are now sensitive to the need for better management of their capital assets. On the whole, a focus on the balance sheet together with a capital charge has encouraged the government departments to extract maximum value from the use of their assets and to review whether the assets they currently hold are necessary to produce outputs.[18]

In order to assess the impact of the reforms, it may be useful to refer to the findings of two independent reviews and two surveys.

LOGAN'S REVIEW

When the National Party came to power in 1990, it appointed a steering group to assess the effectiveness of the reforms. The convenor of the steering group was Basil Logan, the former chief executive of IBM New Zealand. The review set out to answer three questions posed by the prime minister.

1. What were the reforms intended to achieve?
2. What has happened so far? What benefits are being realized and what ongoing costs are being incurred?

3. What more needs to be done to realize the objectives of the reforms and minimize their costs?

Based on interviews, discussions with ministers and senior civil servants, surveys of public service managers, consultations with the major public service unions, and submissions received from a variety of interested parties, the steering group reported its review of public sector reforms in November 1991. The review's overall conclusion was positive.[19] From the accounting perspective, none of the people consulted—the list included virtually all the ministers, chief executives, and members of the senior executive service—doubted the usefulness of the accrual method of accounting.[20]

SCHICK'S REVIEW

Allan Schick conducted an independent review of the reforms in August 1996. Schick's review concluded that the accounting reforms had lived up to expectations, except that additional work had to be done on the costing of outputs.[21]

SURVEYS

A survey of civil servants in the government revealed that of the many public sector reforms that had been undertaken in New Zealand, accounting reform received the highest grade. The survey noted that, 'Accrual accounting is being adopted increasingly by a number of nations, developed and developing, and the New Zealand reforms appear to have improved the ability to identify inefficiencies in the costing and provision of public services and enhanced accountability.'[22]

Another study found that the reforms helped New Zealand improve its compliance with measurements of aggregate fiscal discipline from 26 per cent in 1984 to 94 per cent in 1994. According to the study, 'Prior to the reforms, most public financial statements and budgetary documents were not available to the general public for scrutiny and, even if they were made available, they could not easily be understood even by accountants and financial experts in the private sector. Consequently, government performance was largely nontransparent. The adoption of accrual accounting changed this dramatically.'[23]

CONCLUSION

All evidence point out that introduction of accrual accounting has succeeded in achieving its objectives. New Zealand Inc. now publishes government accounts in a manner similar to those of a private company, the first government in the world to do so. More generally, the accounting reforms in New Zealand have enabled the debate to focus on the nature of the various services being delivered by a department, what the government is paying for them, and how effective is the management of the department delivering them. The reforms have helped to set priorities, both within areas of expenditure and across them, by reference to the government's broader strategic goals. They have also enabled the government to manage its finances on the basis of high quality financial information.

NOTES

1. Douglas (1993).
2. The following discussion on public sector reforms is based on Auditor General of Canada (2001).
3. World Bank (1994) p. 174.
4. Scott and Ball (1993), pp. 6–7.
5. Simpkins (1998), p. 5.
6. Scott and Ball (1993), pp. 14–17.
7. Scott (1994), pp. 176–7.
8. Hepworth (2002), pp. 4–5.
9. Holmes and Wileman (2001), pp. 17–18.
10. Ball, Dale, Eggers, and Saco (2000), p. 21.
11. Holmes and Wileman (2001), p. 34.
12. Ibid., pp. 48–9.
13. Ibid., p. 13.
14. Little (1993), p. 9.
15. Das (1998), p. 96.
16. State Services Commission (1994), p. 18.
17. Holmes and Wileman (2001), p. 34.
18. OECD (1993), pp. 44–5.
19. Holmes and Wileman (2001), p. 29.
20. Das (1998), p. 97n .
21. Simpkins (1998), p. 7.
22. Ball, Dale, Eggers, and Sacco (2000), pp. 10–11.
23. Ibid., p. 11.

4

Accrual Accounting in the Australian Government

Like in New Zealand, Australia experienced (during the 1970s) declining international competitiveness and mounting fiscal deficits that translated into substantial foreign and public debts by the early 1980s. In fact, the history of government indebtedness in Australia has an interesting story to tell. By the end of World War II, the government debt was about 110 per cent of the GDP. Because of the robust economic growth that Australia experienced during the post-war years, indebtedness of the government was progressively reduced, and by the early 1970s the government had achieved a net creditor position. However, in the subsequent quarter century, the position of government indebtedness showed a deteriorating trend. By the early 1980s, current account deficits were at unsustainable levels and there was massive accumulation of public and foreign debt.

PUBLIC SECTOR REFORMS

In 1983 the Australian Labour Party (ALP) was elected to power by a slim margin. During the electoral campaign itself, the ALP had talked about redressing the worsening economic situation by building a strong budgetary position and undertaking public sector reforms. After coming to power, it introduced wide-ranging reforms seeking to improve the efficiency and effectiveness of the public sector and its accountability to the legislature. The reforms aimed to achieve

- a strong budgetary position through expenditure restraint and concentration on core business;
- a devolved financial, employment, and workplace relations framework that allows greater flexibility and places greater responsibility on individual agencies to develop strategies to meet their particular business needs; and
- a range of incentives to ensure that managers manage for results, by

focusing on outputs and developing indicators to measure performance in terms of outcomes for clients.[1]

FINANCIAL MANAGEMENT FRAMEWORK

Reforms in the financial management framework in the Commonwealth government came through three new acts, which replaced the Audit Act 1901 with effect from 1 January 1998.

The Financial Management and Accountability Act 1997

It provides the accountability and accounting framework for Commonwealth bodies. Under the new arrangements, the chief executives are given greater flexibility and autonomy in their financial management: They are also required to promote efficient, effective, and ethical use of public resources.

The Commonwealth Authorities and Companies Act 1997

It provides standardized accountability for those Commonwealth bodies that are separate legal entities and hold money in their own account. The act replaced the diverse accountability and financial and auditing processes for the Commonwealth authorities with a single set of core reporting and auditing requirements. Many of these requirements were modelled on the corporations law and applied the standards and principles applicable to private sector companies.

The Auditor General Act 1997

It describes the powers and responsibilities of the auditor general, contains a much more streamlined set of auditing provisions, and focuses on audit goals rather than processes. The act also sets out the mandate and powers of the auditor general, including the establishment of the auditor general as an independent officer of the Parliament.[2]

EMPLOYMENT FRAMEWORK

A Public Service Bill was presented to the Parliament in June 1997. The Bill sought to

- set up an apolitical civil service that is efficient and effective in serving the government and the Australian public;
- provide a legal framework for the effective and fair employment, management, and leadership of the Australian Public Service (APS) employees; and

- establish the rights and obligations of APS employees.

More importantly, the bill defined public expectations of what a civil service should be, and distinguished the public interest of citizens from the private interest of the APS employees. On the whole the bill created an employment framework that ensured that the APS was in a position to provide both better policy advice to the government as well as higher quality of service to the Australian community.[3]

Workplace Relations Framework

The objective of enacting the Workplace Relations Act 1996 was primarily to modernize Australia's industrial relations system. The act provides for more direct and productive workplace relations between employers and employees, and for freedom of association and more choices to achieve mutually beneficial agreements. Following the Workplace Relations Act, the government authorized the heads of the agencies to settle their employees' terms and conditions of employment.

Management Framework

The new framework for employment and workplace made it possible for a large number of complementary initiatives to be undertaken to cater to the needs of the clients. The framework provided for a system of outputs and outcomes, a system of performance-improvement cycle, and introduction of customer service reforms.

Outputs and Outcomes

In April 1997, the government decided to implement an accrual-based outputs framework for managing resources.[4] The objective was to put in place a management framework that would manage for results by developing robust indicators to assess the performance of the government departments in terms of outcomes for clients. In the past, the systems in the Australian government had been preoccupied with process, and performance was evaluated in terms of the quantity of resources consumed rather than the quality of outcomes.

Performance Improvement Cycle

The main idea of the performance improvement cycle was to ensure that all the departments and agencies reviewed their activities in order to ensure that attention was focused on those activities that were the primary responsibility of the government. In terms of the performance improvement cycle, the Commonwealth agencies were required to

- review their activities;
- assess the costs and effectiveness of government activities in order to improve performance; and
- consider tools, such as benchmarking, business process reengineering, purchaser-provider arrangements, and competitive tendering and contracting performance.[5]

Customer Service Reforms

All Commonwealth departments and agencies that had dealings with members of the public were required to develop a service charter. These charters provided a substitute for competition where no competition existed, and promoted competition where similar services were provided.[6]

INFORMATION REQUIREMENTS OF PUBLIC SECTOR REFORMS

The environment that was created in Australia as a result of the implementation of public sector reforms, demanded better information to assess the effectiveness of programmes and more efficient allocation and management of resources. More comprehensive information on revenues and expenses, and assets and liabilities was a subset of such information. As a part of the reforms, the government decided that in a number of key areas, civil servants should pursue cost-effective options—consistent with value-for-money objectives. For instance, the government specifically instructed that production of goods and services should be taken up in-house only if there was a justification after taking into account the full cost of in-house production. This required that the departments should take into account all economic costs, including superannuation and depreciation, in their assessment. Similarly, departments were required to test the market for outsourcing of both new and existing information technology requirements as an alternative to the maintenance of in-house capabilities. The intention was that the departments should achieve maximum outsourcing, subject to value for money, efficiency, and public policy considerations.[7] That being the case, comprehensive financial information was needed for evaluating programmes and proposals, determining prices for goods and services, lease-buy alternatives, and benchmarking and outsourcing.

ACCOUNTING REFORMS

In May 1992, a joint federal-state working party was established to consider issues associated with government accounting, reporting, and budgeting. The working party recommended that:

- governments examine the decisions that managers and users of financial statements need to make about departments and authorities that operate on cash-accounting systems and, where information derived from accrual systems would assist in the management of resources, assessment of performance and financial position, and the discharge of accountability, and pursue the introduction of such systems and financial statements
- financial statements that are prepared on an accrual basis should be prepared in accordance with the Australian Accounting Standards and the Statements of Accounting Concepts.[8]

The other development was the release of an exposure draft on financial reporting by government departments by the Australian Accounting Research Federation—a body jointly established by the Australian Society of Certified Practising Accountants and the Institute of Chartered Accountants in Australia—to improve the quality of financial reporting and auditing. The exposure draft recommended that government departments should prepare financial reports in accordance with the Australian Accounting Standards and Statements of Accounting Concepts in other words, requiring adoption of accrual-based reporting.

The Department of Finance initiated a pilot study in 1992 to assess the value of both these reports—the report of the working party and the exposure draft of the Australian Research Foundation. The pilot study, while endorsing the findings of both these reports, suggested the preparation of supplementary financial statements for the departments of finance and administration, along accrual lines. The supplementary financial statements consisted of

- an operating statement
- a statement of assets and liabilities
- a programme statement
- a statement of cash flows
- notes.

These statements, together with their underlying structure and accounting policies, provided the basis for extension of accrual accounting to all government departments. On 4 November 1992, the minister for finance announced that federal government departments would move to financial reporting on an accrual basis as the next step in the government's public sector reforms. The announcements indicated that the departments would move to financial reporting on an accrual basis for the financial year ending 30 June 1995.[9]

TRANSITION TO ACCRUAL ACCOUNTING

The States

New South Wales was the first state in Australia to move to accrual accounting. Between 1990 and 1994, 70 agencies moved to accrual accounting. Interestingly, New South Wales adopted accrual accounting without adopting accrual output budgeting (AOB).

Victorian budgets had traditionally been presented, managed, and reported on a cash basis. It was for the first time in 1993–4 that Victoria included in the budget, output measures for each department. Actual data for 1992–3 and estimated data for 1993–4 were presented. A major shift occurred in 1996–7 with improved definitions and performance measures in the reporting of outputs. A comprehensive output budgeting reporting regime for 1998–9 budget cycle was implemented, including parliamentary appropriations and expansion of the capital asset charge regime.

The Australian Capital Territory prepared an accrual-based output budget for 1996–7 and 1997–8, with improvements in output definition and quality of performance measures over that period.

Queensland published outputs as an appendix to the programme statements in its 1998–9 input-based budget. Full accrual accounting was introduced in 1999–2000.

In South Australia, output-based accrual budgeting was fully implemented in 1999–2000. The 1998–9 budget was prepared on an accrual-outputs basis for the first time. The budget provided figures at the output-class level, which was an aggregation of individual outputs. In 1999–2000, the budget was presented for the first time at the level of outputs.

In Tasmania, a cash-based output budget was published in 1996–7 and 1997–8. In 1999–2000, Tasmania implemented an output-based accrual budget.

Western Australia's experience with output budgeting began with all-new funding for the financial year 1997–8 and extended to full funding in 1998–9. A full accrual-based budget was implemented for 1998–9.[10]

THE COMMONWEALTH

The Commonwealth government had made a commitment to move towards accrual budgeting in its coalition policy document launched during the 1996 election campaign. Following the discussion of Australian fiscal reporting practices, which occurred after the release of the 1995–6 budget in May 1995 and in the run up to the 1996 federal election, calls for reforms had emanated from a number of quarters. Demands had been made that the government should present a clear picture of its use of resources and whole-of-government financial position.

The need for an improved financial accounting framework for the Commonwealth government was emphasized by the National Commission of Audit, in the Management Advisory Board's *Beyond Bean Counting*, and in reports by parliamentary committees.

The government began implementing the first accrual budgeting system in April 1997 supported by a Charter of Budget Honesty. The Department of Finance and Administration (DoFA) was made responsible for planning and overseeing its introduction on behalf of the government. This included consultation with Parliament on the implications of the move to an integrated accrual framework, in particular the shift from cash to accrual appropriations, and changing the structure of the appropriation bills. A timetable was also adopted for putting in place the accrual accounting arrangements.

TABLE 4.1: TIMETABLE FOR ACCRUAL ACCOUNTING

October 1997	Major policy issues addressed concerning agency system implementation
March 1998	First audited whole-of-government financial statements for 1996–7
July–September 1998	Trial budget in self-nominating agencies
October 1998	Accrual budget policies, processes and systems in place
May 1998	First full-accrual budget

Source: Reforms to the APS (1998).

DoFA was given the job of developing the policies, principles, and practical issues involved. This included methodology for the specification of outcomes and outputs, form and content of the budget and appropriation documentation, and the treatment of depreciation and other non-cash items. DoFA also evolved a strategy in terms of which consultation had to be carried out with all the stakeholders. The process of consultation was combined with communication and training strategies not only to provide the stakeholders with information and knowledge required but also to develop the understanding and skills necessary to operate in an accrual environment.

On 20 March 1998, the government tabled its first audited accrual-based financial statement. This represented completion of the initial phase of implementation of the Commonwealth's accrual financial management framework. The financial statements showed the operating results and cash flows for the year ending 30 June 1997 and the financial position as on 30 June 1997 for the Commonwealth as a whole. An outcomes and outputs budgeting framework based on accrual accounting was introduced, with the first accrual budget delivered in May 1999. It was a complex task; it involved more than 160 government departments and 120,000 people across the nation, making it one of the largest change-management projects ever undertaken in the Australian government. The exercise was described as 'the most significant budget reform since the wartime tax compact between the Commonwealth and the states'.[11]

REPORTING FRAMEWORK

There are now two accrual-based standards for government accounting and reporting.

- Australian Accounting Standard (AAS31)
- Australian Bureau of Statistics' Government Finance Statistics (GFS) standard.

AUSTRALIAN ACCOUNTING STANDARD

The Public Sector Accounting Standards Board issued AAS31 in 1996, setting out standards for financial reporting by the federal, state, and territory governments. AAS31 requires the adoption of a full-accrual basis of accounting. It prescribes model, general-purpose reports that can be modified to suit the particular needs of a reporting entity. These statements, usually audited by the auditor general, present whole-of-government accounts using GAAP. The accounts, accompanied by various explanatory notes, are presented in the forms of: an operating statement, statement of financial position, and a cash flow statement.

GOVERNMENT FINANCE STATISTICS (GFS)

The GFS system, employed by the Australian Bureau of Statistics (ABS), is designed to provide statistics for all government departments, statutory authorities, government businesses and local government authorities. The GFS is based on two international standards: (a) the United Nation's System of National Accounts (revised in 1993)—SNA93 and (b) the Manual on Government Finance Statistics of the International Monetary Fund. The statistics reported by the ABS show

- consolidated transactions of the various institutional sectors from an economic viewpoint
- roles of the different levels of government in undertaking and financing their expenditure programmes
- transactions of the Commonwealth government and individual state and local governments and universities, indicating the comparative standing of each government in relation to its expenditure, its sources of revenue, its financing transactions, and its holding of assets and liabilities.

The Commonwealth Budget 1999–2000

The Commonwealth government's 1999–2000 budget completed the transition from cash to accruals. The move to accrual budgeting has resulted in several changes.

- Budget reporting has adopted a consolidated framework, by shifting from budget-sector to general-government reporting.
- Consistent with both accounting and GFS, the Commonwealth has produced a complete set of accrual statements.
- In order to promote greater efficiency in the management of its assets, the Commonwealth government has produced a capital budget statement that accounts for all capital expenditure and funding.

THE STATEMENTS

The Commonwealth government now produces a series of statements on an accrual GFS basis (consistent with international standards) including an operating statement, a statement of financial position, and a cash flow statement. These statements are similar to accounting-standard statements. The GFS operating statement's main summary measure is the net operating result. The net operating result, like the accounting operating result, equals revenue less expenses—although classification differences cause the two to diverge. The operating statement identifies the revenues generated and expenses incurred during the reporting period, and any differences therein.

In essence, the balance of the operating statement represents the government's profit or loss for a given year.

The statement of financial position reports the assets and liabilities of the government, and thereby provides information about the resources controlled by and the obligations of the government. This statement includes infrastructure (for example, transport systems), heritage (for example, historic buildings and monuments), and community assets (for example, parks and recreational reserves) that can be measured reliably. Liabilities measure the future sacrifices of economic benefit that the government is presently obliged to make to other entities. The balance of the statement of financial position (assets less liabilities) is net assets.

The cash flow statement indicates the source of cash inflows and how cash was applied by agencies during the financial year. The statement classifies cash flows according to whether they relate to operating, investing, or financing activities. The balance of the cash flow statement is the net increase or decrease in cash held. The GFS cash flow statement also records the underlying cash balance.

DIFFERENCES BETWEEN CASH AND ACCRUAL ACCOUNTING

TIMING OF TRANSACTIONS

In the cash-accounting system, transactions were recorded in the reporting period in which cash changed hands. The accrual system now records transactions in the period in which the income is earned or expenses incurred, subject to the important caveat that the transactions were capable of being reliably measured at that time. Assets, liabilities, revenues, and expenses arising from the transactions or other events are recognized in the financial statements when they have an economic impact on the government, regardless of when the cash flows occur. In the case of the Commonwealth government, accrual reporting has covered some significant financial items that were not included in cash-based statistics because they did not have an associated cash flow. For example, the budget now records the accruing pension expense whether the liability is funded or unfunded. The pension expense in the operating statement, in a given year, is equal to pension accruing to current employees as well as the interest or growth on the outstanding liability while calculating changes in the stock of unfunded pension liabilities, the actuary takes into account the number of salary earners and assumptions relating to growth in wages, inflation, and the expected rate of return on investment.[12]

PUBLIC DEBT INTEREST (PDI)

In the cash accounting system, PDI was recorded as the interest paid during the year. Under accrual accounting, allowance is also made for interest accrued but not actually paid during the period. A further difference between cash and accrual accounting for PDI relates to the treatment of premia and discounts, when debt is issued or when it is repurchased.

TAXATION REVENUE

The preparation of accrual estimates has required a reliable method of recognizing when the taxation revenue accrues to the Commonwealth. For example, the Commonwealth could record an accrual of revenue at the time the economic transactions resulting in a taxation liability took place. It is difficult, however, to know when all such transactions take place. As a result, at this stage, revenue is recognized as accruing at the time the relevant tax law indicates the existence of a requirement to pay an amount in tax, or when a tax liability assessment is raised by the Australian Taxation Office or the Australian Customs Service. In other words, revenue is recognized when the taxpayer makes a self-assessment, or the Australian Taxation Office or the Australian Customs Office issues an assessment.

CAPITAL

Accrual accounting records capital use (depreciation) in the operating statement, whereas the cash accounting system recorded capital expenditure. However, the Australian government's primary fiscal target—fiscal balance—continues to record capital expenditure instead of depreciation. This was considered necessary by the Australian government because the fiscal balance is intended to measure the difference between savings and investment expenditure. The fiscal balance detects the cash investment in a given year, not the capital used. The cash flow statement outlines most of the capital expenditure in the purchase of property, plant and equipment, and intangibles; while total capital expenditure is published in the Commonwealth's capital budget statement.[13]

HOW HAS IT WORKED?

The introduction of accounting reform in Australia was a response to:

- the need for product costing

- the desire to run government departments as businesses
- the need to increase effectiveness, efficiency and transparency of public services, and ensure increased accountability for results.

Have these objectives been achieved?

PRODUCT COSTING

The primary benefit of accounting reforms has been in the area of product (output) costing. When accrual accounting was introduced in the departments, it was combined with output costing systems to enable the departments to measure the full costs of each of the products they delivered to the community. The information provided by accrual accounting is a powerful tool to drive efficiency improvement, in the sense that, it now delivers the unit product cost information that is then used for performance measurement and benchmarking or market-testing purposes.[14]

With the introduction of an output-based accrual budgeting framework, agencies now assign a price to the outputs they produce; the government did, in fact, ask agencies to review the pricing of their outputs. These reviews were intended to establish the basis upon which agencies capture and attribute costs to the outputs, in order to assess whether the prices of outputs are reasonable. As a result of these reviews, the agencies were in a position to:

- produce better information for the ministers, on the pricing of outputs as well as promoting greater transparency in the way they priced their outputs
- improve costing systems to support the accurate pricing of outputs.[15]

The use of accrual accounting has also made it possible to levy a capital use charge. For the first time, the departments and agencies paid back to the budget 12 per cent of their asset base accumulated since federation. The capital use charge aims to place a cost on the Commonwealth for the assets held by departments and agencies. It also provides an incentive for agencies and departments to take stock of the assets held by them and sell off surplus assets.[16]

GOVERNMENT DEPARTMENTS AS BUSINESSES

The traditional cash accounting system measured financial flows in terms of outlays (money paid out) and revenue actually received. The basic cash budget balance equalled outlays minus cash revenue, and in stock terms, was equal to the change in net debt from one year to the next. Over the years, the flawed nature of a cash-budget balance as a measure of fiscal policy stance resulted in a number of quasi-accrual adjustments being made, leading ultimately to an underlying cash-budget balance measure which excluded privatization receipts. With the adoption of accrual accounting, government now reports financial flows in terms of an operating statement equivalent to a business profit-and-loss statement. If the budget operating balance is zero, the year's operating expenses are fully covered by the year's revenue.[17]

In the new accrual output budgeting system, which has been adopted right across Australia, departments are seen as business units with their own operating statements.[18] Like in the private sector, departmental performance in the AOB is now measured with reference to the bottom line of profit and loss. This is in contrast to the traditional thinking in the Australian government in which surplus/deficit measures were seen as meaningless at the level of the individual government departments, which were regarded as inherently loss-making units. The move from cash to accruals is an important step in the Australian government's financial management reform programme to develop a more business-like reporting, which incorporates the full cost of service delivery and a whole-of-government approach.

TRANSPARENCY, EFFECTIVENESS, EFFICIENCY, AND ACCOUNTABILITY

Australia's reforms have contributed to more transparent and informative government accounts and greater efficiency in the management of public resources.[19] The process of specifying outcomes has meant that the departments now determine a series of outputs—deliverable goods and services—relating to these outcomes. The extent to which these are realized—and the efficiency of outputs—is documented in the annual reports. There are indicators of effectiveness and efficiency in the reports, with effectiveness indicators identifying a causal link between outputs and outcomes. Costed outputs with causal links to outcomes are published by the departments, thus enhancing accountability.[20]

NEW FISCAL POLICY INDICATOR

Prior to the introduction of accrual accounting, the cash–budget result was regarded as the headline fiscal policy indicator. The government aimed to achieve balanced or surplus cash budgets, the reason being that a structurally balanced cash–budget was seen as crucial to raising national savings. For more than a decade, Australian macroeconomic policy had been preoccupied with the country's low savings ratio and large deficits on the current account of balance of payments. The dominant view amongst policymakers was that the appropriate fiscal response to this problem should be for the government to stop drawing upon private savings. This called for an end to budget deficits.

With the adoption of accrual accounting, the idea of cash–budget balance has been replaced by a new headline fiscal policy indicator—the fiscal balance. The key fiscal-policy objective has now been reformulated to be the required fiscal balance on average over the course of the business cycle. Fiscal balance equals the operating balance minus net investment. If the fiscal balance is zero, then enough revenue is being raised not only to cover the costs of production of all goods and services delivered to the community, but also to fully pay for the increases in government's capital stock. Fiscal balance is thus a measure of net lending to the government from the private sector.[21] If fiscal balance is zero, government is not drawing on private sector savings to cover either its capital outlays or its operating costs. In other words, if the fiscal balance is zero, government savings equal government net investment.

The concept of fiscal balance is useful, when viewed from a stock perspective. The operating balance equals the change in net worth. Net investment, on the other hand, equals the change in capital stock, that is, the change in non-financial assets. Because the fiscal balance is defined as operating balance minus net investment, it is equal to the change in net worth minus the change in non-financial assets. Since net worth equals non-financial assets plus net financial worth, it follows that fiscal balance equals the change in net financial worth. A deficit on the fiscal balance means an increase in net financial liabilities; in other words, in debt.

Such a concept helps one to understand why the fiscal balance based on accrual accounting is an improvement over the cash–budget balance. Prior to the introduction of accrual accounting, it was considered that the cash–budget balance was a good measure of government's net lending, for the obvious reason that a cash deficit meant a commensurate increase in net debt. However, to use the cash–budget result as a measure of government savings is, in effect, to count as part of the savings any financial assets which the government accumulates to fund increases in non-debt liabilities, for example, full funding of pension obligations. However, putting aside reserves to meet an obligation, when it becomes due, is not saving. This mistake is avoided if one uses the fiscal balance measure, which only counts increases in asset holdings as savings in so far as they are not offset by increases in liabilities. Fiscal balance therefore measures government's net lending with greater precision than did the cash–budget result.

Introduction of the fiscal balance concept has been immensely useful, given the current fiscal policy of the Australian government. It is now the accepted view that for boosting national savings, the government should not borrow at all from the private sector. In other words, the present policy requires that government should save, but that the magnitude of government savings should equal net public investment.

Obviously, accrual accounting has brought significant fiscal policy benefits but there are certain areas in respect of which doubts have been expressed about the efficacy of the accrual accounting system.

DOES ACCRUAL ACCOUNTING CREATE CONFUSION?

It is contended that the introduction of accrual accounting has created confusion. The supposed confusion has arisen because the Australian government has adopted two accrual accounting frameworks. As we discussed, there is one framework based on the AAS31 and the other framework is the GFS developed by the Australian Bureau of Statistics in conformity with international standards developed by the International Monetary Fund and the United Nations. The numbers generated by these two systems can differ significantly. For example, the 1999–2000 Commonwealth budget operating balance was $13.5 billion on a GFS basis. In contrast, the AAS31 operating balance, before abnormals, was $9.5 billion. According to GFS, net worth was minus $11.6 billion, while AAS31 net worth was minus $52.9 billion.

The question arises—why have two frameworks? The explanation is that the two frameworks have two different foci. While AAS31 reflects the accounting focus, the GFS reflects the economic focus. AAS31 is driven by the idea that government accounting should operate just like private sector accounting, whereas GFS is customized for government policy purposes. In the Australian scheme of things, both the accounting frameworks are necessary. The GFS excludes revaluation income and expenses because they are outside the control of the government. The GFS framework yields the net lending or the fiscal balance measure that is important in assessing the impact of the government's policies on the economy. This concept is not found in AAS31 standards. More generally, GFS data is broadly consistent with the data on government transactions in the Australian national accounts and is reflected in the measures of economic activity.

DOES ACCRUAL ACCOUNTING COMPROMISE ACCOUNTABILITY?

It is also contended that accrual accounting has diminished the capacity of the legislature to scrutinize activities of the executive. In a submission to the joint committee of public accounts and audit, Maurie Kennedy, a former senior executive in DoFA, argued that appropriations by high-level outcomes might have a systemic potential to permit payments by executive actions, which could be hidden from the Parliament. Frances Miley and Andrew Read, authors of *Comparing Government Reporting: Looking For Accountability*, suggest that there has been a significant erosion in the quality of government financial accountability because the operating statements have unacceptably low levels of disclosure.[22] Lindsay Tanner, the Shadow Minister for Finance, had this to say in an article entitled 'Restoring Openness in Government', 'The introduction of accrual budgeting has been accompanied by a serious reduction in the amount and quality of budget information made available to parliament. As a result, parliament's ability to ensure that government programmes are delivered honestly and efficiently is being seriously eroded.'[23]

Are these contentions valid? The auditor-general of Australia has defined accountability as the process whereby government departments and the functionaries within them are responsible for their decisions and actions and submit themselves to appropriate external scrutiny. The Commonwealth government currently provides a level of disclosure that exceeds the levels required by the accounting standards. The rule of thumb principle for disclosure of items in the operating statements is based on an amount of $100 million. In many instances, this exceeds the current disclosure requirements in relation to materiality as defined by the accounting standards. The accounting standards require disclosure of revenues and expenses either by nature or by function. The consolidated financial statements of the Australian government provide full disclosure of an operating statement by both nature and function.[24]

THE VERTIGAN REVIEW

An independent review was commissioned by the Australian government, following the 1999–2000 budget. Michael Vertigan, former secretary of the department of treasury and finance in Victoria and Tasmania, headed the review. The Vertigan review concluded that delivery of the 1999–2000 budget in terms of accrual-based outcomes and outputs framework was a major achievement and that the new framework constituted international best practices. According to Vertigan review, the 1999–2000 budget was 'a very considerable achievement' that would 'position Australia at the forefront of public sector budget and financial management internationally.'[25]

CONCLUSION

The adoption of accrual reporting by governments in Australia represents an important step in Australia's reform initiative to develop a more business-like reporting model for the government departments—a model that accounts for the full cost of service delivery. Accrual accounting has provided a more comprehensive measure, over cash accounting, of the total activity of the government and the long-term effects of current policy, thereby enhancing governments' fiscal transparency and accountability. Accrual accounting has also been responsible for bringing about sustainability and sound fiscal management, and providing policymakers with information about the financial effects of current policies on future generations. Accrual information has also allowed markets, businesses, and consumers to more effectively assess governments' fiscal performance over time.

NOTES

1. Moore-Wilton (1999), p. 1.
2. Commonwealth of Australia, Reforms to the APS (1998), pp. 8–9.
3. Ibid., pp. 6–7.
4. Moore-Wilton (1999), p. 5.
5. Commonwealth of Australia, Reforms to the APS (1998), p. 10.
6. Ibid.
7. OECD (1993), p. 26.
8. Ibid., pp. 27–8 .
9. Ibid., p. 28.
10. Carlin and Guthrie (2000), p. 3.
11. Bartos (2000a), p. 5.
12. Treasury (1999b), pp. 12–13.
13. Ibid., p. 13.
14. Robinson (2001), pp. 5–6.
15. Bartos (2000a), p. 4.
16. Ibid.
17. Robinson (2001), pp. 1–2.
18. Ibid., p. 6.
19. Treasury (1999b), p. 2.
20. Rose (2003), p. 22.
21. Robinson (2001), pp. 2–3 .
22. Miley and Read (2000), p. 1.
23. Tanner (2000), p. 1.
24. Bartos (2000b), p. 16.
25. Vertigan (1999), p. 35.

5

Resource Accounting in the UK Government

Accounting in the core departments of the UK government was traditionally on a cash basis. Money was brought to account at the time they were paid and received. Such an accounting practice was consistent with the arrangements whereby the British Parliament voted government departments' supply of funds in cash—with cash being the basis of its planning and control systems. The position in commercial parts of the government was, however, different. Even before they were privatized, the nationalized industries in the UK had prepared their accounts on an accrual basis, along private sector lines, reflecting the commercial nature of their activities. Similarly, the government departments engaged in activities such as ship repairing, engineering, manufacturing, trading, and other commercial or quasi-commercial activities had prepared their accounts on an accrual basis for many years. The Trading Funds established in the 1970s did likewise.[1] It is only in the core, budget-dependent departments of the government, that cash formed the basis of accounting. Attempts to introduce accrual accounting in these core departments started only with the introduction of public sector reforms.[2]

PUBLIC SECTOR REFORMS

In the late 1960s, the Fulton Committee had asked for an accountable system of management with clearly defined responsibilities and staff equipped to carry them out.[3] Acting on the recommendations of the committee, the government initiated a number of reform measures in the 1980s and 1990s. These measures aimed at:

- separating the role of the government in policy making and purchasing of goods and services from that of providing such services,
- providing public services of the quality the citizens deserve at a price that the taxpayers can afford,

- restructuring the administrative setup with the creation of executive agencies within the government,
- introducing transparency into the working of the government within the constitutional principle that it is the ministers who are accountable to Parliament for all that the departments and agencies do, and
- delegating management responsibilities to the departments and agencies.[4]

FINANCIAL MANAGEMENT INITIATIVE

Thatcher government's Financial Management Initiative (FMI) launched in 1982 marked the beginning of a coordinated strategy to improve financial management in government departments. The efficiency scrutinies, conducted by the government in the late 1970s and early 1980s, suggested that the government should provide:

- a clear view of the objectives of the departments and an assessment of outputs and performances with reference to these objectives,
- well-defined responsibilities for making the best use of the resources including a critical scrutiny of output and value for money, and
- information particularly about costs and achievement of objectives, training, and access to expert advice which the departments need to exercise their responsibilities effectively.[5]

The financial management information that the scrutinies yielded provided the basis for the development of delegated budgeted responsibility, and the scrutinies were incorporated in 1982 into the Financial Management Initiative. The FMI was important as an initiative because it suggested radical changes in the internal structure and operations of the line departments. In terms of the FMI, objectives were to be assigned to responsibility centres, costs were to be systematically identified and measured on an accrual basis (in other words, matching the resources consumed to the services delivered), and the costs included not only the direct costs of service delivery but overheads also. This was crucial to hold civil servants accountable for the resources that were used by the departments.

NEXT STEPS

The Efficiency Unit conducted an efficiency scrutiny of management across the government as a whole in 1986. The report of this scrutiny, *Improving Management in Government: The Next Steps* recommended three priorities for reforms.

1. The work of each department must be organized in a way that focuses on the job to be done. The systems and the structures must enhance the effective delivery of policies and services.
2. The management of each department must ensure that its staff has the relevant experience and skills needed to do the tasks that are essential to effective government.
3. There must be sustained pressure, on and within each department, for continuous improvement in the value for money obtained in the delivery of policies and services.

The report recommended that, in order to achieve these priorities, agencies should be established to carry out the executive functions within a policy-and-resource framework set up by the government. The recommendation was based on the assumption that management change was more easily possible within distinctly identified units, headed by civil servants with clear responsibilities rather than in a larger, more diversified organization. An agency was defined as a distinct area of work with a single, named individual—a chief executive—in charge, with personal responsibility to the minister for day-to-day management. An agency was structured around and focused on the task to be completed. The minister allocated resources and set annual performance targets on the results to be achieved. The minister also delegated managerial responsibilities to the chief executive, who decided on how best to run the organization and get the work done with resources allocated to him.

A large number of executive agencies were set up. The main features of these agencies are as follows:

- defined responsibilities and clear aims and objectives, set out in a published framework document
- day-to-day responsibility for running an agency is delegated to its chief executive with personal responsibility and managerial authority for the job to be done
- the chief executive answered directly to the minister
- key performance targets—covering quality of service, financial performance, and efficiency—are set up by ministers and announced to the Parliament
- greater openness, where performance against these targets is reported each year and published in the agency's annual reports and accounts, and in the Next Steps Report
- the basis of ministerial accountability remains unchanged by agency's status. Those working in agencies—including the chief executive—

remain civil servants, reporting to ministers, who are accountable to Parliament. The Next Steps initiative has clarified responsibilities within departments and made them much more transparent than they were before

- The publication of framework documents, key annual performance targets, annual reports, and accounts provides greater transparency to Parliament and the public.[6]

Competing for Quality

The Competing for Quality programme was launched in 1991, with the objective of introducing more competition into government work and achieving the best combination of cost and quality; in other words, value-for-money. The process sought to establish a form of public–private partnership.

The programme encompassed a wide range of efficiency techniques including benchmarking and restructuring but most notably, it paid attention to market testing and contracting out, which were expected to generate substantial savings. Under the programme, four prior options questions were asked of a government activity.

- Whether it needed to be done at all?
- Whether the government had to maintain responsibility for it (if not, privatize it)?
- If the government needed to maintain responsibility for it, would the activity be managed more cost effectively by the private or public sector? (If so, put the activity out to private sector competition—statutory contracting out—or invite the existing employees to compete with the private sector market testing.)
- If the work has to be carried out within the government, is the organization properly structured and focused on the task? (The Next Steps principles of clear accountability and delegation should be properly applied.)[7]

Citizen's Charter

The citizen's charter programme was launched by the prime minister in July 1991. The charter is based on the principle that all public services are paid for by citizens, either directly or through their taxes, therefore citizens are entitled to expect high-quality services that are responsive to their needs and are provided efficiently at a reasonable cost. The aim of the charter was to empower the citizens. It was a statement of the belief that citizens had a right to be informed and to choose for themselves. It was essentially a tool-kit of initiatives and ideas to raise standards in a way appropriate to each service.

COMPREHENSIVE SPENDING REVIEW

The government set up a comprehensive spending review (CSR) in 1997 to bring public spending programmes into line with its own priorities and a coherent set of objectives, and more importantly, to set medium- and long-term plans for the next Parliament, instead of concentrating on short-term issues—which was one of the criticisms of the annual public spending survey process. The white paper *Modern Public Services* (July 1998) set out the results of the CSR; it also announces the intention to introduce public service agreements between each department and HM Treasury, setting out measurable efficiency and effectiveness targets against which progress could be monitored. The core principles that govern the initiative are coordinated access across different parts of the government, greater efficiency and greater incentives, and responsiveness to users and more information on quality and efficiency.[8]

The public sector reform initiatives, starting with the FMI in 1982, sought to get better results out of the resources provided by the taxpayer, and also to deliver more and better for less. The public sector reforms in the UK, taken as a whole, emphasized

- measuring outcomes and outputs rather than inputs, and the needs of the users and not the interests of the producers
- the government sticking to essentials and doing these well
- using partnerships with the private sector where appropriate
- addressing particular tasks, designing the shape of the organization which best meets it, and delegating responsibility for delivery to that organization.

DEVELOPMENTS IN ACCOUNTING

The reform initiatives in the UK represented fundamental steps leading to a refinement of existing, and development of new, financial management procedures. As soon as the implementation of public sector reforms commenced in right earnest, it became clear that there were difficulties in reflecting the essential concerns of the reform initiatives in a cash accounting system—the primary purpose of which was to secure funds from the legislature.

The reason why cash accounting system was found to be lacking was that it did not take into consideration a number of non-cash resource items such as depreciation, cost of capital, debtors, creditors, stock balances, rents, and superannuation; which were considered relevant to the achievement of results-oriented goals set under the reform initiatives. In particular, the assessment of performance on the basis of the value-for-money criteria required financial management information to indicate how the total resources were applied and managed, in addition to information on cash payments and receipts. So it was essentially an appreciation of the fact that the cash accounting system was not in a position to fully reflect the requirements of the reforms that put the adoption of accrual accounting on the agenda.

It was, however, the establishment of executive agencies in 1988 under the Next Steps initiative, that made it necessary for accrual accounting to be adopted in the government departments. An important objective of the Next Step initiative was improved stewardship reporting to ministers, Parliament and the wider public: stewardship in terms of accountability for the management of public resources. The idea underlying stewardship accountability was that all agencies should produce and publish, with their annual reports, commercial-style accounts on an accrual basis. The adoption of accrual accounting was necessary to ensure that full costs, including the consumption of capital, are charged to customers and that the agencies had the necessary information to manage their affairs in a cost-effective manner and achieve their key financial and performance targets.

RESOURCE ACCOUNTING

In his budget speech of 1993, the Chancellor of the Exchequer announced the decision to introduce resource accounting throughout the government. The term resource accounting was defined as 'a set of accrual-accounting techniques for reporting on the expenditure of central government and a framework for analysing expenditure by departmental aims and objectives, relating those to outputs wherever possible', and 'planning and controlling public expenditure on a resource accounting basis'.[9] In other words, resource accounting is not only an incorporation of accrual-based accounting, but also the provision of a necessary link between inputs and departmental aims, objectives and outputs.

In pursuance of the chancellor's announcement, the treasury published in July 1994 a green (discussion) paper, *Better Accounting for the Taxpayer's*

Money, which set out initial proposals and announced a consultation period ending in January 1995.[10] The green paper proposed to

- implement resource accounting in a majority of the departments by 1 April 1997 and in all departments by 1 April 1998;
- ensure that resource accounts are published and laid before the parliament in 1999–2000;
- introduce, in principle, resource budgeting across the government;
- consult on how a resource-based public expenditure survey would work in practice;
- see that, subject to meeting the target dates for introducing resource accounting and the results of further consultation, the first survey on a resource basis is carried out in the year 2000; and
- consult Parliament and others on how expenditure might be controlled on a resource basis and on its consequent reporting arrangements.[11]

The green paper was followed in July 1995 by a white paper that announced the decisions taken. The white paper announced:

- each department would have an accruals-based resource budget and associated departmental financing requirements
- Overall public spending would be controlled through a resource control total, with an associated total financing requirement
- Departments would produce more systematic analyses of their aims, objectives and outputs
- There would be a better treatment of capital, with charges for depreciation and cost of capital, to encourage its more efficient use
- In-year controls would be the minimum necessary to ensure that plans were reflected in expenditure with a framework tailored to suit departmental circumstances that would allow the maximum flexibility consistent with delivering the overall totals.[12]

In setting out the details of reporting, the white paper announced that there would be five audited statements: a summary of resource outturn, an operating cost statement, a balance sheet, a cash flow statement, and a statement of resources (identifying the resource costs of the department's aims and objectives). A sixth statement—an output and performance analysis—followed the notes to the accounts, but was not a part of the accounts and not supposed to be audited.

The white paper also announced a review of the financial documents presented to Parliament, the creation of a Financial Reporting Advisory Board (FRAB) to advise on the application of accounting principles and standards, and confirm that departments would be charged for the cost of capital employed. For reporting to Parliament, the white paper's proposals were to replace the existing (appropriation driven) accounts by a resource account for each department. There were also proposals for changing the way Parliament approved expenditure. Instead of providing all information in cash, supply estimates—the documents providing information for Parliament to authorize expenditure—would present detailed information in resource terms, with an associated cash requirement.

IMPLEMENTATION OF RESOURCE ACCOUNTS

The 1995 white paper was the culmination of a process of consultation and discussion that had lasted for over 18 months. But with the announcement in July 1995, that resource accounting would be introduced by 1998 and resource budgeting from the year 2000, the matter had reached a degree of finality. The white paper announced that Parliament would be asked to make a similar change to the basis on which approval is given for government expenditure and on which the government reports to Parliament.

Fiscal Policy

The July 1997 budget outlined the two rules that came to govern the new fiscal framework.

1. The golden rule during the economic cycle the government will borrow only to invest and not to fund current expenditure.
2. Public debt as a proportion of national income will be held during the economic cycle at a stable and prudent level.[13]

The new fiscal policy, particularly the golden rule, required the adoption of accrual accounting. In respect of the golden rule, the accrual operating balance was of great importance because it was a useful indicator of the intergenerational equity stance of fiscal policy. The golden rule required that the government achieved a balanced accrual budget—in other words, a zero operating balance—on average over the business cycle. In addition, it is only accrual accounting that underpins the golden rule by making a clear structural distinction between current and capital spending, which are no longer treated as if they were equivalent economic categories.

Asset Valuation

An initial national asset register, listing all assets held by the central government departments and their sponsored bodies in England, was published on 24

November 1997. The national asset register, feeding on existing information already gathered for resource accounts, gave the clearest indication of the extent and coverage of the assets the government owned. According to the initial National Asset Register, the public sector was estimated to hold tangible assets of £405 billion and net financial liabilities of £340 billion, placing the public sector's net wealth at £65 billion. The compilation of the National Asset Register of 1997, however preliminary, was decidedly a significant achievement; as the finance committee of Parliament observed, 'This is the first publication of a register of assets held since the publication of the *Domesday Book* in 1087'.[14]

Progress in Implementation

In order to monitor the progress in the implementation of resource accounts, the government drew up a trigger point strategy. Basically, there were four trigger points against which progress was monitored. They were:

1. stage 1 approval requiring satisfactory accounting systems and policies in place to enable production of resources accounts (all the implementing departments achieved this)
2. assessment of departments' opening balance sheets for 1999–2000 (this was targeted for mid-1999)
3. National Audit Office's audit of departments' dry run 1998–9 resource accounts (which was targeted for mid-1999). Part of this requirement was an assurance by the accounting officer on the training arrangements for resource accounting and budgeting, to be given in the autumn of that year. A checklist of the mechanisms, key stages, and checks that needed to be in place, had been provided to departments, together with guidance on how to give the necessary assurance
4. department's dry run and resource-based estimates for 2000–1 to their select committees (which was targeted for early summer 2000).[15]

PARLIAMENTARY APPROVAL

In August 2000, Parliament gave its approval to proceed with the implementation of resource accounting and budgeting (RAB), in accordance with the original project timetable. The Government Resources and Accounts Act 2000, which received royal assent on 28 July 2000, provided the statutory basis for the new framework.

GOVERNMENT RESOURCES AND ACCOUNTS ACT 2000

The purpose of the act was to enable departmental estimates and accounts to be prepared on an accrual rather than a cash basis. The main purposes of the act are:

- to replace and/or amend the existing legislation on government accounts, to enable the introduction of RAB
- to put in place enabling legislation for the preparation and audit of consolidated accounts for the whole of public sector (whole-of-government accounts)
- To enable the treasury to incur expenditure in respect of the establishment of a new body for the purpose of carrying on public–private partnership business and investment in other financial provisions of that body.[16]

How the resource accounts are to be prepared is set out in Section 5 of the act. Section 5 provides for the treasury to determine the form of the accounts and requires the treasury to appoint accounting officers to be responsible for preparation of the accounts. Subsection (1) requires a department, for which Parliament has approved an estimate for a particular financial year to prepare a resource account for that year. Also according to Subsection (1), the resource accounts should describe in financial terms the use by departments of resources during the year, including their acquisition and disposal.

Subsections (2) to (4) of Section 5 provide that the treasury shall direct the form of resource accounts subject to the requirement that they shall present a true and fair view and conform to GAAP, amended as necessary in the context of departmental accounts. In doing so, the treasury will take into consideration the guidance issued by the Accounting Standard Board or any successor. In practice, this means that the resource accounts will follow the normal accounting standards and conventions used in the private sector and elsewhere in the public sector, modified only where necessary, to take account of the particular requirements of departmental accounts. In addition, Subsection (3) requires that the treasury should issue accounts directions to require that the treasury guidance is followed with a view to ensuring that resource accounts contain explanations of differences between items appearing in the estimates and the actual amounts appearing in the resource accounts.

The act also provides that the accounting policies underlying resource accounts, which will form the basis of the treasury directions, should be set out in the Resource Accounting Manual. The FRAB, which brings together representatives from the treasury, departments, the National Audit Office

(NAO), the Audit Commission, the Accounting Standards Board, industry and academia, should be consulted on all additions and changes, including proposals not to follow the standard practice, to the Resource Accounting Manual.

Subsection (4) of Section 5 also requires the accounts to include three main statements.

1. A statement of financial performance
2. A statement of financial position
3. A cash flow statement.

The act requires that resource accounts should consist of five major statements together with supporting notes.

1. A statement of out-turn (showing actual out-turn against the estimate)
2. An operating-cost statement which is analogous to a profit and loss account in company accounts (the statement of financial performance)
3. A balance sheet (the statement of financial position)
4. A cash flow statement
5. A statement relating costs to objectives.

The resource accounts for public sector pension schemes are expected to adopt a different format, based on the requirements of private sector pension scheme accounts. The requirements for those resource accounts were detailed in the Resource Accounting Manual, in consultation with the FRAB. In addition to accounting information, resource accounts will also have to include information necessary to satisfy parliamentary propriety. This will include a note of adjustments between estimated and actual outturn.

Subsection (5) of Section 5 requires all departments preparing resource accounts to send the accounts to CAG for audit by 30 November of the financial year following that to which the accounts relate. Subsection (6) requires the treasury to appoint an official of a department as the department's accounting officer. Subsection (7) places a responsibility on the accounting officer for preparing the departmental resource accounts and transmitting them to the CAG for audit. Subsection (8) enables the treasury to appoint other officials in a department as accounting officers, for parts of the resource account. The objective is to continue the treasury's current power of appointing accounts officers and to remain responsible for departmental accounts.

Subsection 6 also sets out the modalities for audit of the resource accounts by CAG and the procedures for laying the accounts, together with the CAG report there on, before the Parliament. In addition, the treasury's current power to check unauthorized spending by departments is modernized to take account of the RAB.

Subsection (1) of Section 6 requires the CAG to audit any resource account sent to it by a department. CAG's audit certificate is required to state whether in its opinion the accounts show

- a true and fair view,
- that money provided by Parliament has been expended for the purpose intended,
- that resources authorized by Parliament have been used towards the purpose for which the use was authorized, and
- that financial transactions covered by the accounts are in accordance with the relevant authority that governs them.

The first assertion (the true and fair opinion) is the same as that given by auditors on company accounts. This differs from the opinion currently given (properly presents) on the appropriation accounts and reflects the change from a cash to an accrual basis. The second part of the audit opinion is the regularity assertion (that money has been spent and resources used as Parliament intended and that all financial transactions have been undertaken in accordance with the authority that governs them) and is very similar to the assurance given in the audit opinion on appropriation accounts.

Subsection (2) of Section 6 provides that when, in the course of audit, the CAG discovers a material use of resources that required but did not receive treasury authorization, it shall inform the treasury and the treasury may retrospectively authorize the expenditure. Subsection 3 requires the CAG to issue a certificate (which contains its audit opinion) and report on each resource account. Subsection (4) requires the treasury to lay the resource accounts, together with the CAG's certificate and report, before the House of Commons.

Section 9 places a duty on the treasury to prepare consolidated accounts for the public sector (whole-of-government-accounts (WGA) in order to meet the commitment given in the Code for Fiscal Stability. Section 10 provides the treasury with the necessary powers to obtain the information for preparing WGA. Section 11 provides for the CAG to audit the WGA and for these to be laid before Parliament.

OPERATION OF THE RAB

RAB became fully operational on 2 April 2001. As a result, there are significant changes in the accounting system.[17]

Timing Differences

The accrual budget now records costs as they are incurred. The accounts do not include prepayments for goods and services not consumed that year but they do include accrued costs for resources consumed but paid later. Stock consumption is recorded in resource accounting while the spending on adding to stocks is not.

Depreciation

Resource accounts record a charge for depreciation on the assets being used by each department—measuring capital consumption in each year. They measure depreciation more accurately and attribute the cost transparently to individual programmes.

Capital Charge

A cost of capital charge is calculated at the rate of 6 per cent on the net assets employed by each department—measuring the opportunity cost of holding the assets. Depreciation and the cost of capital charge together are referred to as 'capital costs—both are non-cash items.

Capital Charge on Civil Estate Holdings

These are charges on the administrative buildings of the departments. Unlike other capital charges, these are applied in the departmental expenditure limits as the departments already have experience in controlling these as part of running cost controls.

Provision for Bad Debts and Future Liabilities

A provision is made for bad debts and future liabilities.

Changes in Accounting for Capital Spending

The capital spending of public corporations such as NHS trusts is included in the capital spending of the departments rather than in departments' external finance of these bodies. Under the cash accounting system, capital spending of public corporations was included in the accounting adjustments in the annually managed expenditure. In resource accounting, the capital spending of public corporations is effectively switched into Departmental Expenditure Limits. Some items which used to be recorded as current accounts under national accounts are recorded now as capital under resource accounting, notably the Defence Ministry's fighting equipment.

Whole-of-Government Accounts

The code for fiscal stability requires the government to produce accounts for the whole public sector on a consolidated basis. It also requires the government to apply the best-practice accounting methods—UK GAAP adapted for the public sector—in the production of its accounts.[18] The WGA, as prepared now, are commercial-style accounts covering the whole of public sector. These accounts are prepared on an accrual basis rather than on a cash basis, using commercial accounting standards and practices, adapted where necessary for the public sector context.[19] WGA presents a true and fair view of government's activities and is audited against this criterion alone, with no option on regularity. Regularity continues to be covered in each of the underlying accounts. In fact, WGA are intended to provide additional information on the government's overall finances, and not to replace any existing requirements. What matters, however, is that the GAAP-based WGA are fully auditable, yielding additional confidence in their reliability and are based on established accounting practice—providing a true and fair view of the government's financial performance. In effect, the WGA provide better transparency and accountability to Parliament as well as greater certitude in respect of fiscal planning.

New National Asset Register

In July 2001, the treasury published an updated and improved national asset register (NAR), providing for the first time a comprehensive list and valuation of all assets owned by government departments and their executive agencies. The NAR includes

- all tangible fixed assets (including military and heritage assets)
- all intangible fixed assets (such as intellectual property rights)
- all fixed asset investments (such as share holdings) owned by departments. Departments have followed normal accounting rules for the recognition of assets in deciding whether an asset should be included.

The government in UK has broken new ground with the updated NAR, which includes valuations of all assets and describes changes in asset holding since 1997. The NAR is a clear, tangible, benefit arising from the adoption of resource accounting and is a key tool in the management of public assets. This is because resource accounting measures the full costs of holding and using assets, and the departments have to meet these costs, rather than be encouraged to overlook them as under the cash accounting system, thereby giving a clear incentive to sell off costly non-productive assets. This encourages the departments to get the best value from the assets they are responsible for, and makes them more clearly accountable for their stewardship. The NAR shows the progress made in improving asset management; for example, the total value of assets listed in 1999–2000 was £274 billion while surplus properties worth £1.3 billion were sold off during the year, unlocking resources which can be used more productively elsewhere.[20]

CULTURE CHANGE AND TRAINING

The adoption of accrual accounting in the Government of UK called for a cultural change on the part of civil servants through an understanding and acceptance of how to use the additional information generated by accrual accounting and of the potential benefits it offers, and also, a commitment to change. It also meant that for initiatives of this kind to succeed, adequate training has to be given for the use of the additional information to enable analysis, interpretation, and subsequent decision-making to take place.

This was done by requiring the departmental accounting officers to give an assurance that adequate arrangements exist for training resource accounting to be carried out as a part of the trigger point strategy. As we noted, the third trigger point was NAO's audit of departments' dry run of 1998–9 resource accounts, which was scheduled for the autumn of 1999. Part of this trigger requirement was the assurance by the accounting officer on resource accounts training arrangements, to be given in the autumn of that year.

One important aspect of the RAB training structure was to address how the departments had outlined their expectations of the new resource accounting systems (especially in relation to defining and measuring progress towards the achievement of departmental aims and objectives) and how subsequent training messages were designed to realize these expectations. The other aspect that was addressed by the RAB training structure was to meet the skill needs created by

- systems operations and accounting system changes,
- accounting policy changes in terms of staff understanding and applying changes in requirements,
- changes resulting from the introduction of resource-based reviews and resource baselines, together with an understanding of how RAB fits into the government's fiscal framework and the impact this will have on planning processes within departments, and
- wider changes, such as the need for analysis and interpretation of

information generated by RAB for decision-making purposes, that is, financial awareness.[21]

The accounting officer, when giving his assurance on the arrangement for RAB training, had to certify that all these implications had been addressed.

Accounting Technicians

A key development in the introduction of RAB was the employment and training of accounting technicians within the government; this was the finding of a survey conducted by the Development of Accountancy Resource Team (DART)[22] that looked at the employment and training of accounting technicians. The survey showed that there were about 300 qualified accounting technicians working in the Government of UK with customs and excise; HM Prison Service; department for the environment, transport, and the regions (DETR); the National Insurance Contributions Agency; and the ministry of defence being the key employers. According to the survey, there were 1000 technicians under training in different departments. In addition, a diploma course in government finance with major focus on RAB was started in September 1998, with 150 trainees training for the diploma, and a further intake of 150 for each of the subsequent years. The departments and agencies that were keen on inducting these diploma holders included the ministry of defence, HM Prison Service, DETR, Ministry of Agriculture, Fisheries and Food (MAFF), the Child Support Agency, and the Inland Revenue. The survey found that increase in the number of technicians had not only contributed towards raising the profile of accountancy and finance within the departments and agencies, but was also an indication of the enhanced skills brought to accounting and finance within government through major training initiatives.

The International Dimension

DART also carried out a study of lessons learned by the governments in Australia and Canada in implementing accrual accounting. The key questions in the study were:

- how these two countries had defined their training needs and related these to business planning processes in the government departments
- how these needs were quantified and stratified
- what steps were taken to translate these quantified needs into a specification which the training providers could deliver
- what training solutions were provided (for example, type of courses and the duration)
- how delivery programmes were constructed and carried out

- how training was linked to gauging the overall effectiveness of both the individual and the organization.[23]

The key findings of the study were:

- senior civil servants needed to be made aware of the benefits and possibilities of the new information flow, but any training needs to be carefully timed to ensure that it takes place just before the information first becomes available
- the departments should be encouraged to outline their expectations of the new systems in resource accounting and budgeting terms which will then enable training needs to be quantified and stratified throughout the departments
- all targets and objectives set by senior management should be output-outcome related with built-in incentives to ensure their achievement; training can then be given on aspects of performance measurement and quantifying the outputs and outcomes.[24]

Clearly, a great deal of activity took place on the training front in the UK, and the accounting officer's assurance on the adequacy of RAB training was the focal point of this activity. But what is particularly instructive is how the government, through a comprehensively designed training structure, tried to induce a culture change through an understanding and acceptance of how to use the benefits of accrual accounting.

HOW HAS IT WORKED?

The introduction of resource accounting in the UK was in response to demands for

- more accurate and relevant management information with which the departments can cost the resources they use and decide on the mix of resources they need with the outputs they deliver;
- securing economy, efficiency, and effectiveness of public services;
- better asset management; and
- improvement in public expenditure so as to increase stability, responsibility, and fairness.

Have these objectives been achieved?

Management Information

The RAB has been a trigger for departments to re-assess and invest in new management information systems in order to utilize the new resource information. RAB has required expenses and income to be allocated to each of department's objectives. The benefit from costing the objectives has been that government is now in a position to demonstrate to the taxpayers the relative resources consumed by the services it provides.[25]

Economy, Efficiency, and Effectiveness of Public Services

A system of comprehensive performance assessment review has been introduced. A department is given a rating; higher the rating, greater are the flexibilities the department is given— which means increased funding. Poorly rated departments are subjected to intervention by central government. Public service agreements have been introduced for each of the 18 main government departments and five cross-departmental areas of policy. These include statements of the aims and objectives of each department together with the outcome-focused performance measures and targets. Evaluation of the impact of public service agreements shows that departments have developed better links with local service providers and there is resource reallocation with a view to improved programme effectiveness.[26] Performance assessment in the Government of UK has evolved from being a simple evaluation of a department's performance against a set of national performance indicators to being a more rigorous assessment of a department's ability and capacity to improve the services it delivers. Performance against a set of output-based measures is critical to the performance assessment process, but of equal importance is the assessment of the department's performance management system; in particular, its resources, management, and capacity to improve service delivery.[27]

Better Asset Management

One of the distinct benefits of RAB has been that assets in use by government departments, but which were invisible in financial terms under the cash accounting system, have acquired distinct values. At a minimum, the existence of such valuations has helped to raise the consciousness of the departments delivering public services to the assets they have control over and to overcome the impression, which was created by the operation of cash accounting system, that assets were free goods. Better asset management has undeniably been the single largest benefit of adopting resource accounting. This, in turn, has generated some direct benefits and some indirect ones too as detailed below.

- Availability of an asset register providing details of what a department owns with a view to scrutinizing whether the use of all the assets are necessary for delivering outputs.
- Availability of asset valuations providing details of the replacement cost.

- Full costs of the outputs are available.
- Departmental activities are appraised in a realistic manner so as to assign costs for them.
- Stock control systems are tested for their robustness.

Although the RAB has been adopted only recently, there are already a number of visible benefits. For example, student loans are more transparent, with cash flows now separated from the cost of making the loan. More generally, across all departments, working capital is now fully accounted for, whereas previously billions of pounds were merely held in suspense accounts. The near elimination of suspense accounts as a result of resource accounting and a clearer accounting for capital has, at the same time, brought about better management of cash.[28]

Fiscal Policy

As we noted, the government's approach to public expenditure is governed by the following rules.

- *The Golden Rule:* During the economic cycle, the government will borrow only to invest and not to fund current spending
- *The Sustainable Investment Rule:* Borrowing to finance investment will be set so as to ensure that net public debt, as a proportion of GDP, will be held during the economic cycle at a stable and prudent level.

These rules have ensured that public finances have remained in a sound position and, more importantly, these rules have also promoted fairness between generations. The adoption of accrual accounting has supported these fiscal rules through the separate identification of capital and revenue expenditure; an act of separation that is incapable of being delimited under the cash accounting system.[29]

On the whole, the new system has

- ensured that the full economic costs of government activity are now measured properly by (a) including non-cash costs and (b) matching them to the right period;
- helped to end the historic bias against investment by clearly separating capital and revenue expenditure and has improved the management of capital by measuring, for the first time, the full costs of holding and using assets (including depreciation and a cost for capital charge); and
- given the government, the Parliament, and the public better information on how resources are helping to achieve government objectives.

CONCLUSION

The Chancellor of the Exchequer, in his foreword to the green paper described the accounting changes as, 'probably the most important reform of civil service accounting and budgeting arrangements this century'.[30] M. Wright noted that, 'Not since the 1960s has a change of such magnitude been introduced unprovoked by either a financial or an economic crisis'.[31] The development of resource accounting and budgeting has introduced best-practice financial management into the government. In the process, the Government of UK has been able to achieve substantial improvement in the efficiency and effectiveness of the services delivered by the government.

NOTES

1. HM Government (1994a), p. 40.
2. OECD (1993), p. 49.
3. Fulton Committee Report (1975), p. 1.
4. Das (1998), pp. 102–3.
5. Ibid., p. 103 .
6. OECD (1999), pp. 2–3 .
7. Ibid., p. 3.
8. HM Government (1996a), p. 1.
9. Likierman (1997), p. 19.
10. HM Government (1994a), p. 2.
11. Ibid., p. 2.
12. For details, see Likierman (1997).
13. HMSO (1997b).
14. Scottish Parliament (2001), p. 21.
15. Ross (1999), p. 8.
16. HMSO (2000), p. 2.
17. Based on HM Treasury (2000a).
18. HM Treasury (2001b), p. 1.
19. HM Treasury (2000a), p. 1.
20. HM Treasury (2000c), p. 1.
21. Ross (1999), p. 10.
22. Ibid.
23. Ibid.
24. Ibid., pp. 10–11.
25. Hepworth (2002), p. 8.
26. National Audit Office (2001), p. 6.
27. Rose (2003), p. 32.
28. OECD (1993), p. 21.

29. Hepworth (2002), p. 14.
30. HMSO (1994a), p. 2.
31. Wright (1995), p. 1.

6

Accrual Accounting in the Swedish Government

The administrative setup in Sweden consists of the central government and a large number of independent agencies. There are about 300 agencies in Sweden; they vary greatly in size—the small agencies having as few as 10 civil servants while the large agencies employ as many as tens of thousands. Approximately 99 per cent of civil servants in Sweden are employed by the agencies while the remaining 1 per cent work with the ministries.[1] Actual operations of the government are conducted in the agencies.

The size, structure, and types of operations vary from one agency to another but what distinguishes these agencies from the line departments of the government in other countries is the independence that the agencies in Swedish government enjoy. They are independent to take their own decisions, and they are free from any control and regulation by the central government. There is a very clear separation between the ministries on the one hand and the agencies on the other. Such separation of policy and operational functions has been a hallmark of the Swedish government's functioning for over 200 years.[2]

Personnel management in Sweden has historically been marked by a great deal of decentralization, the only exceptions being the collective bargaining arrangements and provision of accommodation.

Collective Bargaining

Collective bargaining arrangements have historically been centralized. There is a National Collective Bargaining Office that negotiates and concludes all pay agreements centrally with the unions representing the staff of the agencies. The agreements are then approved by the cabinet and sent to the finance committee of the Parliament for approval. Typically, the agencies are not allowed to offer a compensation package that is different from the centrally determined pay agreements.[3] Agencies had no control over the resources used for meeting requirements of the wage settlements, which accounted for a substantial portion of the total resources at the disposal of the agencies.

Accommodation

Supply of accommodation to government organizations was centrally controlled. An organization of the central government was responsible for supplying all government organizations with offices and other accommodation. Typically, rent was charged by this central organization for the services it offered to the agencies, but in case of increase in the rentals, the agencies were compensated by the central government.[4]

PUBLIC SECTOR REFORMS

Structural Changes

Structural changes in the functioning of the public sector in Sweden were introduced in the early 1980s. The changes included abolition, amalgamation, and corporatization of organizations in the state structure. At the time of making these changes, the Swedish government decided that these should take place in the agency form. In cases where the agency form was not appropriate, the government chose to introduce the structure of limited companies or non-profit making associations.

Corporatization was introduced in a major way. Several of the state-owned enterprises were converted into limited companies, including Swedish National Defence Factories, Swedish State Power Board, Swedish Telecom, and Sweden Post. Approximately 100,000 employees were affected in the process. Corporatization in Sweden was intended to create a competitive environment, to make government activities more efficient and to get better returns from the capital invested. To guarantee competitive neutrality, independent supervisory agencies were created in the areas of telecommunications, postal service, and electricity markets.

A caveat is in order. Unlike in other countries where fairly fundamental changes in the state structure were effected as a part of public sector reforms, there was no major change in the Swedish government's structure apart from corporatization. For example, the process of radical restructuring—that took place in New Zealand, Australia, and the UK by way of separating policy making from operational functions—was not necessary in Sweden because, as we noted earlier, such structural separation had already been in place for over 200 years. In fact, the governments in these three countries were taking a leaf out of Sweden's experience while restructuring their public sector.[5]

Delegation of Decision-Making

In 1988, the government decided to shift from management by resources to management by results. This meant that the consumption of resources—not the acquisition or cash payments—became the important consideration in assessing the performance of agencies. It also meant that civil servants in the agencies were given the necessary flexibility in implementing programmes. But there is a quid pro quo for the increased flexibility: managers are held accountable for the results. The reforms envisioned a fundamental change holding managers responsible for what they do, not how they do it. Instead of controlling inputs, the focus is now on outcomes and outputs. The accountability regime is based on ministries specifying the results they expect of their agencies, and the agencies then reporting to the ministries on the results they have achieved.[6]

Collective Bargaining

In 1994, the process of collective bargaining was totally devolved to the agencies and is now the responsibility of the agencies. The agreements are negotiated entirely by the agencies themselves.

Accommodation

The central control in respect of provision of accommodation was abolished in 1993. The agencies are now free to choose their accommodation—they can also get their accommodation supplied by the private sector. The government organization in the central government responsible for supplying accommodation was abolished.

Accountability for Results

The results expected of the agencies are now specified in the letter of instruction (Regleringsbrev) which the ministries issue to each agency immediately following the approval of the budget by Riksadagen (the Swedish legislature). As per the guidelines issued by the ministry of finance, the contents of the letter of instruction should include a review of how the agency's work contributes to the government's desired outcomes, a specification of objectives and targets at an operational level and how the agency is to report back on the results achieved, and the specification of any special assignment that the agency is supposed to carry out.

ACCOUNTING REFORMS

The historical development of government accounting in Sweden has an interesting story to tell.[7] In the nineteenth century, government expenditure was recorded when the government decided to incur expenditure rather than when the expenditure was incurred. As a result, it was not possible to establish the cash position of the State. There was a fraud in the office of the paymaster general in the beginning of the twentieth century and, because of the fraud, the government decided to create a cheque account with the Bank of Sweden, and accounting principles were laid down on a cash basis. Under this system, only actual payments were to be recorded, and accounts were arranged in accordance with the budget structure of the State. This meant gross accounting: separating income from expenditure. Only at the end of the financial period, the agencies were allowed to record their debts and claims, so that the outcome of the State budget did not have to depend upon late payments. In respect of public enterprises, assets were shown in a separate system of funds but only if they carried a surplus yield to the budget of the State.

INTRODUCTION OF ACCRUAL ACCOUNTING

As the State sector expanded in the 1960s, there were increasing demands for accounting information. As a result, the Programme Budget Scheme was introduced, in which the cost of staff (including a roughly calculated social security fee), office premises, and (in some cases) interest on capital were distributed to the various programme activities of the government departments so as to enable the parliamentary appropriations to cover the total cost of programme activities. The Programme Budget Scheme was only partly successful; this was because the concept of depreciation was not included in the scheme. However, with a central computerized accounting system, responsibility was increasingly delegated to the agencies. A postal giro system was also established, in which all agencies received payments and made disbursements for which they were responsible, and the balances were cleared with the government's cheque account with the Bank of Sweden on a daily basis. On the whole, the system established clear responsibility for cash management at the agency level, and the utilization of the savings potential at the central level. Although accounting took place at the agency level, the ministries were treated for all accounting purposes as separate agencies.

In 1979, the Government Accounting Ordinance was issued, introducing accrual accounting in the agencies. The ordinance, however, contained provisions for granting exemptions to the agencies from adopting accrual accounting. In practice, exemptions were granted to a large number of agencies, allowing them to use cash-based accounting. In 1991, the ordinance was amended providing for gradual abolition of the exemptions given, and roughly one-third of the agencies changed their accounting every year until finally, the last exemptions were abolished in 1994.[8]

ACCOUNTING ORGANIZATION AND REGULATION

The Agency as an Independent Accounting Unit

The annual accounts in Sweden are prepared only in the agencies. Each agency is responsible for its own accounts. Even though the agencies are an integral part of the central government, and therefore, not independent legal entities, the accounting methods are designed as if the agencies were completely independent units. For Sweden as a whole, the Swedish National Financial Management Authority (ESV) is the agency responsible for the development of generally accepted accounting practice and for consolidation of accounting information.

Each agency is required to generate financial information every month and send it electronically to a database in ESV. Part of the information is aggregated monthly, while other parts of the information are aggregated quarterly or annually. After careful analysis, the aggregated information is transferred to the ministries and to other organizations such as Statistics Sweden and the National Institute of Economic Research. The agencies' statements of financial performance and financial position are consolidated once a year into a central government annual report. Each agency pays its bills and expenses, and the payments are made by a giro system connected to banks. Each agency has its own bank accounts, but these bank accounts are all connected to the government's central current account. The system is similar to a corporate account system.

Each agency has its own accounting system. ESV distributes and supports a commercial accounting system called Agresso, which the agencies are recommended to use. However, if an agency wants to use another system, it is allowed to buy any system that is offered on the open market. Each agency is also responsible for its own internal control system. Actually, it is stipulated that the head of the agency is responsible for 'the organization being structured in a way that ensures that the accounting, the handling of funds and the management of other assets as well as the agency's operations are controlled in an adequate way'.[9]

Accounting for All Financial Transactions

The activities of the agencies are financed from different sources: appropriations from the state, fees, charges, grants and donations, as well as internal loans issued by the Swedish National Debt Office, and leasing. Some agencies also collect taxes and legal fees. All such income, as well as related expenditure, are recognized in the agencies' accounts. Taxes and legal fees are normally collected by the agency on behalf of the State and subsequently transferred to the government central current account. The way the accounting model is designed, an agency receiving taxes accounts for the revenue and includes the revenue in a specific section of its statement of financial performance.

Appropriations from the State budget, however, constitute the most important source of financing for the agencies. Frame appropriation is the most common type of appropriation, wherein the agencies are permitted to save unused amounts and use them in the following year, and there is a credit facility that enables using a portion of the following years' appropriation in advance. One-twelfth of the total appropriation is normally paid into the agency's bank account each month.

Agencies in Sweden are permitted to charge user fees for providing public services and products. The Swedish constitution stipulates that in matters of determining the size of user fee, the principle of full cost recovery should be the general pricing policy.[10] What this means is that the user fee, in the long run, should neither exceed nor be below the full cost of the service provided. Some agencies such as the universities, receive grants and donations to finance their operations. The government has prescribed a framework of rules that regulates the circumstances under which the agencies are permitted to receive donations and how assets created out of such donations are to be treated. The agencies are allowed to use internal loans to finance investment in fixed assets other than infrastructure; they are also allowed to enter into agreements to finance through leasing. However, certain conditions have been stipulated in respect of such leasing agreements: the agency has to prove that it is less expensive for the State as a whole to lease an asset rather than purchasing it or financing the purchase with the aid of an internal loan.

THE ACCOUNTING MODEL

The accounting model followed by the government is very similar to the accounting principles used by private sector companies in Sweden. The key features of the accounting model are:

- double entry recording
- a chart of accounts
- a chart of object codes
- accrual accounting
- financial statements—such as a statement of financial performance and a statement of financial position.

The accounting model integrates external and management accounting through the chart of accounts and the chart of object codes. The model also comprises both general accounting (irrespective of the source of finance) and State budget accounting, including appropriations and general income such as taxes. As the general accounting is on an accrual basis and the State budgeting accounting is partly on cash basis, the accounting model needs to take this into consideration. For example, special accounts are used for cut-off items such as accrued expenses or deferred expenditure. These accounts are either included or excluded, depending on the report produced or the type of analysis required.

ACCOUNTING REGULATIONS

The budget act stipulates, 'Government accounting shall be performed according to generally accepted accounting practice, and further regulations on accounting shall be issued by the government or an agency designated by the government. Reports shall give a true and fair view of operations, financial performance and position, and the stewardship of financial and other assets.'[11] The Swedish government has issued several ordinances relating to government accounting. In addition, the ESV has the authority to issue supplementary regulations to the agencies. On the whole, accounting regulations in Sweden are patterned on the rules and standards as prevailing in the private sector, the only difference being that wherever necessary, the government regulations should accommodate the special characteristics of the public sector. As private sector accounting principles in Sweden are similar to International Accounting Standards Committee (IASC) standards, government accounting principles in Sweden also bear a very close resemblance to the IASC standards. Following are the ordinances and regulations that have been issued by the Swedish government.

ORDINANCE ON ANNUAL REPORT AND BUDGET DOCUMENTATION

The ordinance on annual report and budget documentation describes the budget and accountability documents that an agency should submit to the cabinet, the contents of the documents, and the time at which they are due. The documents stipulated are the annual report, the interim report, and the budget documentation. The ordinance also sets out the valuation principles to be followed while valuing different types of assets. In structure and content, the ordinance is patterned on the Annual Accounts Act, which is followed by private sector companies in Sweden.

BOOKKEEPING ORDINANCE

The bookkeeping ordinance provides:

- definition of generally accepted accounting practice
- current recording of transactions
- accounting vouchers
- the closing of books
- reporting requirements for consolidation purposes.

So far as the contents are concerned, the ordinance is very similar to the Bookkeeping Act in the private sector.

Supplementary Regulations

There are several regulations issued by the ESV that lay down detailed rules and clarifications in the areas covered by the ordinances. While laying down these regulations, ESV has followed the recommendations made by the Swedish Financial Accounting Standards Council and the Swedish Accounting Standards Board, IASC, and International Federation of Accountants—Public Sector Committee (IFAC-PSC). The ESV has also taken note of the standards set by the International Standard System of National Accounts and the International Monetary Fund's Government Finance Statistics (GFS). ESV makes additions and changes to the regulations, by way of amendments, once a year. The general principle informing the ordinances and regulations is that each agency should follow generally accepted accounting principles (GAAP). The ordinances and regulations follow the rules and standards for private sector companies, except in areas relating to taxation and protection of the interest of shareholders and creditors. The explanation for such exception is that since the agencies do not pay tax on profit, and since the State is one legal entity, adequate guarantee for the claims of the creditors has already been provided.

On the whole, Swedish government and its agencies follow, to a very considerable extent, the same rules and regulations as the private sector companies in Sweden. What it means is that, for the purposes of solving accounting problems, the same methods as are followed in the private sector are also followed in the Swedish government. Since the Riksadagen has consented to the accounting ordinances and regulations, the same accounting principles are now observed throughout the State sector in Sweden. In other words, since 1 July 1993, the Swedish State sector is using full accruals as the general basis for accounting. As a consequence, it is now possible to draw up annual accounts for the state of Sweden, based upon generally accepted accounting principles, consisting of an operational statement, a balance sheet, and a statement of source and application of funds.

ACCOUNTING AT THE AGENCY LEVEL

The agencies are required, under the provisions of the accounting ordinance to record all economic events on a current basis. Economic events are defined as in the following.

- *Payments:* receipts and disbursements on a cash basis.
- *Claims and liabilities:* income and expenditure to be recorded currently on a modified accrual basis.
- *Settlements:* these transactions typically include the use of appropriations or accounting for revenue on the State budget or settlements with the government's cheque account.

Before the books are closed, and this happens when the annual accounts are prepared, economic events are recorded in the accounts. This is needed so that the relevant revenues and costs relating to that fiscal year are shown. Examples of such periodization items are cut-off (accrued) items such as the part of invoiced office rents relating to another year. The value of assets and debts is assessed, and depreciation cost is recorded. This results in full accrual accounting. However, such items need not necessarily be recorded on an annual basis; in fact, the periodization items can also be recorded more frequently. Some agencies do it even on a monthly basis.

The economic events are said to be external if they relate to an entity outside the agency; this includes other agencies in the State structure as well as private companies or organizations. Settlements with the State budget or with the government's cheque account are also considered to be external, from the agency's point of view. The accounts reflecting these external economic events are arranged so as to facilitate the production of an operational statement and a balance sheet according to the fixed schedules. Therefore, a standard chart of accounts can be used by most agencies, without alteration.

THE ANNUAL REPORT OF THE AGENCY

The annual report of an agency has the following statements and reports.

- *Statement of financial performance:* the statement covers all revenues and expenses.

- *Statement of financial position:* the statement includes current assets and fixed assets as well as liabilities and capital.
- *Cash flow statement:* the statement provides a summary of cash receipts and cash payments during the year. In the cash flow statement of an agency, information is provided under various subheads such as operations, investments and collection of taxes, and transfers. The statement shows how operations and investments have been financed.
- *Appropriation report:* The report includes the outcome of appropriations and general State budget incomes. The outcome is compared with the amount of appropriation placed at the disposal of the agency and with the calculated amount for State budget income.
- *Performance report:* The report compares results actually achieved with the goals and objectives of the agency. If the ministry concerned has not specified any reporting requirements, trends in respect of volume, incomes, costs, and quality of the outputs are presented and commented upon.

The annual report also includes notes with information on the accounting and valuation principles applied and other information necessary to understand the report.

THE STATEMENT OF FINANCIAL PERFORMANCE

The main functions of the statement of financial performance in an agency are to:

- provide an account of the cost of operations
- account for resources made available for operations and to account for the extent to which this revenue is derived from appropriations or from other sources respectively
- account for the change in an agency's net capital and to show how this change has occurred.

TABLE 6.1: THE DESIGN OF THE STATEMENT OF FINANCIAL PERFORMANCE

Operating Revenue
Revenue from appropriations
Revenue from fees and other charges
Revenue from grants
Financial income
Total

Operating Costs

Cost of staff
Cost of premises
Other operating costs
Financial expenses
Depreciation and write-downs

Total
Net surplus/Deficit from operations

Profit or loss on holdings in associated
   companies and subsidiary companies

Collection of general income

Revenue from fees and other revenues that
may not be used by the agency
Revenue from taxes
General revenue transferred to the government budget

Balance

Transfers

Appropriations for grants/allowances
Contributions from other agencies to finance
   grants and allowances
Other funds received to finance grants/allowances
Financial income
Financial expenses
Allocations to/withdrawals from funds, etc., for
   transfer purposes
Grants/allowances provided

Balance

Change in capital for the year

Source: ESV (2001).

The statement of financial performance starts with revenue from operations (although there was a great deal of discussion at the time the accounting model was developed as to whether it would be more appropriate in the government sector to start with expenses). In the Swedish case, however, in respect of the matching principle, the expression 'reversed matching' is used in the sense that revenue for the period is matched against cost instead of vice versa. Appropriations are regarded as a source of financing. It differs from other sources of financing (revenue from grants, fees, charges, etc.), but which are treated as operating revenues.

The statement has broadly the same layout as the income statement of a private sector company, but with a significant difference. In the statement of financial performance, the main source of income is revenue from appropriations, which is recorded when an agency utilizes its rights to incur expenditure to the State budget. An expenditure that is to be covered by the State budget arises when the invoice is received and recorded, irrespective of the date of payment of the invoice. The transaction results in a revenue from appropriation (credit) and a claim on the government (debit). The claim is settled when the money is transferred from the government's cheque account to the agency, either daily or monthly.[12]

Another feature of the statement of financial performance are the sections on revenue from fees and taxes (which are not at the agency's disposal), and transfers (funds from the State budget paid to individuals or organizations). In such cases, the agency acts merely as a conduit for funds, to or from the State budget such as with income tax or pensions.

When the new accounting model was being developed in Sweden, there were discussions whether collections of taxes and transfers should be included as items in the statement of financial performance of the agency concerned or accounted for in the agency's statement of financial position. It was argued that taxes and transfers are outside the legitimate operations of the agency because their payment has nothing to do with the costs of production of an agency's services. Finally, it was decided that collections of taxes and transfers were to be accounted for in specific sections in the agency's statement of financial performance and should be regarded as revenue and expenses. The argument being that this would be the best way to collect and consolidate information on taxes and transfers. In the section 'Collection of general income', agencies recognize taxes received as revenue, and the tax income forwarded to the central government's current account is recognized as expense. As a result, the net balance of the section is often zero. The same principle is also used for transfers. Collection of taxes is normally recognized as income when a tax liability is issued to the taxpayer. Government transfers are normally recognized as expenses when the payment is made, the reason being that payment is regarded as discretionary until the payment is made.

The change in net capital for the year is often very close to zero in an agency's statement of financial performance. The reasons are:

- for operations financed by user charges and fees, the full cost of recovery principle is applied. This means that, in the long run, revenue and expenses are of the same size

- grants received from donors are allocated to specific periods, that is, only the grants used to finance a period's costs are recognized as revenue. Other grants are accounted for in the statement of financial position. In the long run, grants are fully spent in operations and therefore there is normally a zero net balance
- the appropriation amount recognized as revenue is normally very close to the period's expenses.[13]

THE STATEMENT OF FINANCIAL POSITION

The Statement of Financial Position gives a summary account of assets, capital and liabilities. The important role of the Statement of Financial Position is to distribute costs to different periods. The design of the Statement of Financial Position is as in Table 6.2.

TABLE 6.2: ASSETS CAPITAL AND LIABILITIES

Assets	Capital and liabilities
Intangible fixed assets	*Agency capital*
Capitalized expenditure on research and development	Government capital
Rights and other intangible assets	Revaluation capital
Advances for tangible fixed assets	Gifts and donations
	Shares in profits of subsidiary and associated companies
Tangible fixed assets	Change in capital brought forward
Buildings, land, and other real estate	Change in capital in statement of financial performance
Improvements to real estate owned by others	
Machinery, plant, and equipment	*Funds*
Construction in progress	Funds
Reserve stock for war or emergencies	
Advances for tangible fixed assets	*Provisions*
	Provision for pensions and similar commitments
Financial fixed assets	Other provisions
Shares in subsidiary and associated companies	
Other long-term securities and bonds	*Liabilities, etc.*
Long-term claims on other agencies	Loans at the Swedish National Debt Office (SNDO)
Other long-term claims	Other loans
	Interest account credit
Lending	Other credits at the SNDO
Lending	Debts to other agencies

Stock
Stock and stores
Work in progress
Properties
Advances to suppliers

Receivables
Accounts receivable
Claims on other agencies
Other claims

Periodization items
Prepaid expenses
Accrued revenue from grants
Other accrued revenue

Settlement with the government
Settlement with the government

Short-term investments
Securities and shares

Cash and bank balances
Balance on interest-bearing account at
 SNDO
Other balances at SNDO
Other cash and bank balances

Accounts payable
Other liabilities
Cash deposits
Advances from customers

Cut-off items
Accrued expenses
Unused grants
Other deferred revenue

Contingent Liabilities

Source: ESV (2001).

The statement of financial position has the same main layout as the balance sheet of private companies, the only difference being in respect of the sections of settlements with the government and Agency Capital, which correspond to equity in a private company. Assets are recorded at acquisition value, with straight-line depreciation according to the expected lifetime of particular assets.

Definition of Assets

In defining assets, the IFAC-PSC definition is used: 'A resource controlled by an entity as a result of past events and from which future economic benefits or service potential are expected to flow to the entity.'[14] The main rule followed is that all assets are shown on the face of the statement of financial position. The assets are classified into two groups—current assets and fixed assets. There is also a section for loans that can be both short-term and long-term.

Fixed Assets

A fixed asset is an asset that is intended for permanent use or possession. Fixed assets—financial, physical, and intangible assets—are valued at the acquisition cost, less accumulated depreciation. A fixed asset that is received free of charge is recognized at its market value. Depreciation is based on the economic life of each asset. If the value of an asset has decreased by more than the depreciation made, and if the decrease in value of the asset is judged to be permanent, the value of the asset is written down. Fixed assets, with a value that considerably and permanently exceeds their recorded value, are stated at an amount not in excess of that value, that is, they may be appreciated. Shares in subsidiaries and associated companies are regarded as fixed assets and are valued using the equity method.

Current Assets

Current assets are not intended for permanent use or possession. With few exceptions, current assets are recognized either at acquisition value or at fair value, if the latter is lower. Fair value refers to the sale value less estimated selling expenses. The value of stock or similar assets, is estimated on the basis of first in first out (FIFO) principle of weighted average prices or of some other similar principles. The last in first out principle is not used. Doubtful receivables are recognized at the value that is expected to be received. Claims and debts in foreign currency are valued at the exchange rate prevailing at the end of the accounting year.

ACQUISITION VALUE

Acquisition value (the historical cost) is the main valuation principle used in the Swedish government. As an important role of the statement of financial position is to distribute costs to different periods, acquisition value is the valuation method that is normally used, because it reflects the resources sacrificed for acquisition of the asset, and the sacrifice should be distributed over a period of time. Moreover, acquisition cost (less depreciation, if applicable) is the value on which interest or yield should be placed if the intention is to let each generation pay for the use of resources, including the borrowing cost of investments. Decisions on replacement have to be taken by each generation. The underlying logic is that the government is accountable not only for the management of administration but also for economic situation of the entire society.

DEPRECIATION METHOD

Fixed assets with a limited economic life are depreciated systematically during their lifetime. There is no specified limit to economic life, it depends on how the asset is used by different agencies. Consequently, each agency decides on its own depreciation period. The supplementary regulations of the ESV require that the depreciation period should normally be taken at three to seven years for computers; 5 to 10 years for machines, vehicles and inventories; and 30 to 40 years for buildings and roads. Expenditure on research and development is depreciated over less than five years. The depreciation method used is normally straight-line but other methods are used if appropriate.

Obligations

In the central government sector in Sweden, obligations are divided into liabilities, provisions, and contingent liabilities; in the same structure as used by the IASC. A liability is recognized on the face of the statement of financial position when it is probable that an obligation will have to be met. Where provisions are concerned, the IASC definition is used, that is, liabilities of uncertain timing or amount; for example, some organizations account for the provisions for pensions and for restructuring costs. However, as a basic principle, provisions for pensions are accounted for by the National Government Employees Pensions Board. The pension cost is spread annually through pension fees that the agencies have to pay to the board. Contingent liabilities are defined as per standards laid down by IASC and they are disclosed in the annual report of each agency; for example, government guarantees are regarded as contingent liabilities.

Capital

Capital is recorded when an agency receives appropriations to be used for investments such as in infrastructure, but that are not financed through internal loans. The capital is decreased in accordance with depreciation made. If an agency receives donations with the provision that only returns on the donation may be used in operations, the amount received is recorded in donation capital.[15]

THE CASH FLOW STATEMENT

Information from the statement of financial performance and the statement of financial position is combined to produce the cash flow statement. It has five sections—operations, investment, loaning, collection of taxes, and transfers. Each section is adjusted for short-term claims and liabilities, whereby the cash flow from the section is shown. The appropriation report describes in detail the settlements with the government; the Report is, in fact, a specification to the item in the balance sheet entitled Settlements with the

Government. In the report, outcome is shown against allocated appropriations and estimated State budget revenue.

THE PERFORMANCE REPORT

The most important document in an agency's annual report is the performance report. In this report, the agency accounts for its major types of output with cost per unit, quality, and measurable effects. The development of costs per branch of operations is accounted for and commented upon. This information is taken from management accounting of the agency, in which internal economic events show the distribution of cost and revenue between various objects in the agency. It is obtained through the use of object codes in various structures—organizational units, output, branch of operation, projects—attached to the accounts.

The annual report of an agency, including the five reports and statements, is sent to the ministry concerned and is examined by the Swedish National Audit Office (SNAO), which issues an audit report on every agency.

ACCOUNTING AT THE LEVEL OF THE GOVERNMENT

Accounting information of the agencies is transmitted electronically to the SNAO, which is the organization responsible for preparing aggregated accounts of the State. The agencies are required to submit information every month on:

- outcome of appropriations and State budget revenue—this is required for forecasts of the State budget outcome
- income and expenditure according to economic categories—this is required for macroeconomic analyses and financial statistics
- payments—this is required for reconciliation purposes at the State level.[16]

Annually and semi-annually, the agencies are required to submit their statements of financial position and statements of financial performance to the national audit office; the idea is to consolidate the annual accounts of the State. Such a consolidation requires the specifications of transactions with other government agencies. The annual accounts of the State cover the legal entity of the State of Sweden except the national bank, which is treated as a separate legal entity. Public utilities and government agencies financed with fees are also included, although they are considered as belonging to the private sector in the National Accounts of Sweden.

Additional information is provided about the areas where government exercises a decisive influence such as limited companies partly owned by the State, and about funds that are a concern of the State although not formally a part of that legal entity such as the public pension funds. In case the true value of an asset—the market value, the replacement cost—differs considerably from what is shown in the balance sheet, it is provided in the note. Combined with a cash flow statement for the whole State, this gives a much better overall picture than the State budget alone does. More importantly, it includes all state activities, not just those financed out of the State budget, and the annual accounts show the assets owned by the State to be considered when the state debt is analysed.

SPECIAL ACCOUNTING ISSUES

INFRASTRUCTURE

Investment in infrastructure is treated as an asset. Roads are depreciated over forty years. Maintenance and upkeep expenditure to retain their service potential is treated as expense for the period. Before 1993, investments in infrastructure such as roads was treated as an expense but is now recognized at acquisition value less depreciation. When the new accounting model was introduced, road investments for the period 1955–94 were valued retroactively. A conversion was made with the help of special indices. A similar method has been used for the railways. Old roads and railways have been valued at historical cost less accumulated depreciation and recognized in the statement of financial position, with a special item under capital, as counter value. This gives an overall picture of each year's cost of infrastructure, depreciation, upkeep, etc., and makes it possible to analyse the position in respect of government's debt, while taking into consideration what has been used for investment and what has been spent on consumption. Civil airports, electric grids and waterways are built by public utilities and therefore treated as assets.

EMERGENCY ASSETS INCLUDING MILITARY ASSETS

Emergency assets are assets that are kept in stock for use in an emergency or a war situation. They are divided into three groups:

- emergency assets, which are sold and replaced on a current basis such as food supplies
- emergency assets which are kept for their total economic life
- emergency assets under construction.

All emergency assets are classified and valued as fixed assets. Emergency assets that are sold and replaced on a current basis are valued according to the FIFO method. Accordingly, defence material—such as real estate, vehicles, weapons and other equipment—are, in principle, accounted for as assets. This principle has been in effect since 1998. Before that, a distinction was made between material used for training of military staff on the one hand and materials kept in reserve, to be used in the event of war, on the other. There are two reasons why all military equipments are treated on a par with other assets. One is a practical consideration. It is difficult to distinguish the equipment used for training purposes from that kept in stock. The other consideration is more theoretical. Keeping military equipment in stock can be regarded as an insurance for providing a service potential for each generation of citizens, and the expense should be recognized in the years when people enjoy such a benefit.

HERITAGE ASSETS

Heritage assets are the only exemptions from the rule that all assets shall be accounted for. Heritage sites were excluded from the accounts—when the agencies constructed their statements of financial position in 1993—because, in many cases, information on acquisition cost did not exist or was irrelevant because of the change in prices. The heritage assets were considered to be of no relevance in respect of contributing to better financial management which, in any case, was the primary objective of the reforms. Even the heritage assets acquired after 1993 were excluded from recognition. The regulations supplementing the ordinance on annual report and budget documentation states that, 'Land, buildings, and other real estate with predominantly historical or cultural value, as well as museum objects for which there is normally no market, may be excluded from recognition.'[17]

ASSETS ACQUIRED THROUGH DONATIONS

These are recorded at a value that corresponds to the market value at the time of acquisition.

FINANCIAL LEASING

Assets acquired under finance leases are capitalized and included in the accounts together with a liability to pay future rentals.

INTANGIBLE ASSETS

The accounting rule for expenditure on research and development requires that the expenditure be recognized as a fixed asset if that asset may be of considerable value to the operations during the years to come. Due to the use of the word 'may', some agencies recognize expenditure on computer programmes etc., as an asset, while other agencies do not. From 2002, the accounting rules have been changed in order to achieve uniformity between agencies. The position now is that expenditure on research is treated as an expense while expenditure on development is to be recognized as a fixed asset if the asset is expected to be of considerable value to operations during years to come.

EVOLUTION OF STATEMENTS OF FINANCIAL POSITION WHEN THE NEW ACCOUNTING MODEL WAS INTRODUCED

Even before the accounting reforms were taken up, most agencies had asset registers and therefore, it was possible to establish acquisition cost of the assets. In such cases, the asset was recognized on the face of the statement of financial position along with the accumulated depreciation at amounts that would have been shown if the new principles had been followed from the beginning. The corresponding credit amount was recorded as capital and during subsequent years, the annual depreciation of these assets reduced the capital until the assets were fully depreciated. This resulted in annual expenses that included depreciation of the assets acquired before the accounting reforms. As a transitory rule, assets with a remaining economic life of less than three years did not have to be recognized nor did assets with a minor value, such as furniture.

PENSION LIABILITIES

Pensions for government employees are recorded as a cost by each agency, as they are accrued. The cost is distributed through fees from the National Government Employee Pensions Board. The expenditures are recognized on an actuarial basis. The employees pensions board handles administration of the pensions and accounts for the pension liability, with exceptions for smaller amounts that are accounted for by a few agencies themselves.

NATIONAL DEBT

Swedish national debt is the largest liability on the central government's consolidated statement of financial position. Treasury bonds with coupons are recognized at nominal value. Treasury bills and treasury bonds without annual coupons are recognized at the amount received at the time of issue. The foreign currency debt is recognized at the exchange rate—as at the end of the year. Accrued interest is recorded as a cut-off item (accrual) and is therefore not included in the definition of national debt.

UNSPENT GRANTS

Unspent grants are the grants received but not yet spent for their intended purpose. They are recorded as a cut-off item (prepaid revenue) in the statement of financial position. This means that only the grants that are actually spent during the year are regarded as revenue, the reason being that the matching principle is applied in this context. Consequently, accrued grants are recognized as an asset in cases where the promised grants are spent before they are received.

CONTINGENCIES UNDER SOCIAL INSURANCE PROGRAMMES AND OTHER TRANSFER PROGRAMMES

Future contingencies regarding social insurance programmes are normally not taken into account as obligations or contingencies, and are therefore not reported on the face of the statement of financial position.[18]

ACCOUNTING AND REPORTING PLANS

CHART OF ACCOUNTS

The chart of accounts is based on a concept that is used by many private companies in Sweden. With private sector standards as the point of departure, the ESV has developed a standard chart of accounts that can be used by the agencies; the chart is recommended but its use is not compulsory. As regards the detailed accounts, it is quite common for the agencies to make modifications and add new accounts so the chart better suits their specific needs.

The structure of the chart of accounts is based on a decimal classification with hierarchically categorized levels (digit positions). The first digit of the account number indicates the class of account; the second, the group of accounts; the third, fourth, and fifth, indicate the account. The chart includes nine account classes, numbered 1–9. The classes of accounts 1–8 are used for external transactions, accounts class 9 is used for internal transactions (internal cost allocations etc.). Separate account classes are provided for revenue and for the major types of costs for material and labour. Separate account classes are also provided for assets, liabilities, and equity. The following is the basic format for the chart of accounts.

TABLE 6.3

ACCOUNT
Class
1 Assets
2 Liabilities and capital
3 Revenue
4 Cost of staff
5 Cost of premises, office services, external services
6 Depreciation
7 Collection of taxes, transfers
8 Change in capital
9 Internal revenue and expenses (within an agency)

Source: ESV (2001), p. 22.

Sweden has a double entry accounting system and consequently one account is debited and another account is credited. The chart of accounts for agencies differs from the private sector's standard chart of accounts in some respects. These differences stem from the differences between government and private sector accounting. For example, a separate account class has been created for collections and transfers of agencies. There are other transactions too that are specific to government agencies.

PLAN OF REPORTING CODES

The plan of reporting codes, which is compulsory, is based on the plan of accounts. However, it is less detailed. It is used for reporting and consolidation, and for facilitation of monitoring of different types of financial information, such as:

- type of expenditure and income (salaries, cost of premises, etc.),
- economic category (consumption or investment), and
- type of asset and liability.

The structure is designed in a manner that makes it possible to keep items referring to specific periods—such as depreciation as well as accrued and deferred items—separate from other expenditures and incomes. This allows information to be analysed on a full accrual basis as well as on a modified accrual basis. This is necessary because budgeting in Sweden is not on a full accrual basis.

CHART OF OBJECT CODES

By having a chart of object codes, it is possible to store and retrieve information in various dimensions in order to follow up and evaluate the results of operations. As a result, the chart of object codes is crucial to performance reporting and monitoring the cost of different activities in an agency as well as the cost of products and different kinds of services. The chart is also used for management accounting. For example, it is used to allocate costs between different organizational units in an agency. There is no compulsory structure of the chart of object codes. The agencies are at liberty to include additional object codes such as areas of activity, products, projects, and organizational units. Also, the chart of object codes is not static. It is adjustable over time as the operations of an agency and the information changes. On the whole, the chart of object codes and the chart of accounts form the accounting plan of an agency in Sweden.

REPORTING AND CONSOLIDATION

Monthly Reporting

All agencies are required to produce financial information on a monthly basis and send it electronically to ESV; in any case, not later than twelve days after the end of the month. The information is structured according to the plan of reporting codes. After compilation and analysis, the information is transferred to the ministries and sometimes to other organizations such as Statistics Sweden and the National Institute of Economic Research. The monthly report includes information on

- the use of appropriations,
- the collection of general income such as taxes, and
- payments made.

The State budget, which includes the use of appropriations and the collection of State budget revenue, is used to follow up budget forecasts and State budget ceilings. Information on payments made is used for reconciliation of the central government's corporate bank account system.

Quarterly Reporting

Financial statistics are reported by the agencies once in a quarter. The information is used for compiling national accounts as well as government finance statistics. The ESV compiles information from the agencies and then transfers it to Statistics Sweden.

Semi-annual Reporting

An interim report is submitted by 15 August each year. It covers the first six months of the year and consists of almost the same financial reports as in the annual report. However, the reporting requirements of the interim report are somewhat less detailed, as neither a cash flow statement nor the votes have to be included. On the other hand, forecasts of the expected State budget income and expenditure at the year end are included.

Annual Reporting

The annual report is to be submitted by 22 February.

PERIODIZATION

Periodization is regarded as a process by which revenue and cost items are divided into two parts. One that affects the present period's statement of financial performance, and another part that is carried forward to one or more subsequent periods through the statement of financial position. According to the current accounting rules, correct periodization is required for the semi-annual and annual reporting. In principle, there are three types of periodizations. These are:

- periodization of stocks, stores, and the like (periodization of the current assets)
- depreciation (periodization of fixed assets)
- accrued and deferred items such as accrued and prepaid revenue and expense.

ELIMINATION OF INTERNAL TRANSACTIONS

When consolidating accounting information from the agencies, it becomes necessary to eliminate internal transactions such as sales from one agency to another as well as government-internal receivables and liabilities. Previously, such elimination was done only at the end of the year. From the year 2000, the accounting information from the agencies makes it possible to make eliminations in the semi-annual reporting. In respect of the elimination of internal receivables and liabilities, the requirements have recently been intensified—to improve quality of the elimination process. This means that now, in their reports, the agencies often need to refer the receivables and liabilities to specified counterparts in the central government. The agencies also need to check their balances against each other.

IMPLEMENTATION

After gradual implementation over a period of two years, accrual accounting was fully implemented in the Swedish central government from 1 July 1993. The process of implementation required accrual accounting to be adjusted or replaced; accounting policies to be developed; routines to be changed; and a great deal of information, education, and training.

ACCOUNTING SYSTEMS

An important prerequisite for implementation of accrual accounting was the availability of accounting systems that could handle accrual accounting. Prior to the implementation of accounting reforms, most agencies were using a centralized system, which had been used since the late 1960s. This system was modified to handle accruals. A new system was also made available to the agencies. The new system, called Agresso, is a commercial system that is used by many private companies worldwide. Through the introduction of the new system, it was possible to make the transition from centralization to decentralization.

ACCOUNTING POLICIES

In the 1980s, accounting policies were formulated in a way that moved the government closer to private sector practices in respect of accounting principles. But even then, most agencies were neither required to follow accrual accounting principles nor to submit financial statements like what is being done now. So the accounting policies had to be developed further. The point of departure was the adoption of accounting policies applicable to the private sector in Sweden. Certain adaptations were however necessary, keeping in view the peculiar requirements of the public sector.

EDUCATION AND TRAINING

A great deal of activities—by way of education, training, and information dissemination—had to be undertaken before accrual accounting was actually implemented. Printed material had to be generated for providing an overview of changes in the process and explaining the reasons for changing to accrual accounting. Training, mainly through seminars, was an important way of disseminating information. Seminars were conducted for personnel working with financial administration at the agencies. A contact person was nominated at the ESV, to be approached when there were questions about the implementation of accrual accounting.

On the whole, the transition to accrual accounting in Sweden was smooth. The process is instructive in the way care was taken to see that the essential differences in the functioning of the government and the private sector were kept in mind while implementing the change to accrual accounting.

THE BUDGET AND THE ACCOUNTING PRINCIPLE

While the Swedish government, including its agencies, account on a full accrual basis, the budget is presented partly on a cash basis and partly on a modified accrual basis. As a result, it is considered necessary to keep the accounts in a structure that enables analysis on both accrual and cash basis, and in many cases also on a modified accrual basis. But such a combination of accounting practices has complicated the accounting model; it has also resulted in problems of defining when an event is to be recognized in the different types of reports. A further problem is that the accrual-based financial statements do not receive the attention they should receive. In the follow-up process, it is often the budget that is considered the most important. Riksadagen decides on appropriations in the budget. When monitoring operations, the appropriations—on a cash or modified accrual basis—are naturally the most important follow-up items.

Due to substantial budget deficits in the first part of 1990s, a new budget process was introduced in 1996 in which expenditure ceilings were introduced as a tool to strengthen the process. Expenditure ceilings were monitored very closely. The new budget process also focuses on macrorestrictions. As these restrictions are often on a cash basis, the accrual basis of accounting has not been accorded the kind of importance it should have received.

HOW HAS IT WORKED?

As we discussed, the main reason for implementing accrual accounting in the Swedish government was to facilitate the implementation of management by results. It is a fact that the implementation of management by results has been greatly helped by the adoption of accrual accounting. The agencies now account for major types of output with cost per unit, quality, and measurable effects. Because the government in Sweden has shifted from management by resources to management by results, such information has been of key importance, both for the ministries' and for the agencies' own management and control. In addition, because the accrual model enables accounting for fixed assets, there have been improvements in financial control and decision-making on investments.

The capitalization of assets, such as computers and machines, has made it possible for the agencies to calculate depreciations and account for them in each period during which the machines were used. As a result, there is complete cost accounting now, especially in combination with the implementation of a system for interest allocation. With complete cost accounting, it is now possible to distribute costs to various products or activities. Consequently, consumption of resources—not the cash payments—is now weighed against the performance of an agency, and evaluation of the results of an agency's different programmes and activities is the basis for implementing management by results.[19] In that sense, the adoption of accrual accounting was, in fact, a precondition for the implementation of management by results.

The introduction of accrual accounting has increased financial awareness. More concretely, it has led to the realization that accounting information is a tool that can be used to solve financial difficulties in the Swedish state sector and make government activities more efficient.[20] It has led to the introduction of accounting methods similar to those applied in the private sector companies and there have been many benefits from this; for instance, in the matter of recruiting and training personnel. It has also facilitated the use of standard accounting systems.[21]

With the introduction of accrual accounting, the information on assets has improved greatly. The improved information is used partly as a basis for allocating resources and costs, and partly for keeping track of government property. In Sweden, a great deal of importance is attached to allocation of resources and costs. Of course, it is also considered important to keep track of government property, but even before accrual accounting was implemented, government agencies were already maintaining some form of asset registers for most types of assets.

In addition, the new forms of control, which accrual accounting has enabled, have provided a better basis for the government's continuous monitoring of the activities of agencies. Management by results has been most effective in the government's control of agencies' administrative appropriations within the framework of the budgetary process. Attempts are currently under way in Sweden to apply management by results to transfers and other specific-purpose appropriations in a more meaningful manner.

There are, however, two negative aspects. The first is that accounting has become very complicated. This is due to the conflicting demands for information from politicians, ministries, statisticians, and agency managers at various levels. Second, the accounting model is neutral to the different ways of financing activities through appropriations, internal loans, sales income, grants or capital yield. The similarity with private sector accounting has sometimes led to misinterpretation of the meaning of an agency's annual report. But, on the whole, these are minor operational problems.

The adoption of accrual accounting has called for massive efforts at all levels of the government. Accounting systems have been modified. The professional skills of the accounting staff have been raised. New accounting methods have been developed. The balance sheets of the agencies have been reconstructed to include assets formerly recorded only as expenditure, such as office machines or national roads.[22]

CONCLUSION

It is important to note that the transition to accrual accounting in the Swedish government was achieved rather smoothly. One reason for this was that no organizational changes were called for; this, as we noted, was because of the fact that the Swedish administrative structure already had a comprehensive network of agencies functioning autonomously and this was compatible with the adoption of accrual accounting. The other reason for smooth transition was that accrual accounting was implemented only in the agencies and in the whole of government financial statements, but not in the budgetary process. As a result, only minor changes were necessary so far as the budgetary process and the involvement of parliament was concerned.[23] Conversely, because budgets in Sweden are presented partly on a cash basis and partly on a modified accrual basis, the result is a duality of system, which has created confusion. In fact, the Swedish experience begs the conclusion that introducing accrual accounting and changing over to an accrual budgeting and legislative approval system should go hand in hand. On the whole, however, the gains of adopting accrual accounting in the Swedish government and the agencies have been immense. In fact, the accounting reforms have been described as the 'most important change in government administration in Sweden since the 17th century.'[24]

NOTES

1. ESV (2001), p. 29.
2. Blondal (2001), p. 43.
3. Ibid., p. 45 .
4. Ibid., p. 45.
5. Ibid., p. 43.
6. Ibid., p. 49.
7. Strom (1997), pp. 25–6.
8. Ibid.
9. ESV (2001), p. 9.
10. Ibid., p. 10.
11. Ibid., p. 11.
12. Strom (1997), p. 27.
13. ESV (2001), p. 15 .
14. Ibid., p. 17.
15. Ibid., pp. 17–18.
16. Strom (1997), p. 28.
17. ESV (2001), pp. 19–20 .
18. Ibid., pp. 19–21.
19. Ibid., pp. 7–8.
20. Strom (1997), p. 28.
21. ESV (2001), p. 8.
22. Strom (1997), p. 28.
23. ESV (1997), p. 26.
24. Strom (1997), p. 25.

Comparative Experience
The Issues

The adoption process of accrual accounting in these four countries has varied considerably, but it has also highlighted a set of common issues.[1] First, government departments have certain assets that are not found in the private sector and therefore, have to be treated differently. Second, transition to accruals requires decisions on how these assets should be valued. Third, there are issues about the accounting standards to be adopted. Fourth, the question arises as to who should set the accounting standards. Fifth, there are a number of implementational issues such as change management and sequencing of the reforms.

ASSETS

The kind of assets that are found only in the government, but not in the private sector, can be broadly categorized into heritage assets, emergency assets, and infrastructure assets.[2]

HERITAGE ASSETS

Heritage assets include historical buildings, monuments, archaeological sites, museums, and galleries. Several issues arise in the treatment of heritage assets. Their acquisition costs are generally not available. In any case, most of these assets are not marketable because the laws of the land prohibit their sale and they do not have any replacement value. Contents of museums and galleries are another special issue. New Zealand, for example, values the contents of its national archives on the same lines as done by international auction houses. Sweden, on the other hand, excluded heritage assets from the accounts when the agencies in the Swedish government prepared their statements of financial position in 1993; even the heritage assets acquired after 1993 were excluded from recognition. The Swedish government decided that land, buildings, and, other real estate with predominantly historical and cultural value as well as museum objects should be excluded from recognition.

There is also the emotional aspect. While considering the recognition of heritage assets, one has to account for the emotional values while attaching market value to a nation's heritage and treasures. It is also felt that valuation of the heritage assets should logically have no relevance in contributing to better financial management, which is the primary objective of financial reforms.

EMERGENCY ASSETS

Emergency assets, including military assets can be defined as assets that are kept in stock for use in an emergency or war-like situation. These assets can be divided into six categories.

1. Emergency assets that are sold and replaced on a current basis such as food supplies.
2. Emergency assets that are kept for their total economic life.
3. Emergency assets under construction.
4. Research and development efforts of the military.
5. Surplus assets such as decommissioned facilities.
6. Military's earmarked radio frequency for communications.

Based on the experience of the countries we studied, there seems to be general agreement on including emergency assets in the accrual accounting process. There is also agreement on the fact that all emergency equipments should be capitalized and depreciated. It is accepted that military assets are prone to premature destruction, but the approach is to depreciate them on a normal basis and then write them off as extraordinary items if they are lost. In New Zealand, dedicated military equipment is recorded at depreciated replacement cost; valuations are made through specialist assessment by the New Zealand Defence Force advisers. In Sweden, all emergency assets are classified and valued as fixed assets. The emergency assets that are sold and replaced on a current basis are valued according to the FIFO method.

Defence material such as real estate, weapons, and other equipment are accounted for as assets in the Swedish government. In fact, in Sweden, before 1998 there was a distinction between material used for training of military staff and material kept in reserve (to be used at the time of war). Such a distinction has now been given up, and all military equipment is treated on a par with other assets. This is for two reasons.

1. It is difficult to distinguish the equipment used for training from that kept in stock.
2. Military equipment in stock is for the benefit of future generations and therefore, the expense should be recognized only when the future generations use the benefit.

It is recognized that capitalization of research done by the military is difficult, particularly when such research is carried out in-house for developing new military systems. This is because such information is kept confidential and therefore, it is not easily available.

Regarding the treatment of surplus assets, such as decommissioned facilities, the practice is to carry them at nil value. However, a negative value has to be assigned because of the cost of holding the decommissioned assets.

In respect of radio frequency spectrum which is exclusively used by the military for meeting its dedicated communications needs, it is agreed that such exclusive use of the airspace represents a huge opportunity cost for the government because it would otherwise have great commercial value. The practice, therefore, is to include such spectrum used by the military.

Infrastructure Assets

Infrastructure assets generally consist of highways and other network assets, which often have very high value. The issues with infrastructure assets are mainly two.

1. The impact of long useful lives of these assets on deciding depreciation schedules for them. Some countries do not depreciate these assets, rather they certify that the maintenance of these assets is such that they have an infinite life span.
2. It is often difficult to estimate the acquisition cost of infrastructure assets. This is because of the age of these assets and also because of the difficulties in separating the original acquisition cost from the subsequent maintenance expenditure.

VALUATION ISSUES

Valuation issues relate to

- the kind of valuation: current, historic, or replacement cost;
- the valuation methodology; and
- periodic revaluation.

Historic cost has been the traditional basis of valuation; this is based on assets valued at their acquisition cost with subsequent depreciation. There are problems, however, with historical cost. Asset's values are generally outdated because of the passage of time since the asset was acquired. There may also be inconsistencies in the treatment of individual assets; for example, two identical buildings can be valued differently if they were acquired at different times. In addition, it is difficult in the government to arrive at the original cost due to lack of proper documentation.

The solution to these problems is proposed by current valuation. Information provided by current valuation is not outdated. Current valuation also provides a reliable indication of the resources locked up in an entity and therefore, it becomes possible to calculate the true cost of services. On the whole, it provides a better basis for assessing the performance of a government department. But the problem with current valuations is that it can fluctuate significantly from one year to another. As a result, windfalls are created when values go up and shortfalls created when values go down. Also, fiscal discipline is undermined if the windfalls from such fluctuations are used to effect increases in other expenditures.

Some of the countries whose experiences we studied, found it necessary to revalue assets periodically to take account of the changing prices. Such periodic revaluation was necessary to use accrual information for setting performance targets in the government departments and assessing whether they had been achieved. Strategic targets of returns on capital, or net assets, as well as information on costs—which were factored into considerations of efficiency, setting charges, and market testing—would be meaningless if consumption of these resources was not accounted at their current value. Seen objectively, historical cost in the context of government introduces a downward bias on costs that, in turn, can produce false notions of efficiency. Therefore, countries such as New Zealand and Australia incorporate a stipulation for periodic revaluation of assets in their accounting policies.

In Sweden, however, doubts were raised about using market or replacement values while accounting for government departments. This is because only a very small part of the assets owned by a government can really be sold and therefore, there are problems with establishing a market value for these assets. In addition, market values may not be relevant for the purposes of government. For example, attributing market value to heritage assets of a country is not relevant: from the perspective of management and control, the value of these assets does not matter as they are not intended to be sold.

Typically, the content of a balance sheet can be defined on the basis of an indirect or direct method. If an indirect method is used, greater importance is attached to content of the income statement. If a transaction does not fulfil the cost definition, an asset is shown in the balance sheet. If a direct method is used, the content of the balance sheet is emphasized. In Sweden, an indirect view of assets is used. The main aim is to produce the costs of operations; in other words, the balance sheet permits costs to be scrutinized. This means that the management and control of operations is of primary importance and capital has only a supportive purpose.

ACCOUNTING STANDARDS

In designing accrual accounting arrangements for government departments, the key issue is development of specific accounting standards. As we noted, countries implementing accrual accounting have based their definitions of accrual accounting upon the accounting standards applicable to the private sector in their countries. Private sector experience and practices have provided valuable insights and these have been embodied in the establishment of accounting standards.

Private sector accounting standards are designed to generate a true and fair view, and identify the profit and return on capital. Therefore, the design, it is argued, is inappropriate for a government that is concerned with equity and the delivery of non-market services. But the fact remains that governments, as a part of liberalization measures, are now asking the private sector to deliver public services, either wholly or partially. Therefore, it makes sense to adopt accounting standards that can generate cost comparisons between the government provision of services and the private sector providing them. It would also be extremely expensive for the government to develop its own accounting standards *de novo*.[3]

That being the case, it makes sense to base the definition of government's accounting standards on the standards prevailing in private sector, adapted, wherever necessary, to meet the special requirements of government operations. In New Zealand, the Public Finance Act 1989 and the Financial Reporting Act 1993 stipulate that the standards should conform to GAAP. In the United Kingdom, the standards are based on UK GAAP adapted, where appropriate, to take account of the governmental context. In Sweden, the accounting regulations are patterned on the rules and standards prevailing in the private sector, with the only difference that, wherever necessary, the accounting regulations have accommodated the special needs of the government.

WHO SETS THE STANDARDS?

This question is particularly important in an accrual environment where many judgements have to be made for the treatment of individual transactions, more so than with a cash system of accounting. Independence of the standard setter therefore becomes a key issue. In New Zealand and Australia, there is one professional standard setter, totally independent, for both public and private sector, and the governments follow the decisions of the independent standard setter. In the United Kingdom, the body is chaired by an independent person and enjoys considerable freedom. It includes members who are fully independent of the treasury and one who is the representative of the CAG. Sweden is the only exception because the ESV (the Swedish National Financial Management Authority) is a government body.

ACCRUAL REPORTING

There are different ways in which accrual-based information can be reported in financial statements, ranging from simple lists of assets, liabilities, revenues, and expenditure, to articulated financial statements that show a financial position, changes in that position, operating results, and cash flows. All the four countries, whose experience we studied, have chosen a model involving the preparation of articulated financial statements, very similar to the formats prevailing in the private sector. At a minimum, these countries have required the preparation of the following statements:

- operating statement reflecting revenues and expenses and showing net operating position
- statement of assets and liabilities
- cash-flow statement showing the flow of cash in respect of operating, investing, and financing activities
- notes or schedules that clarify or show additional information on a disaggregated basis for users seeking more details.

While the reporting models adopted by all the four countries are generally similar to those in the private sector, the fact to be noted is that no country has been governed by private sector practices *in toto*. In all these countries, the reporting format has been suitably modified to recognize the important differences between the nature of government and private sector activities, and their objectives and modes of financing. Operating statements (as opposed to profit and loss statements) have been developed, which focus on the gross and net cost of government activities. The statements have been designed to:

enhance the ability to assess performance by showing the full cost of resources consumed in programme delivery, identifying the extent to which costs are recovered through user charges, and the net cost of programme delivery. These statements facilitate efficiency assessment by enabling an appreciation of the relationship of outputs to the full cost of resources consumed.

Only in Australia have two reporting frameworks been adopted: one framework based on the Australian Accounting Standard (the AAS31, which is generally based on private sector practices), and the other framework being the GFS, which is in conformity with international standards developed by the International Monetary Fund (IMF) and the United Nations (UN). These two frameworks have two different foci: while AAS31 is driven by the idea that government accounting should operate just like private sector accounting, the GFS reflects the economic focus; in particular assessing the impact of government's policies on the economy.

The balance of advantage would lie in adopting the two frameworks, as in the Australian government, but the numbers generated by these two frameworks can be startlingly different. For example, for the Australian government, the 1999–2000 Commonwealth budget operating balance was $13.5 billion on a GFS basis, while the AAS31 operating balance before abnormals was $9.5 billion. In respect of computing the net worth, the contrast was even more striking: while the GFS net worth for the same year was minus $11.6 billion, AAS31 net worth was minus $52.9 billion. This is only to suggest that when both the frameworks are adopted, a great deal of harmonization between them would be necessary.

WHOLE-OF-GOVERNMENT REPORTING

All the countries, whose experiences we studied, generated whole-of-government accounts in some form or the other. As we have seen, the whole-of-government accounting in these countries is in the form of commercial-style accounts and reports covering the entire government, that is, the government in its widest sense. The accounts are prepared on an accrual basis, using commercial accounting standards and practices suitably modified to fit the governmental context.

A number of concerns have been raised about accounting and reporting on a whole-of-government basis. These include issues such as:

- defining the reporting entity,
- establishing whether elements of financial statements at whole-of-government level should be expressed in terms of statistical and economic data to facilitate comparison between governments and countries,

- whether whole-of-government balance sheets should be limited to reporting financial assets and liabilities, and establishing reporting formats which are user-friendly.

The countries whose experience we looked at, have responded to these issues in ways that they considered most useful depending on their requirements. The major benefit of aggregate government reporting has been in assessing the macroeconomic impact. As we have seen in the case of New Zealand, which was the first country in the world to prepare aggregate financial information on an accrual basis for the government as a whole, an estimate of the overall net worth of the government made it possible to evaluate the effects of governmental action on the public sector's health. Such aggregate information about the health of public sector in New Zealand, has been used constructively to interpret such indicators as debt accumulation and the build-up of contingent liabilities, and whether the government's financial assets and liabilities have been managed (in the total context of the government's balance sheet) in the same manner as a large private company is managed.

IMPLEMENTATION ISSUES

There are a number of implementation issues as well. They relate to culture change and sequencing of the reforms.

CHANGE MANAGEMENT

Experiences of the countries studied indicate that implementation of accrual accounting is as much a process of change management as it is of implementing new policies, procedures, and systems. Ideally, the process of conversion to accrual accounting should include a component of change management, if only to ensure that there is an understanding of the potential benefits that it provides, how to use the information generated, and above all else, to induce a commitment to the reforms. As we have seen, the conversion to accrual accounting in these four countries included a strong component of change management.

The culture change does not come about automatically. It has to be promoted aggressively at all levels of the government, including the policy makers and senior civil servants.[4] The important point to note is that, for accrual accounting to succeed in the government environment, the departments need to be prepared culturally for the introduction of accrual accounting: they should be willing to recognize and accept the changes it will bring about. In fact, the success of accrual accounting will depend upon the willingness to accept that the accounting reforms would typically alter the roles of those responsible for financial management in government by changing their influence and responsibilities.[5]

SHOULD THE CHANGE TO ACCRUALS BE IN PHASES?

It is possible to implement accrual accounting in phases with a certain proportion of the ministries and departments changing to accrual accounting each year. While such a phased process is more manageable administratively, it runs the risk of impeding the process of culture change that is such an important part of the transition to accrual accounting.[6] On the other hand, the change to accruals can be achieved in what is described as a big bang: all the ministries and departments changing over to accruals at the same time. The merit of a big bang is that it helps the process of culture change. In the ultimate analysis, whether the change should be effected in a phased manner or follow the big bang, would depend upon circumstances of the particular country and the preconditions to be met for the adoption of accrual accounting—a subject we discuss later in the book.

On the whole, it is not desirable to adopt private sector accrual practices to the government *in toto*. Since private sector norms are not in a position to fully reflect the requirements of government departments; the need arises to develop special accounting policies and standards that reflect the unique nature of the government, the services it provides, the special characteristics of its assets, and above all else, the typical requirements of government departments.

NOTES

1. OECD (2003), p. 22.
2. Proceedings of the Senior Budget Officials of OECD (2002), pp. 3–7.
3. Hepworth (2002), p. 16.
4. Proceedings of OECD Senior Budget Officials (2002), p. 8.
5. Hepworth (2002), pp 18–19.
6. Proceedings of OECD Senior Budget Officials (2002), p. 9.

8

Comparative Experience
The Gains

The experiences of the four countries, with adoption of accrual accounting in the core departments of government, clearly affirms that there is a range of specific, incremental gains that accrual accounting has to offer.[1] The gains are in the areas of:

(a) devolution of authority and increased accountability
(b) provision of government services
(c) resource management
(d) assessment of long-term effects of government policies.

DEVOLUTION OF AUTHORITY AND INCREASED ACCOUNTABILITY

Devolution of authority to the line departments, in respect of resource allocation, has been a common gain in all the four countries (New Zealand, Australia, UK, Sweden). Accrual accounting has provided information on the full costs of departmental activities, thereby enhancing accountability for resource allocation decisions (New Zealand, Australia, UK, Sweden).

EFFICIENT PROVISION OF GOVERNMENT SERVICES

Accrual accounting has made increased private sector participation possible in provision of public services (New Zealand, Australia, UK, Sweden). Decisions on contracting out (New Zealand, Australia, UK) and market testing (UK) require accrual information to make comparisons between full costs of similar services provided by the government and the private sector. Information of comprehensive costing which accrual accounting provided, has made it possible for all four governments to levy user charges.

BETTER RESOURCE MANAGEMENT

Accrual accounting has provided information on the value of under-utilized assets. On the basis of such information, decisions have been taken that have led to better management of assets (New Zealand, Australia, UK). Information generated by accrual accounting has made it possible for the governments to levy a capital charge, leading to better asset management and putting efficiency pressures on the line departments (New Zealand, Australia, UK). Accrual accounting has provided information on full input costs as compared to outputs, and such information has enabled all the four governments to quantify the efficiency of their activities, resulting in better resource management. By generating information on accounts payable and receivable and inventories—which have reduced working capital requirements—accrual accounting has enabled better cash management (New Zealand, Australia, UK, Sweden).

CAPABILITY TO ASSESS LONG-TERM EFFECTS OF GOVERNMENT POLICIES

Accrual accounting has highlighted issues about financial policy and performance, for the government as a whole, including assessment of the government's net worth and changes in it over time. It has also provided information on long-term sustainability of policies, taking into account the future expenditure implications of the decisions. By recording unfunded pension liabilities and taking them into account while presenting the financial position of the government, accrual accounting has made transparent the transfer of costs to future generations. By providing such information, accrual accounting has been able to underpin intergenerational equity issues.

The gains from accounting reforms in these four countries are indeed impressive, but the question is: have these gains resulted in an improvement in the fiscal positions in these countries? The answer is in the positive, as Table 8.1 shows.

There are, of course, several reasons for the favourable fiscal outcomes, but the most important reason is adoption of reforms. In Table 8.1, if one looks at the countries that have experienced budgetary surpluses, they are the ones who have been at the forefront of reforms. Interestingly, those countries which started the reforms earlier, were the first ones to achieve budgetary surplus. The countries that undertook the most comprehensive reforms are the ones who have achieved the most sustainable surplus.[2] On the whole, the four countries whose experience with reforms we studied were able to achieve favourable fiscal outcomes.

Admittedly, the gains from adoption of accrual accounting have been comprehensive but one has to consider how relevant they are to the Indian situation. Can they address the shortcomings we had pointed out in Chapter 2? Are there specific instances of successful reform elements that are relevant to the Indian situation and can be replicated?

TABLE 8.1: GENERAL GOVERNMENT FINANCIAL BALANCE SURPLUS OR DEFICIT AS A PERCENTAGE OF NOMINAL GDP

	1993	1994	1995	1996	1997	1998	1999	2000	2001
USA	−5.0	−3.6	−3.1	−2.2	−0.9	0.3	0.8	1.7	0.5
Japan	−2.4	−2.8	−4.2	−4.9	−3.7	−5.5	−7.1	−7.4	−7.1
Germany	−3.1	−2.4	−3.3	−3.4	−2.7	−2.2	−1.6	1.2	−2.7
France	−6.0	−5.5	−5.5	−4.1	−3.0	−2.7	−1.6	−1.4	−1.4
UK	−7.9	−6.7	−5.8	−4.4	−2.2	0.4	1.1	1.6	1.0
Italy	−10.3	−9.3	−7.6	−7.1	−2.7	−3.1	−1.8	−0.6	−1.5
Canada	−8.7	−6.7	−5.3	−2.8	0.2	0.5	1.6	3.2	2.4
Australia	−5.6	−4.6	−3.7	−2.2	−0.5	0.6	1.6	0.1	0.0
New Zealand	−0.4	3.1	2.9	2.9	1.6	−0.2	0.9	1.9	0.9
Netherlands	−3.6	−4.2	−4.2	−1.8	−1.1	−0.8	0.4	2.2	0.3
Finland	−7.3	−5.7	−3.7	−3.2	−1.5	1.3	1.9	7.0	4.9
Sweden	−11.9	−10.8	−7.7	−3.1	−1.6	2.1	1.3	3.7	4.8

Source: OECD.

We found in Chapter 2 that the main shortcomings of the accounting system in the Indian government were:

- it does not help in the management of assets and cash
- it distorts the true cost of government
- it concentrates on control of inputs rather than the outputs produced and the outcomes achieved
- it does not address intergenerational equity issues
- it provides opportunities for fiscal trickery.

ASSET AND CASH MANAGEMENT

As discussed in Chapter 2, accounting system in the Indian government has not helped in asset management. This is primarily because expenditure on capital assets, which are used over many years, is recorded only in the year when the expenditure is incurred. No subsequent account is taken of whether the assets created are still in use and what are the returns to the government on account of their use. In respect of cash management, the principle of lapse has encouraged departments to spend their full annual appropriations often by recourse to means that are not exactly exemplary.

ASSET MANAGEMENT

The reforms introduced by the Government of New Zealand address the shortcoming we discussed in respect of asset management. Prior to 1990, the departments in the New Zealand government were as negligent in their stewardship of public assets as the departments in the Indian government are now. They viewed capital as a free good, and once an asset was in place there was no mechanism to track and charge for the capital tied up in the asset. The following observation by Allan Gibbs, a private businessman who was associated with several state-run corporations, describes the state of affairs that existed in New Zealand prior to the introduction of reforms.

> The Government was extremely extravagant with capital. One of the first things we did was collect up the excess bulldozers, bits of machinery and gear and toys that the Forest Service had accumulated with the extra money it was getting, and we put it in a big yard . . . there was acres and acres of it—and we had a huge auction. This was equipment that would make your eyes fall out, it was beautiful new plant and it was totally unnecessary.[3]

As a part of the reforms, the New Zealand government levied a capital charge—a charge on the cost of capital tied up in the assets of an agency. Amount of the capital charge was derived by applying a rate to the agency's capital base, which is typically the net amount of taxpayers' funds invested in the agency. The capital charge applied an interest rate to all capital, creating an actual cost for the capital. By introducing a system for recovery of the cost of capital, the government ensured that the agencies reveal the full cost of producing outputs. To that extent, the system of capital charging encouraged them to maximize on their employment of capital. In addition, the levy of capital charge provided an incentive to the agencies to sell their surplus assets, otherwise they would have to pay the charge even on surplus assets. It was an added incentive that the agencies were allowed to retain the proceeds from disposal of their surplus assets.

The introduction of capital charge led to better asset management, rationalization of capital, and decline in requests for capital.[4]

Better Asset Management

Capital charge provided the necessary incentive for the agencies to:

- extract the greatest value from their assets
- review whether the assets owned by the agency were necessary for realization of the agency's mission.

In 1993, Price Waterhouse was commissioned by the treasury of New

Zealand to assess impact of the system of capital charge. The conclusion of Price Waterhouse's study was that 'the capital charge regime has been very successful in making explicit to chief executives the costs of owning assets.' And, 'there are sufficient examples of the way in which the charge has influenced the behaviour to state unequivocally that the concept has been successful and that it is important to continue the regime and, where possible, improve upon it.'[5]

Rationalization of Capital

The levy of capital charge encouraged civil servants to critically examine benefits of the assets, relative to their cost. For example, it led to significant improvements in the foreign affairs ministry. When capital was seen as a free good in the pre-reforms era, the ministry had accumulated assets to the order of $400 million overseas. With the introduction of capital charge, the ambassadors had to pay interest on the expensive properties and they were forced to undertake economy measures.

Decline in Requests for Capital

With the introduction of capital charging, there has been a significant reduction in requests from the agencies for injection of capital. Since the agencies have to pay capital charge on the capital injection they ask for, they are unwilling to request additional capital unless they expect strong productivity gains in the process.

The benefits that have flowed out of the system of capital charging in the New Zealand government are as follows:[6]

- it has reduced the levels of investment and the asset holdings of agencies
- it has made explicit the cost of capital invested in the agencies
- resources are now managed at the agency level instead of such matters being referred to higher levels in the government
- the prices for services delivered by the agency reflect full production costs.

CASH MANAGEMENT

As a part of the reforms, the Swedish government introduced a scheme of cash management that is very successful. Under the scheme, appropriations for operating costs are deposited into the agency's interest-bearing account at the rate of one-twelfth each month. If an agency spends its appropriations at a slower rate, it is paid interest on the balance in its account. If it spends its appropriations at a faster rate, it pays interest to reflect the government's cost of borrowing. The experience of Swedish government with this scheme has been that it has increased awareness in the agencies regarding judicious management of cash.

Another element of the scheme is, in allowing the agencies to carry forward their unused appropriations. Under the scheme, up to three per cent of the annual appropriation for operating costs is automatically carried over. However, larger amounts need approval of the ministry of finance on a case-by-case basis. This has served three important purposes.

- It has prevented reckless spending by the agencies at the end of a financial year.
- It has contributed to financial discipline because any overspending in the year has to be repaid from future appropriations.
- There is an incentive for the agencies to achieve efficiency gains, because the scheme permits such gains to be retained by the agency itself. Before the carry-forward scheme was implemented, there was practically no incentive to achieve efficiency gains in the agency's operations.

The Swedish government has also introduced a facility for borrowing against future appropriations, permissible up to the level of three per cent, but this borrowing facility has rarely been used. The facility is used only by agencies overspending their appropriations, and any such overspending has to be paid back from future appropriations.

The Swedish government has also put in place a scheme of mandatory borrowing. The scheme provides for loans to buy computers and other administrative equipment. The creation of mandatory borrowing facility is intended to rationalize investment decisions and foster better management of administrative equipment by evenly spreading their cost over the useful life. This is consistent with accrual accounting practices in which the length of a loan is coterminus with the useful life of the equipment. The loans given out under this scheme carry interest at market rate.

On the whole, the scheme of cash management introduced by the Swedish government has contributed significantly to the maintenance of aggregate fiscal discipline. More importantly, it has put an end to the reckless spending by agencies by the end of the financial year.[7]

TRUE COST OF GOVERNMENT

As we noted in Chapter 2, a major shortcoming of the functioning of accounting system in the Indian government is that the focus on 'cash only' has distorted the true cost of government operations. This, as we discussed, is because of three reasons. First, the syste m treats pension costs of government employees as an unrelated, and therefore, uncontrollable item of expenditure occurring when the government employees retire, instead of attributing the pension costs to the time period when the employees were working with the government. Second, expenditure on a capital asset, which is used over many years is recorded only in the year when the capital expenditure is incurred. Third, in cases of government providing guarantees for loan repayment, the system does not reflect the long-term costs involved.

Reforms in the Australian government show how such shortcomings can be addressed. Accrual reporting now covers financial items that do not have an associated cash flow. For example, the Australian budget now records the accruing pension expense in the operating statement that, in a given year, is equal to pension accruing to current employees as well as the interest or growth on the outstanding liability. In calculating changes in the stock of unfunded pension liabilities, the actuary takes into account the number of salary earners and assumptions relating to growth in wages, inflation, and the expected rate of return on investment. In fact, it was only after the recording of accrual pension costs that the Australian government made plans to fund these liabilities, which included renegotiating their terms with its employees and developing realistic employee and employer contribution patterns.

In respect of capital, the accrual accounting framework in the Australian government records capital use (depreciation) in the operating statement instead of capital expenditure.

All significant contingent liabilities whose budgetary impact is dependent on future events—that may or may not occur— are disclosed in the budget, classified by major categories reflecting their nature, and historical information on defaults for each category. In cases where contingent liabilities cannot be quantified, they are listed and described.

The Australian government has gone even further in reflecting the true cost of governmental activities. For example, it has specifically directed that the production of goods and services should be taken up in-house only if there is a justification for the same after taking into account the full cost of in-house production. This requires that the departments in Australian government take into account all economic costs including pension and depreciation, while working out the full in-house cost. The departments are also required to test the market for outsourcing of both new and existing information technology requirements as an alternative to the maintenance of in-house capabilities. That being the case, departments have to prepare full financial information for evaluating programmes and proposals, determining prices for goods and services, lease/buy alternatives, benchmarking, and outsourcing.

INPUTS VERSUS OUTPUTS

As discussed in Chapter 2, the Indian government has an input focus of control and accountability: the rules and procedures operate only to control the acquiring of inputs. This leads to a situation where no attention is paid to the outputs that are produced using these inputs, and the departments are not held accountable for the outputs they produce.

This is a very serious shortcoming, but the New Zealand government has shown a way to address this. As part of the reforms, it has moved from an input to an output focus of control and accountability. Outputs are services delivered by a government department while inputs are money, staff, and procedures that are used to produce the department's services. Outcomes are the benefits accruing to the community, as a result of government's actions, while planned output are those benefits that the government wishes to achieve.

Outputs in the New Zealand government are viewed in exactly the same way as the products or services produced by a private company, and are also priced in a manner similar to market transactions. The minister in charge of a department chooses outputs that will lead to the desired outcomes, and negotiates a price for these outputs. The chief executive in charge of a department is held accountable for the delivery of outputs. A performance agreement is signed between the minister and the chief executive every year. It defines the outputs in terms of quantity, quality, cost, and when relevant, location and timeliness.

The performance agreement is in three parts. First part describes the key result areas and the expected results, which are expressed in verifiable terms and include output-related tasks. Second part sets out detailed information about the outputs to be purchased. It provides the minister with information to assess the value of departmental outputs, so that he is in a position to make comparisons with similar outputs produced in the private sector. Third part provides information on the stewardship of public assets.

The output system has led to changes in budgetary appropriations. The New Zealand government has replaced the previous line-item system which consisted of single departmental votes subdivided into programmes, and within programmes into the category of inputs, with an accrual appropriation system based on outputs. Separate appropriations are now voted, authorizing resources for the purchase of outputs. The resources voted by New Zealand's parliament are based on costing provided by the departments, and are in terms of the outputs as agreed to in the performance agreements. The output system has led to two important changes: informed decision-making and the end of politically motivated spending.[8]

Informed Decision-Making

The focus on outputs means that ministers now have access to useful information about the services produced by their departments and therefore, are in a position to take informed decisions after considering the competing alternatives. In addition, the system of output appropriation in New Zealand has provided a sound basis for both departmental management and governmental decision-making.

End of Politically Motivated Spending

Budgeting based on outputs—combined with performance agreements that specify the quality, quantity, price, and timeliness of each output—has eliminated politically motivated spending in New Zealand. Because the chief executive in charge of a department has complete control over the mix of inputs he uses to produce outputs, the projects to be taken up are selected on the basis of cost–benefit analysis and not on the basis of political influence. Stuart Milne, chief executive of the ministry of transport, Government of New Zealand has this to say, 'With our system, there is no political inter- ference on where the money goes for roads.'[9] Simon Upton, an MP, agrees, 'I couldn't imagine having people coming through this office all day lobbying for special favours. Our new system is a good security against corruption in politics.'[10]

The benefits that have accrued from the output system are several.[11]

- It has allowed greater discretion and innovation in the choice of how much and what kinds of inputs to use for provision of public services.
- It has increased the focus on achieving policy goals.
- It has reduced the ability of politicians to indulge in politically motivated public spending.
- It has provided government departments the incentives to charge for services.

INTERGENERATIONAL EQUITY ISSUES

As discussed in Chapter 2, accounting system of the Indian government does not address intergenerational equity issues. Intergenerational equity is primarily concerned with the appropriate balance between taxes and borrowings to finance current expenses today and capital expenditure. In other words, the taxpayers in each time period (current and future) should as a group contribute to public expenditures from which they derive benefits, in accordance with their share of the benefits generated by those expenditures. It means that while future taxpayers should pay for the benefits generated for them, costs should not be transferred from the current taxpayers to future taxpayers when there is an increase in current expenditure.

In the accounting system as it operates in the Indian government, all capital expenditure is treated as a debit in the financial year in which it takes place. In other words, even the capital expenditure that generates benefits for the future taxpayers is being totally financed by the current taxpayers. On the other hand, future taxpayers are being made to pay for pension liabilities that should rightfully be discharged by the current taxpayers. These are serious intergenerational equity issues.

The UK government has addressed these issues. It promulgated two rules in July 1997 that now govern the fiscal policy:

- golden rule: over the economic cycle, the government only borrows to invest and not to fund current expenditure
- sustainable investment rule: borrowing to finance investment is fixed so as to ensure that net public debt, as a proportion of GDP, is held over the economic cycle at a stable and prudent level.

What the golden rule essentially means is that the current expenditure is financed through taxation and investment is financed through borrowing. This implies very clearly that current taxpayers pay for current public spending but the future generations bear the cost of the borrowings that finances investment, as it will be they who gain from that investment. It also means that a clear structural distinction is being made between current and capital expenditure, which are no longer treated as if they are equivalent economic categories; an act of structural separation which addresses the shortcoming of a cash accounting system. Clearly, the golden rule promotes fairness between generations. In addition, the sustainable investment rule, which stipulates the stable debt ratio requirement, places a constraint on the amount of investment that can be financed by borrowing and prevents an escalation of public debt.

OPPORTUNITIES FOR FISCAL TRICKERY

In Chapter 2, we had pointed out how the accounting system in the Indian government provides ample opportunities for indulging in fiscal trickery in that it allows the government to show a financial position and performance that is better than what it really is.

The reforms undertaken by the New Zealand government are instructive in the way this shortcoming can be overcome. The Public Finance Act, while making the adoption of accrual accounting a statutory requirement, stipulated that financial statements of the departments and for the government as a whole should conform to GAAP. Such a stipulation ensures that government reporting is in accordance with externally imposed rules and standards. Opportunities for the government to indulge in fiscal trickery are greatly reduced when the financial reporting is in accordance with externally imposed rules and standards that stipulate how activities and transactions in the government should be accounted for.

It is an additional safeguard that the maintenance and enforcement of the accounting standards in the Government of New Zealand is entrusted to a private entity that is independent of the government. With such a practice, the Government of New Zealand has subjected its governmental financial reporting to scrutiny by an independent private agency. To that extent, the government does not have the opportunity to engage in self-serving interpretations of financial transactions to show a position and performance that is different than what it really is.

By using accrual accounting to prepare government accounts, which are also independently audited, the Government of New Zealand has totally eliminated the scope for fiscal trickery. The result is, the integrity and reliability of reported information have been enhanced. Credibility of the government is also enhanced in the process, and members of the public now have greater confidence in the New Zealand government's financial management ability.[12]

CONCLUSION

These were some of the important reform measures that these four countries implemented with very strong gains. More importantly these gains have particular relevance to the Indian situation. It is important to note that the conditions that prevail in India now are not very dissimilar to the conditions that prevailed in these four countries when they undertook reforms. For example, these countries faced budgetary deficit and debt situations that required them to undertake reforms. The present situation in India is no better in respect of deficit and debt. In addition, position in the Indian government, in respect of liabilities on account of pension and government guarantees is no better than what prevailed in these countries when they undertook accounting reforms. That being the case, there is a very strong

case for the Indian government to undertake accounting reforms on the lines
that these four countries have done.

NOTES

1. OECD (1993), p. 5.
2. OECD (2003), p. 2.
3. Ball, Dale, Eggers, and Sacco (2000), p. 13.
4. Ibid., pp. 14–15.
5. Ibid., p. 15.
6. Ibid., p. 13.
7. Blondal (2001), pp. 48–9.
8. Ball, Dale, Eggers, and Sacco (2000), pp. 18–19.
9. Ibid., p. 19.
10. Ibid.
11. Ibid., p. 13.
12. Richardson (1997), p. 9.

9

Introducing Accrual Accounting in the Indian Government

While recognizing the need for accounting reforms in the Indian government, the question is: what are the preconditions that are to be met for introducing these reforms in India? Professor Allan Schick, for example, counsels the developing countries to take 'basic steps to strengthen rule-based government and pave the way for robust markets', which he sees as a precondition of public service modernization of the New Zealand type.[1] Schick suggests that the following preconditions have to be satisfied.

- They need to develop and formalize the market economy.
- They need to establish reliable external controls including financial management, a skilled civil service, and real budgets.
- They need to establish some basic approaches to public management, such as, input control and reliable internal controls.
- They need skilled human resources.

In particular, Schick points to the investment that is required to be made in human resources; he says, 'Managers must have disciplines and skills necessary to operate in a devolved management structure before gradually loosening the bonds of central control.'[2]

Noel Hepworth sets a number of conditions for success in introducing accrual accounting.[3] Some of the important ones are

- participation of the accountancy profession and joint development of accounting standards
- an appropriate cultural approach
- a robust audit process
- an IT capacity.

Are these preconditions capable of being met in the Indian context? Most of Schick's preconditions, though qualitatively more rigorous, are easily met in India.

MARKET ECONOMY

India has always had a market economy. However, thanks to the liberalization measures of 1991 and the resultant rule-based measures, the market economy now is thriving and is—more importantly—quite robust in its functioning.

FINANCIAL MANAGEMENT STRUCTURE

We have a well-established financial management structure, basic principles of which are firmly established in the working of the Indian government. Reliable external control mechanisms, such as an institution of external and independent audit, are enshrined in the Constitution itself. We have real budgets, which are formulated and executed in accordance with rules and procedures prescribed in the Constitution. There is an established government–cultural ethic that has internalized the requirements of a neutral, non-political civil service along with a strong, well-regarded central agency— the Ministry of Finance—which is responsible for the management of government finances. The ministry exercises well-understood and accepted systems of financial control over other ministries and departments of the Indian government.

INPUT CONTROLS AND RELIABLE INTERNAL CONTROLS

The Indian government also observes the basic approaches to public management, such as input control and reliable internal controls. As we discussed in Chapter 2, the system of input control is exercised very rigorously. The Indian government has in place a reliable system of internal control, which functions rather efficiently. India boasts of an old civil service; in fact, the oldest covenanted civil service in the world, having been established as early as 1854. It is skilled too, but its skills extend primarily to exercising a system of rigid controls in a centralized milieu.

It is in such a context that Schick's stipulation for civil servants having the ability to operate in a devolved management structure before gradually loosening the bonds of internal control, assumes critical importance. As we discussed, for the accounting reforms to succeed, there has to be a strong component of change management. Members of the civil service in India need to be persuaded to recognize and accept that the implementation of accounting reforms will typically alter their roles, influence, and responsibilities by asking them to work more productively in a devolved management structure.

PARTICIPATION OF THE ACCOUNTANCY PROFESSION

Hepworth stipulates that the accountancy profession in a reforming country should be professionally competent. It should also be interested in and involved with the development of accounting standards for the government, the application of these standards, and the monitoring of their implementation. India is lucky in having an accounting profession that is not only very competent professionally, but also ready to help government organizations in implementing the accounting reforms. For example, as early as 1999 the accounting standards board of the Institute of Chartered Accountants of India (ICAI), which is responsible for establishing accounting standards for private sector companies in India, had set up a committee to suggest accounting standards for urban local bodies in the government. Based on the deliberations of this committee, ICAI's accounting standards board issued and published a booklet in October 2000, entitled *Technical Guide on Accounting and Financial Reporting by Urban Local Bodies*, for guiding the urban local bodies seeking to introduce accrual accounting.

The technical guide provides important inputs on preparation of notes to accounts, compilation of accounts, and development of appropriate accounting policies in the areas of grants, depreciation, treatment of retirement benefits, and valuation of inventory and fixed assets. The technical guide also provides guidance on how to develop opening balance sheets to help in the transition from cash to an accrual system. Its overall suggestions are:

- financial reporting should be based on accrual basis of accounting
- financial accounting and reporting should conform to accepted accounting standards and policies.[4]

ICAI is also very actively involved in the ongoing exercise of several municipal bodies in India converting to accrual accounting. It has even set up an Accounting Research Foundation (ARF) with a view to developing a knowledge base on the emerging areas of accounting and financial management in order to root the knowledge base in hard core practical experiences. The ARF is mandated to provide consultancy services, in fact, it was asked in April 2002 to design and implement the change to accrual accounting in Delhi's municipal corporation.[5]

Clearly, the Indian government, as and when it decides to undertake accounting reforms, can look forward to enlisting active participation of the accountancy profession in developing accounting standards, their application, and monitoring of their implementation.

A ROBUST AUDIT PROCESS

Schick suggests reliable external controls to financial management as a precondition. Hepworth also suggests that there should be a comprehensive, annual, independent audit of the accounts of each department at the end of the financial year; with reports to Parliament and detailed scrutiny where appropriate. In the Indian government, there is a system of independent audit represented by the CAG. The CAG is an independent authority constituted by the Constitution of India. The independence of its audit is assured by providing it protections and privileges under the Constitution. The powers of the audit institution are also enumerated in a legislative enactment—the Comptroller and Auditor General of India (Duties, Powers, and the Conditions of Service) Act 1971— thereby bolstering its independence.

The functions of audit in the Government of India are very comprehensive. They consist of:

- audit of all government expenditure incurred from the revenues of the central and state governments,
- audit of stores and stocks,
- audit of all receipts,
- audit of appropriation to ensure that government grants are spent for the purpose for which they are provided,
- audit of classification,
- administrative audit to ensure that expenditure is supported by the requisite administrative authority,
- audit of propriety to find out improper exercise of discretion and comment on the propriety of sanctions and expenditure,
- audit of efficiency to ascertain whether the expenditure has achieved the expected results, and
- audit of accountancy to detect fraud, technical errors, and errors of principle in the expenditure.

Article 151 of the Constitution enjoins the CAG to present audit reports to the president of India, who lays them before the Parliament. Public accounts committee of the Indian Parliament discusses these reports—the discussions include examination of witnesses from the executive. A final report is prepared, including action items, and presented to the legislatures. On the whole, the audit of government expenditure in the Indian government is external, independent, and also comprehensive.

AN IT CAPACITY

Hepworth recommends that the country should have an IT capacity that is capable of responding to the new and additional requirements, which the introduction of accrual accounting and budgeting would require. India has the necessary IT capacity that can effectively meet the requirements arising out of implementation of accrual accounting, budgeting, and associated performance measurement initiatives.

INADEQUACY OF THE EXISTING REFORMS

If these preconditions are capable of being met in the Indian situation, why is it that these reforms have not been tried out in the Indian government? Or, for that matter, why is it that the range of public management reforms implemented in the post-liberalization scenario in India has not been as comprehensive in its scope, as in the four countries whose experiences we studied? Is there an institutional explanation? Could it be that this is linked to the type of politico-administrative regime?

Olsen and Peters try to provide an explanation for variations in the pace and direction of public management reforms in different countries. They argue that a distinction needs to be made between the 'statist, public law and legalistic regimes found in Continental Europe', and countries with an 'Anglo-Saxon tradition of separation of the state from civil society, with the latter having claims to primacy over the former'.[6] They contend that the European tradition involves a political culture that asserts the role of the State in managing society, while in Anglo-Saxon countries, the State arises from contract between the citizens and government. That is why, they argue, public management reforms have been more successful in countries like the UK, Canada, Australia, and New Zealand.

In addition, Olsen and Peters argue that the ability to implement public management reforms is a function of the type of politico-administrative regime. According to them, Margaret Thatcher's success in implementing reforms in the 1980s was essentially a function of her working in a parliamentary system. This enabled her to achieve results less likely to be achieved in the divided, presidential regime of the United States. For example, in the cases of Germany, Norway, and Switzerland, the minority or coalition governments may not take kindly to reforms when compared with a majoritarian government such as in the United Kingdom. The ruling politicians in minority or coalition governments may appeal to vague and general values in order to maintain broad coalitions—often rejecting careful, comparative evaluations.

However, such distinctions are difficult to sustain because of empirical evidence to the contrary. For example, Finland has successfully adopted result-based budgeting. Sweden, as we noted, has switched over to accrual accounting. Netherlands has adopted performance auditing. France has implemented an outcome approach to scrutiny of budgets. The successful experience of these countries with public management reforms would testify to the fact that the academic distinctions that are made in the public administration and social policy literature—on the differences between the Anglo-Saxon and European systems on the one hand and the politico-administrative regimes on the other—are not really tenable.[7]

If success of public management reforms does not depend on the type or nature of politico-administrative regime, why is it that such elementary financial management reforms as performance budgeting or zero-based budgeting have been so remarkably unsuccessful in the Indian government? Let us analyse the reasons.

While looking at the functioning of performance budgeting in the departments of the Indian government, Thimmaiah found that factors such as bureaucratic resistance, corruption of public servants, and legislative indifference contributed to the the failure of the scheme.[8] Thimmaiah also found that performance budgets were prepared in the spirit of routine documentation rather than in the spirit of pioneering. Also, the performance budget documents were descriptive, lacking in analysis of progress and performance. Thimmaiah came to the conclusion that India was the victim of having such a traditional budget that is difficult to change.[9]

As we noted, the implementation of zero-based budgeting in the Indian government has not been successful either. It is primarily because bureaucrats manning the ministries and departments have not taken too kindly to it. The reason for bureaucratic resistance is not far to seek. No programme in the Indian government, once undertaken, is ever closed down even if it outlives its utility. A government programme generally creates a complement of permanent staff. If the scheme is scrutinized as rigorously as zero-based budgeting would ideally demand, there is a likelihood of the programme being discarded for non-performance. The Indian bureaucrats would not like this to happen because it would create problems for continuation of the permanent staff. That being the case, the Indian bureaucracy has done its best to ensure that zero-based budgeting is not implemented seriously.

BUREAUCRATIC RESISTANCE

Bureaucratic resistance is the key. Indian bureaucrats are comfortable with the cash accounting system because it gives them the latitude to massage financial information, to show a performance that appears to be better than it really is. Arguably, this is only a subversive gain in the short term. It is therefore necessary to persuade the Indian bureaucrats, engaged in policy-making functions, that accrual accounting would provide them with a more comprehensive database and a reporting framework to develop policies and assess their sustainability in the longer term. Bureaucrats in the implementing departments may view the transition to accrual accounting as laborious work. However, they should be made to understand that it is worth their effort as they will then have more complete information to make decisions and to have their performances assessed on a more objective basis than what it is now.

There is also the need for creating a commitment to reforms on the part of politicians. As we saw with the four countries that changed over to accruals, there was an enviable degree of political commitment to the reforms. How can such political commitment to reforms be garnered in India? The ruling politicians here may not like the idea of changing over to accrual accounting because, for them, the cash system provides a perfect opportunity for indulging in creative accounting. The accrual system will provide no such opportunity. But if the politicians can be persuaded to look beyond the essentially short-term opportunities for fiscal trickery, to the advantages that accrual accounting has to offer, they would not be averse to make the change. Accrual accounting, as we noted, is in a position to generate information which will enable the voters to better assess the performance of the government. This would help politicians, who have done good work, to get the necessary public endorsement at the time of elections. The benefits that accrual accounting offers to politicians are real, otherwise politicians in New Zealand, Sweden, Australia, and the UK would not have agreed to adopt it.

In the ultimate analysis, it is a question of pressurizing the bureaucrats and politicians. That it is a function of pressure, is borne out by an interesting development that is currently taking place in the Indian government's structure. Municipal bodies in the Indian government, which have traditionally accounted on a cash basis, are changing over to accrual accounting. The important thing to note is that these municipal bodies are taking up accounting reforms under pressure from financial institutions and the judiciary, both of whom have insisted on the municipal bodies adopting some form of accrual accounting.

For example, accrual accounting was introduced at the insistence of the World Bank in the 1980s in Mumbai—where the exercise was limited to water supply and a sewerage project—and in Chennai Municipal

Corporation—where an attempt was made to undertake accounting reforms in all its accounting operations. During 1990–5, the World Bank insisted on introduction of accrual accounting in six municipal corporations and one municipal body (Anand) as a part of its funding to Gujarat Urban Development Project. At the behest of the Asian Development Bank, accounting reforms have been taken up in state of Tamil Nadu and in the Tumkur municipality. In the case of Delhi's municipal corporation, accounting reforms were taken up to implement directions of the Supreme Court of India.

There are also instances of Bangalore, Hyderabad, and Indore municipal corporations undertaking accounting reforms as a part of wide-ranging urban reforms. In the next few pages, we discuss the experiences of some of the municipal bodies with accounting reforms in analyses of the key elements, their impact, the issues involved, and the lessons to be learnt.[10]

ACCOUNTING REFORMS IN AHMEDABAD MUNICIPAL CORPORATION

Ahmedabad Municipal Corporation took up accounting reforms at the behest of the World Bank. Prior to the reforms, Ahmedabad Municipal Corporation accounted on a cash basis. Functioning of the cash system left a lot to be desired. The corporation was not in a position to state the real condition of its finances. Its accounts had not been finalized for many years. Its assets had not been valued and it had no information on its total assets. Except for the loans and borrowings, there was no information on its long-term, short-term, and current liabilities. The accounting data it had was generally inadequate and unreliable. There was improper distinction of receipts and payments under different heads such as revenue, capital and extraordinary, and there were problems in tallying and cross-checking of accounts. The accounts were in such a mess that the corporation was not in a position to access market borrowings to finance its development requirements.

SCOPE OF THE ACCOUNTING REFORMS

The accounting reforms sought to:

- introduce accrual-based accounting systems
- make proper distinction between capital and revenue expenditure
- introduce budget monitoring systems
- adopt standard accounting systems to enable inter-corporation comparisons

- standardize forms for publishing annual accounts, balance sheets, and the like
- introduce multi year financing
- conduct training programmes for implementation.

STAGES OF IMPLEMENTATION

The corporation took almost eight years to realize an incomplete but workable accounting system. The phases of implementation were

- 1990–3: Designing the improved accounting system, preparing the training manual, and conducting training for staff
- 1993–5: Manual implementation of the improved system because of difficulties in the manual mode, development of customized accounting software
- 1995–7: Parallel runs of the old and new systems; on the basis of experience from the parallel run, necessary corrections made in the manual system and the software
- 1997: Conversion to a double-entry, accrual-based, computerized accounting system

RESULTS

The results of the accounting reform (December 2003) are:

- The corporation has converted its receipt and payment records from a single-entry to a double-entry accounting system. These entries are computerized online. However, the asset and liability transactions are not part of the online computerized system. They are entered offline when the annual accounts are finalized.
- No accrual-based entry (payable) on the revenue or capital expenditure is passed.
- The existing system fails to automatically generate a balance sheet for the concerned period. Although the inventory has been valued, it cannot be added to the current assets.
- The corporation has not valued all its fixed assets; it has not entered the available information on them into the accounting package. Under the circumstances, it is difficult to ascertain its actual assets position.
- The corporation has not entered the data on liabilities in its accounting package. As a result, information on its outstanding loan liability is not available online.

- The procedure for entering or accounting returned cheques is adequate. The tax demand is raised immediately in the taxpayer's account. But as the balance sheet module is not operational, the accounting system fails to reflect this in the balance sheet.

Because of these deficiencies, the accounting system that the corporation has realized can be described as a double-entry, cash-based receipt and payment accounting system, and not a full accrual-based system.

BENEFITS

Although Ahmedabad Municipal Corporation has not fully converted to accrual accounting and its software-based system is inadequate, the benefits of the new system are several.

- The double-entry system allows scientific recording of accounting transactions, which can be cross-tallied and verified.
- Computerization has improved accuracy of the system. It has improved the timeliness of accounting operations. It has led to savings in manpower costs. It has also made it possible for the corporation to access analysed data while taking decisions.
- The classification of receipts and payments is scientific and follows standard accounting norms.
- Accuracy and reliability of the accounting data has improved to the extent that the data is now acceptable to the financial institutions and the financial market. Financial position of the corporation is now available in a form that is accepted by professional fund managers. As a result, Ahmedabad Municipal Corporation became the first municipal body in South Asia to raise funds from the open market through a public issue of municipal bonds of Rs 1 billion.

ISSUES

There were several issues why the accounting reforms in Ahmedabad Municipal Corporation did not fully fructify.

- Support from the government of Gujarat, for the accounting reforms, was lukewarm. The government never issued formal orders for the implementation of accounting reforms. Also, it did not change the municipal account code.
- Within the Ahmedabad Municipal Corporation itself, implementation

of the reforms did not receive support and encouragement from the top management. As a result, the implementation process ran into roadblocks, such as securing administrative clearances for implement-ation of different phases, implementation of the reports of consultants, provision of adequate staff for training and implementation, and frequent transfers of the trained staff.

- The terms of reference for the project did not contain important components such as computerization and auditing of the improved accounting system.
- No opinion-building exercise was undertaken.
- The accounting reforms were not implemented along with the other reforms; as a result stakeholders were not ready for the reforms.
- The consultants lacked experience and exposure on the working of the government. What the consultants recommended was a modern enterprise accounting system instead of an accrual accounting system adapted to the needs of the government. The result was that municipal officers and the staff had a lot of difficulties in accepting a pure enterprise accounting system.

IMPACT ASSESSMENT

The accounting reforms, though incomplete, have helped Ahmedabad Municipal Corporation to improve the quality, reliability, and credibility of its accounting data. Its financial position has improved. The new accounting system has helped Ahmedabad Municipal Corporation to cut costs and conserve resources. More importantly, it has helped the municipal body to identify sources of resource mobilization. Its credibility has increased so dramatically that the corporation has now raised development funds from the market through the issue of municipal bonds.

MUNICIPAL ACCOUNTING REFORMS IN TAMIL NADU

In Tamil Nadu, all the municipal bodies—five municipal corporations and 102 municipalities—have made the transition to accrual accounting. The reforms came at the behest of the Asian Development Bank. Before the accounting reforms were introduced, municipal bodies in Tamil Nadu could not present a clear picture of their finances. The only thing they did was to prepare receipts and payment statements. The annual accounts of these municipalities showed money actually received and spent, without taking into account their accrued income and outstanding liabilities. They did not prepare statements of assets and liabilities, which could reflect their true financial position.

These municipal bodies badly required funds to develop urban infrastructure, and the state government was not in a position to provide the necessary funding. Although the financial institutions were prepared to provide loans, they were unable to assess the municipal bodies' ability to repay the loans, because the municipal bodies were not in a position to provide financial information in a format that was acceptable to the financial institutions.

SCOPE OF THE ACCOUNTING REFORMS

The reforms sought to

- design new accounting systems
- collect information on municipal properties in order to prepare the opening balance sheet
- recommend the appropriate legislation required to change the municipal accounting system
- prepare an accounting manual
- develop norms for recognizing assets
- provide training
- provide professional support for implementing the new accounting system
- computerize the new accounting system
- conduct a parallel run of the new system along with the old one.

Stages of Implementation

The accounting reforms took three-and-a-half years to implement, with one more year for computerization. Implementation consisted of:

- End of 1997 to January 1999—Conception of the project, preparation of the manual, and securing the government clearances
- February 1999 to March 2000—Implementation of accounting reforms in 12 pilot municipal bodies, updation of the manual, and development of accounting software
- April 2000 to March 2001—Implementation in remaining 95 municipal bodies, and computerization of accounting system in 12 pilot municipal bodies
- April 2001 to March 2002—Computerization of accounting system in the remaining 95 municipal bodies.

RESULTS

All the municipalities in Tamil Nadu have now converted to a computerized accrual accounting system. For the last three years ending December 2003, they have prepared balance sheets in the accrual formats. Here are some other results of the accounting reforms.

- The quality and timeliness of accounting data has improved.
- The accounts are user-friendly.
- It is now possible to provide comprehensive and realistic data on the financial position of these municipal bodies, to secure funding from the market or multilateral agencies.
- The transparency in municipal bodies has raised the comfort level of rating agencies.
- The reforms have brought about qualitative improvement in the auditing system.
- There is better classification of expenditure.

CRITICAL ELEMENTS OF THE REFORMS

The critical elements of accounting reforms in Tamil Nadu were:

- total support from the state government
- total involvement of the top management of municipal bodies in the implementation of reforms
- a comprehensive accounting manual
- elaborate training and opinion-building exercises
- appropriate implementation methodology
- total commitment of the municipal bodies and their staff.

One element that played a key role in the successful implementation of accounting reforms was the accounting manual. A great deal of work went into its preparation. A committee consisting of three members was appointed in 1998, and it undertook the task of preparing a draft. First draft of the manual was ready by June 1998 and submitted to the government. The draft of the manual was discussed with the commissioner of municipal administration, the chief executive officer of the Tamil Nadu Urban Infrastructure and Finance and Services Ltd, and the director of the Local Fund Audit. It was also examined by the finance department of the Tamil Nadu government.

In June 1999, the draft manual was sent to the Institute of Chartered Accountants of India for review. A round table conference was organized in

September 1999 by the Indo-US FIRE project and HUDCO, to discuss the various issues raised by ICAI. Senior civil servants of the Tamil Nadu government, representatives of ICAI, municipal officers and employees, and the local accounting consultants participated in the conference. Based on the suggestions received, amendments were made to the draft and the final accounting manual was brought out.

The accounting manual is in three parts. The first part describes the accounting procedures; the second part provides the chart of accounts; and the third part details the new forms and formats that are to be used in the new accounting system. The procedures, accounts, and forms—that were specifically designed for the new accounting system—were described in detail in the manual. The manual was comprehensive and contributed greatly to the successful implementation of the accounting reforms.

IMPACT ASSESSMENT

The greatest impact of the accounting reforms has been at the level of policy. It has drawn attention of the Government of India, policymakers, donor agencies, and professional organizations like the ICAI to the importance of the accounting reforms in a municipal environment. It has also attracted the attention of the Comptroller and Auditor General of India. Finally, it has provided a model to other municipal bodies in the country and other state governments. On the whole, the experience of municipal accounting reforms in Tamil Nadu is a pointer to the fact that accounting reforms can be successfully implemented if there is effective political and administrative will.

ACCOUNTING REFORMS IN BANGALORE MUNICIPAL CORPORATION

The Bangalore Municipal Corporation undertook accounting reforms to change from a cash accounting system to an accrual, fund-based accounting system. Prior to the reforms, the accounting function was treated as a terminal function in the corporation, and not as a core activity. The recording of transactions was mostly incomplete. There were huge arrears in accounts. The audit work was pending for over five years. Since the accounting system was not in a position to generate accurate and reliable information, it was difficult to present the real financial position and operational performance of the corporation. As a result, it was not possible to establish the creditworthiness of the corporation for securing loans from financial institutions.

SCOPE OF THE ACCOUNTING REFORMS

The reforms sought to

- introduce a fund-based accounting system
- draft and get the accounts and budget regulations passed
- design and introduce a management information system and works management system
- prepare an inventory of the assets
- streamline the payroll
- computerize the accounting system
- train the staff.

STAGES OF IMPLEMENTATION

The corporation took about three years to implement the reforms. The stages of implementation were:

- October 1999 to December 1999—Appointment of consultants
- January 2000 to September 2000—Process mapping of the existing system, understanding of the information flow, assessment of the needs, and the introduction of decentralization initiatives
- October 2000 to March 2001—Reengineering of the information flows, understanding the user requirements, designing the software, creating a development master running test data entries, and formulating accounting regulations and budget processes
- April 2001—Passing of the Bangalore Mahanagar Palika (Accounts) Regulations, with the approval of the government of Karnataka
- April 2001 to March 2002—Carrying out test runs and generating MIS reports, and implementing the works and payroll modules
- April 2002 to March 2003—Preparing asset inventory, generating financial statements, review of the reforms, writing of work reports, and reformulating the budget regulations
- March 2003—Preparation of the opening balance sheet.

RESULTS

Bangalore Municipal Corporation now maintains its accounts on an online, computerized, accrual-based, double-entry, fund-accounting system. The system has been integrated with the budgeting and financial management modules.

The accounting reforms have led to better financial management. As a result of the reforms, accounting regulations are in place. There is a single and unique source of information. Assets have been verified and there is an inventory of assets. The system of making payments to creditors has been streamlined and is more equitable now. The budget variances are analysed department-wise. The capital and revenue concept has been introduced.

The reforms have also resulted in improved organizational functioning. There is now the concept of MIS-enabled decision-making. Employees at the lower level have understood the power of automation. Job definitions, accountability, and responsibility are now fixed and have become the basis for preparing the budget.

The reforms have also led to increased support for stakeholders. The elected representatives are now empowered by MIS reports. Open and transparent information is now available to the citizens.

In addition, there are some specific, incremental benefits, which are listed below.

- The accounts are current. Bangalore Municipal Corporation now presents its accounts for public discussion every quarter, under an initiative known as the Public Record of Operations and Finance (PROOF).
- Due to the integration of bank accounts, the corporation discovered that an amount of Rs 40 crore was lying unused. It has now been put to productive use.
- With all the work being coded (about 13,000 works are listed in the database), it is now possible to monitor the progress of each work. Because of such monitoring, liability of the corporation towards work bills, at any point of time, has decreased to around Rs 40 crore from Rs 200 crore earlier.
- The payment cycle has fallen from the earlier three months to around one month at present. The average age of a bill coming up for payment is eight to ten months now, as against eighteen to twenty-four months earlier.
- The corporation is now in a position to make its loan repayment on due dates.
- The transparency of the new accounting system has made it possible for the corporation to get a credit of Rs 250 crore, without government guarantee.

CRITICAL ELEMENTS OF THE ACCOUNTING REFORMS

The critical elements leading to the success of accounting reforms in the Bangalore Municipal Corporation are:

- overwhelming support of the Government of Karnataka, including that of its political leadership
- creative involvement of citizens' bodies, change agents, experts, and retired government servants in the conceptualization, design, and implementation of the reforms
- active support of the top management and accounting staff of the corporation
- consultants and implementing teams of the corporation worked in tandem, and there was continuity of the team members
- implementation of the reforms was subjected to regular and productive reviews
- broad-based approach characterized the reforms. It covered all aspects linked with the accounting system

A key element that contributed greatly to success of the reforms was the total support of all the stakeholders. The government of Karnataka demonstrated strong political and administrative will for the reforms, with the chief minister of the state initiating the reforms and the various departments of the government extending total support. The entire exercise received continuing support from the staff of the corporation itself, notably from the commissioner and the accounting staff, who came to recognize the accounting function as a core activity and not as a terminal one. The involvement of Bangalore Agenda Task Force, a public–private partnership that oversees the functioning of all the agencies engaged in urban development tasks in Bangalore city, also contributed to the success of the reforms.

IMPACT ASSESSMENT

It needs to be noted that the reforms in Bangalore Municipal Corporation were not limited to accounting issues. They included a broader agenda of budgetary, work management system, and MIS reforms. As a result of the comprehensive nature of the reforms, the impact of accounting reforms is favourable. Top management in the corporation is now in a position to access information on the precise potential of each revenue source and the actual realization against it. As a result, they can explore modalities of increasing the revenue of the corporation. The top management also has access to information on how and where the money has been spent, funds that are not utilized, and the areas which are in need of funds. Consequently, in the last four years, the corporation has increased its revenues by a factor of two; it has also increased its total developmental expenditure at a higher rate than its revenue growth. More importantly, it has improved the quality of its expenditure, for the simple reason that the accounting reforms have made it possible for the corporation to know the exact use to which its money has been put. The ready availability of such information has also made public scrutiny of the corporation's accounts and financial performance possible. This has enhanced the credibility of Bangalore Municipal Corporation in the eyes of its citizens.

ACCOUNTING REFORMS IN HYDERABAD MUNICIPAL CORPORATION

Hyderabad Municipal Corporation undertook accounting reforms to introduce a modified accrual-based, double-entry accounting system in 2001 as a part of its broader agenda to implement urban reforms. The broader agenda aimed at augmenting municipal resources, introducing an area-based property tax system, restructuring the municipal organization, improving the delivery of municipal services, and applying e-governance to provide responsible, responsive, and efficient municipal governance to citizens. Prior to the accounting reforms, the corporation operated a cash accounting system. Under that system, the cashbooks were not closed and the closing final balance was based on receipts and expenses classification. Income due for collection was not known. The corporation was not in a position to determine the money spent on assets and the money available to incur further expenditure. On the whole, it was difficult to ascertain the real financial position of the corporation.

SCOPE OF THE ACCOUNTING REFORMS

The reforms sought to:

- design and develop a modified accrual accounting system
- prepare an accounts manual, and draft a chart of accounts
- develop software to support the computerization of finance and accounts functions, and ensure that there was appropriate interface with other operating modules
- test and implement the improved accounting system
- train employees on the new accounting and software operations

- carry out parallel run and finalize the accounts
- develop a budget manual and redraft budget document under the new system.

STAGES OF IMPLEMENTATION

The reforms were conceptualized in April 2001 and completed in April 2003. It took one more year for stabilizing and fine-tuning the reforms. The stages of implementation were:

- April 2001—conceptualization
- October 2001—consultants commence work
- October 2001 to January 2002—preparation of the accounting manual and its implementation
- February 2002—preparation of the budget document and its reconstruction using revised formats and budget codes
- February 2002 to July 2002—building customized software that meets the needs of the new accounting system
- August 2002—parallel run
- April 2003—preparation of the year-end balance sheet as on March 2003
- 1 April 2003—change-over to the new online computerized accounting system.

RESULTS

The results have been very encouraging.

- The corporation now maintains all its accounts on the online computerized system.
- It has prepared bank reconciliation statements for all its bank statements.
- It has composed an opening balance sheet on the basis of its past annual accounts and subsidiary registers.
- Budgets are integrated with the accounts and the budgetary system supports budgetary controls.
- Preparation of final accounts is easier.
- Quality analysis of financial statements is now possible.
- The reforms have facilitated better financial management practices.
- The average time of realizing cheques and processing bills has been reduced substantially.

CRITICAL ELEMENTS OF THE REFORMS

The critical elements helping the success of accounting reforms at the Hyderabad Municipal Corporation are:

- well conceived and professionally managed computerization and accounting reform efforts
- total commitment of the top management, accounting staff, and audit staff of the corporation
- efficient information technology support
- consultants' understanding of the existing situation and the problems at the micro level
- evolution of appropriate strategies by the consultants to fully ground the systems.

IMPACT ASSESSMENT

The impact of the accounting reforms is positive. The greatest impact has been to address the woes of service providers. They do not have to chase the bills now as they did under the cash accounting system, and the cheques are ready to be collected at the delivery counters of the corporation.

The new accounting system enables an examination of expenditure at the ward level. This, to a very great extent, has helped decentralize the management. The corporation now assesses its financial performance at multiple levels, such as at the corporation, functional or departmental, geographical, functionary, or head of accounts levels. This is a testimony to the fact that a single data source is capable of providing management information that can enable monitoring and decision-making.

The impact of the accounting reforms has also been in the realm of policy. On the basis of the very positive impact the reforms have generated in the Hyderabad Municipal Corporation, the state of Andhra Pradesh has decided to introduce accounting reforms for all the municipal bodies in the state.

THE LESSONS

What are the lessons to be learnt from the experiences of these municipal bodies with accounting reforms? Clearly, the strategies and processes for implementing accounting reforms in these municipal bodies have varied considerably, but there are some common lessons to be learnt.

OWNERSHIP OF THE REFORMS

The most crucial element in determining the outcome of reforms is the ownership of the reforms process. In the case of Ahmedabad Municipal Corporation, there was no ownership of the reforms and that was perhaps the most important reason why the reforms went awry. In the case of the municipal bodies in Tamil Nadu, Bangalore, and Hyderabad there was overwhelming local ownership of the reforms, a fact that partly explains why the reforms succeeded in these municipal bodies.

OPINION BUILDING

It is important that the stakeholders and user groups should own the reforms too. This depends on the participative nature of the reform process. Participation of stakeholders and user groups creates favourable conditions for ownership and willingness to reform. It also makes the reforms more broadbased and ensures their sustainability. Opinion-building exercises are useful in this respect. In the case of Ahmedabad Municipal Corporation, this key feature was absent. On the other hand, there was a high level of participation from all the stakeholders in Tamil Nadu, Bangalore, and Hyderabad.

PROFESSIONAL SUPPORT

Technical assistance of professional bodies should be enlisted in the implementation of the reforms, even if expertise is available in-house. In addition, it needs to be ensured that the terms of reference (ToR) for hiring professional support is drafted comprehensively and that important elements are not lost sight of. In the case of Ahmedabad Municipal Corporation, the ToR did not include auditing and computerization. Thus, while the accounting was modified to double-entry accrual system, the audit procedures, check lists, and auditing practices continued to comply with a single-entry, cash-based system.

ACCOUNTING POLICIES

Accounting policies need to be resolved before the actual conversion takes place. This is especially important because the process affords an excellent opportunity to involve all stakeholders in the implementation and ensure their ownership of the process. In Tamil Nadu, Bangalore, and Hyderabad the resolution of accounting policies was done in a very broadbased manner, involving as many stakeholders and user groups as possible. In the case of Ahmedabad Municipal Corporation, this important aspect was neglected.

THE ACCOUNTING MANUAL

The external consultants are often not in a position to comprehend fully how a municipal body functions. Therefore, it becomes necessary to bring out an accounting manual, which blends the typical experiences of the functioning of municipal bodies with professional expertise. An accounting manual is also necessary to provide guidance to the implementing staff in the new procedures, accounts, forms, and formats. Tamil Nadu was successful in bringing out a comprehensive accounting manual, which elaborated on every procedure, account, and format that was specifically designed for the municipal bodies. The Tamil Nadu experience is also instructive in the way it involved expert bodies, user groups, functionaries of the municipal bodies, and government officials in the preparation of the accounting manual.

CAPACITY BUILDING

Building the capacity of implementing staff is a critical component of the process of conversion. The municipal bodies that built capacity in their staff—by involving them at all stages of the design and implementation of the accounting reforms—were the ones that achieved the most favourable outcomes.

PARALLEL RUN

A parallel run needs to be conducted with both the old and new accounting systems. However, the point to note is that the parallel run should neither be too long nor too brief. If the parallel run is too long, it produces lethargy and constrains the ability of the organization to make the transition to the new form of accounting. In the case of Bangalore Municipal Corporation, for example, the parallel run lasted longer than it should have. In case of Tamil Nadu, the parallel run was conducted over the right period of time.

ACCOUNTING SYSTEM DEVELOPMENT

Computerization contributes greatly to the success of accounting reforms. Different approaches were, however, used to define at what precise point computerization should be introduced. Bangalore Municipal Corporation, for example, introduced computerization right from the beginning of the reform process. In case of Tamil Nadu and Hyderabad, the parallel run and the transition were completed on a manual basis, and computerization was introduced only after that.

THE ISSUES

There are primarily three issues that emerge from the experiences of municipal bodies with accounting reforms. First, each experiment in municipal accounting reform was a stand-alone exercise. This was because there was no uniform accounting system that these municipal bodies could follow. There was no replication of successful innovations, and no attempt to repeat tried and tested reform elements. The result, unfortunately, was a good deal of heterogeneity, presenting a scenario where the accounting data and performance measurements across municipal bodies are largely incomparable.[11]

Second, the present process of municipal bodies changing over to accrual accounting has involved a great deal of delay. Ahmedabad Municipal Corporation took more than seven years to achieve, what turned out to be an incomplete transition. What is needed as a corrective is the evolution of a simple, user-friendly accounting system that is capable of being implemented with least possible delay.[12]

Third, there is a concern as to whether the results of accounting reforms have really been commensurate with the expectations they had aroused. It is a fact that the accounting needs of municipal bodies could have been met by a modified accrual accounting system. Such a system is fully capable of integrating the features of an accrual-based, double-entry accounting system to the characteristics, activities, and purpose of the municipal bodies. A full accrual accounting system, which was not necessary in the first place and took an enormous amount of time to realize, did the disservice of raising expectations that went far beyond what the municipal bodies really needed.

The issues we have highlighted relate essentially to the question whether the appropriate variant of accrual accounting was adopted. They do not, in any way, detract from the relevance and usefulness of accrual accounting to government organizations. In fact, all the municipal bodies whose experience with adoption of accrual accounting we studied, are much better off now than when they used to account on a cash basis. They have been able to achieve strong gains in efficiency, transparency, credibility, user-friendliness, and accountability.

The strongest gain, however, is the mere fact that it has even been possible to implement accounting reforms in the context of municipal bodies. The environment, in which the accounting reforms were implemented, needs to be put in perspective. The present municipal accounting system in India was designed and put in place during the colonial times, to serve regulatory and maintenance functions—and is intrinsically archaic. However, over time, in order to handle new accounting transactions and the growing range of functions, the municipal bodies did add incremental accounting subsystems. However, all this did practically nothing to strengthen the core accounting system, except to make it a heavily distorted system on the whole.[13]

That it was possible for accounting reforms to take place and even fructify in the highly archaic and distorted environment of the municipal bodies, gives us the confidence that adoption of accrual accounting is eminently possible in the core, budget-dependent departments of the Indian government, which can be credited with having qualitatively a much better accounting environment relative to the municipal bodies. In addition, these municipal bodies were able to achieve varying degrees of efficiency, transparency, user-friendliness, credibility, and accountability in their operations as a result of the conversion to accrual accounting. That being the case, there appears to be a very strong case for introducing accrual accounting in the core, budget-dependent departments of the Indian government.

NOTES

1. Schick (1998), p. 123.
2. Rose (2003), p. 14.
3. Hepworth (2002), pp. 18–21.
4. Shiromany (2003), pp. 54–5.
5. Joshi (2003), p. 43n.
6. Olsen and Peters (1996), p. 3.
7. Rose (2003), p. 26.
8. Thimmaiah (1984), p. 49.
9. Ibid., p. 55.
10. The analyses of the accounting reforms in the municipalities are based on Joshi (2003) and (2004).
11. Joshi (2004), p. 5.
12. Ibid.
13. Joshi (2004), p. 15.

Implementation
A Roadmap

A key lesson that emerges from the experiences of the four countries and the Indian municipal bodies, with the adoption of accrual accounting, is that there should be adequate preparation before embarking on the actual conversion. In the case of Ahmedabad Municipal Corporation, the conversion to accrual accounting did not fructify fully because some crucial elements were lost sight of at the planning stage. In the following pages, we draw a roadmap of how the process of conversion to accrual accounting in the ministries and departments of the Indian government should be conceptualized, designed, organized, and implemented.

ALLOCATING ROLES AND RESPONSIBILITIES

THE LEAD AGENCY

As a first step, a ministry or department in the Indian government—which is entrusted with the accounting function—should be designated as the lead agency for implementation of the accounting reforms. The lead agency should be given the following responsibilities.

- developing policy parameters within which the accounting policies of the ministries and departments are to be grounded
- determining the accounting procedures and controls
- developing elements of the accounting reforms
- evolving a standard setting process and establishing an appropriate body for standard setting
- developing a financial reporting policy and establishing an appropriate body for evolving and monitoring the reporting framework
- working out the nature and contents of the enabling legislative framework and piloting the bill through the legislature
- determining the nature of the audit opinion and incorporating appropriate legislative and executive changes to reflect the changed nature of audit opinion
- preparing an accounting manual

- preparing detailed guidelines for the guidance of implementing ministries and departments
- setting out suitable milestones for implementation and evolving a set of trigger points and monitoring them
- selecting appropriate technologies and systems
- evolving communication and training strategies
- developing a strategy for opinion building
- preparing an initial and final 'national asset register'
- conducting a parallel run exercise
- exercising quality control over the implementation process.

In New Zealand, it was the treasury that was the lead agency while in the Australian government it was the department of finance and administration. In Sweden, it was the Swedish National Financial Authority, while in the United Kingdom it was the treasury. In the Indian government, the ministry of finance, and in particular the Controller General of Accounts, could be designated as the lead agency to conceptualize, design, and implement the accounting reforms.

THE MINISTRIES AND DEPARTMENTS

The implementing ministries and departments should be given the responsibility to:

- develop accrual accounting arrangements in a timeframe to be specified centrally
- prepare an opening balance sheet
- Specify the broad classes of outputs which can become the basis for budgetary appropriations in an accrual-based budget
- develop cost-allocation systems to enable the allocation of all departmental costs to outputs
- take full responsibility for the financial management of their departments, including the integrity and reliability of information to be provided
- provide a full set of financial statements (to be centrally prescribed) on an accrual basis as well as a statement on delivery of outputs and a statement of responsibility for the reliability of information in the statements
- make available the accrual statements to audit
- provide information to an integrated financial management information system

- evolve a change management strategy, constitute change management teams, and take up training and opinion-building exercises.

CREATION OF A SPECIAL TASK TEAM

The lead agency should create a special task team to spearhead the implementation efforts for the realization of accounting reforms. It is important that the staff assigned to the special task team should have an understanding of accounting policy issues and also a proven track record of working in a mission mode. The staff chosen for manning the special task team should be allowed to continue with the team for full duration of the reforms. They should not be saddled with other responsibilities and chores that may possibly detract from their commitment to the accounting reforms. Similar special task teams should be created at the levels of implementing ministries and departments.

HIRING PROFESSIONAL SUPPORT

It would be necessary to select a technical consulting firm, that can provide external professional support in (a) the designing of accounting reforms and (b) technical guidance in the implementation. Three important considerations need to be kept in mind while choosing the firm and defining the scope of technical support.

1. The technical consulting firm should have some understanding of how the government functions: the unique nature of the government, the services it provides, special characteristics of its assets, and the typical requirements of government operations. A technical consulting firm without such an understanding may end up suggesting a corporate inspired model that will be singularly inappropriate in the context of government. This happened in the case of Ahmedabad Municipal Corporation, where the technical consulting firm provided a modern, enterprise accounting system without aligning it to the structure and processes of the government. With the result, functionaries of the corporation were hard put to relate the accounting model to their work practices.

2. The scope of the project should be adequately defined. In order to realize the full scope of reforms, the ToR for technical assistance by the consultancy firm should be comprehensive and unambiguous. It should be ensured that no element is lost sight of while defining the ToR. As

we noted, elements such as audit and computerization were missed out when drawing up the ToR for Ahmedabad Municipal Corporation. As a result, while the accounting was modified to an accrual-based system; the audit procedures, check lists, and auditing practices continued to comply with a single-entry, cash-based system.

3. The contract with the technical consulting firm should be for a period that is long enough to cover not merely the designing of accounting reforms but also the parallel run, the actual implementation, and a slight overlap that can help address problems arising out of the post-reform blues. If the contract does not cover all these events, it can cause dislocations. For example, in Ahmedabad Municipal Corporation the contract with the consultants expired long before the accounting reforms were completed. This was responsible, in part, for the corporation achieving an incomplete transition.

DEFINING ACCOUNTING POLICIES AND STANDARDS

It is important that the policies and standards under accrual accounting should be defined, and be in place, before embarking on the process of conversion. The key issue, however, is the development of specific accounting standards. The four countries whose experiences we studied, based their definition of accrual accounting upon the accounting standards applicable to their private sector. Taking a cue from the experience of these countries, it is advisable that—while defining the accounting policies—the standards as prevailing in the Indian private sector could be the base.

This has three distinct advantages.

1. It facilitates free flow of expertise from the Indian private sector, both by way of consulting work for developing new systems and in the deployment of personnel.
2. It obviates the need for Indian government to engage in *de novo* formulation of standards, which can be frightfully expensive both in terms of resources and time.
3. The Indian government, as a part of its liberalizing measures, is now increasingly asking the private sector to deliver quite a few of its public services. It would be logical, therefore, to adopt private sector accounting standards that are capable of generating cost comparisons between the government providing these services and the private sector providing them.

However, it is not desirable to adopt private sector accounting standards *in toto* because private sector norms do not fully address the requirements of government departments. It will be necessary to modify the private sector accounting policies and standards to reflect the unique nature of the government.

The accounting standards (AS) board of ICAI has already set some accounting standards. They relate to:

- disclosure of accounting policies (AS 1)
- valuation of inventories (AS 2)
- cash flow statements (AS 3)
- contingencies and events occurring after the balance sheet (AS 4)
- prior period items and changes in accounting policies (AS 5)
- depreciation accounting (AS 6)
- accounting for construction contracts (AS 7)
- accounting for research and development (AS 8)
- revenue recognition (AS 9)
- accounting for fixed assets (AS 10)
- accounting for the effects of changes in forex rates (AS 11)
- accounting for government grants (AS 12)
- accounting for investments (AS 13)
- accounting for amalgamations (AS 14)
- accounting for retirement benefits (AS 15)
- borrowing costs (AS 16)
- segment reporting (AS 17)
- related party disclosures (AS 18)
- lease (AS 19)
- earning per share (AS 20)
- consolidated financial statements (AS 21)
- accounting for taxes on income (AS 22)
- accounting for investments in associates in consolidated financial statements (AS 23)
- discounting operations (AS 24)
- interim financial reporting (AS 25)
- intangible assets (AS 26)
- financial reporting of interest in joint ventures (AS 27)
- impairment of assets (AS 28).

These standards pertain to accrual system of accounting but are intended for corporate or business enterprises. They have to be suitably modified to include the requirements of government departments.

Benchmark guidance is now available on how to modify private sector accounting standards to include the requirements of government departments. The public sector committee (PSC) of International Federation of Accountants has done comprehensive work on the accounting, auditing, and financial reporting needs of national, regional, and local governments; related government agencies; and the constituencies they serve. The PSC has brought out a set of International Public Sector Accounting Standards (IPSASs) to be used by governments. To date, the PSC has issued 19 accrual IPSASs. They relate to:

- presentation of financial statements
- net surplus or deficit for the period
- the effects of changes in foreign exchange rates
- borrowing costs
- consolidated financial statements
- accounting for investments in associates
- financial reporting of interests in joint ventures
- revenues from exchange transactions
- financial reporting in hyperinflationary economies
- construction contracts
- inventories
- leases
- events after the reporting date
- financial instruments: disclosure and presentation
- investment property
- property, plant, and equipment
- segment reporting
- provisions, contingent liabilities, and contingent assets
- related party disclosures.

What is important about these IPSASs is that they provide benchmark guidance to countries whose governments plan to convert to accrual accounting, and therefore, should be made use of while defining accounting standards for the Indian government.

The key consideration, however, is that accounting policies and standards, suitable for use in the government context, need to be developed and put in place before starting the process of actual conversion. It is necessary that stakeholders and user groups such as taxpayers, legislators, oversight agencies, planners, administrators, bankers, investors, and economic analysts—who have a vital interest in how the government accounts—should be consulted while resolving accounting policies and standards. This provides an excellent opportunity for involving all the concerned stakeholders in the implementation process itself, thereby ensuring their ownership of the reforms. As we noted while looking at the municipal accounting reforms, Tamil Nadu and Bangalore implemented this stage of the reforms in an exemplary manner. They involved all the stakeholders and user groups including the citizens' bodies, their own functionaries, the audit institutions, and ICAI—thereby ensuring a successful transition.

STANDARD SETTING

The question as to who sets the accounting standards is particularly important in an accrual setting because a number of judgements have to be made in respect of the treatment of individual transactions. Therefore, independence of the standard setting body becomes a key issue. As we noted in respect of New Zealand and Australia: there is one professional standard setter, totally independent, which sets standards for both the government and private sector, and the governments in these two countries follow the decisions of the independent standard setter.

The Comptroller and Auditor General of India has set up a standard setting body for the Indian government—the Government Accounting Standards Advisory Board (GASAB). The GASAB came about in order to establish and improve standards of governmental accounting and financial reporting and enhance accountability mechanisms.[1] As per the notification setting up the GASAB, the board is responsible for:

- formulating and proposing standards that improve the usefulness of financial reports based on the needs of the financial report users
- keeping standards current and reflecting changes in the governmental environment
- providing guidance on implementation of standards
- considering significant areas of accounting and financial reporting that can be improved through the standard setting process
- improving the common understanding of the nature and purpose of information contained in financial reports.[2]

To its credit, GASAB has been remarkably diligent. It has already brought out several exposure drafts on guarantees given by governments, accounting and classification of grants-in-aid, cash flow statements, and presentation and components of financial reports. These exposure drafts relate to the cash system of accounting. The present composition of GASAB is as follows.

- Deputy Comptroller and Auditor General—chairperson
- Controller General of Accounts
- Controller General of Defence Accounts
- Financial Commissioner, Indian Railways
- Director General, National Council of Applied Economic Research
- Joint Secretary (Budget), Ministry of Finance, Government of India
- Deputy Governor, Reserve Bank of India
- President, Institute of Chartered Accountants of India
- Principal Secretary (Finance) of four state governments on annual rotation basis
- Director General (Accounts), Office of the Comptroller and Auditor General of India—member secretary.[3]

How representative is the composition of GASAB? Clearly, it is heavily weighted in the favour of government functionaries. Both the chairperson and secretary of the board are from the office of CAG.

The important question is—can GASAB be designated as the standard setter for developing and monitoring accounting standards for conversion to accrual accounting? With its present government-dominated composition, GASAB does not come across as a truly independent body. The accounting standards board of the ICAI—which is responsible for establishing accounting standards for the private sector companies—could be the ideal candidate for the purpose. The merit of having ICAI as the standard setting body would be in the fact that, as an independent agency in charge of formulating and enforcing accounting standards, it can be relied upon to eliminate opportunities for the Indian government to indulge in fiscal trickery.

REPORTING FRAMEWORK

As with the accounting standards, a great deal of preparation needs to go into designing a financial reporting framework. The four countries whose experiences we studied, have chosen a model for the preparation of articulated financial statements very similar to those in the private sector. They have taken care to see that the private sector reporting format is suitably modified to recognize the important differences between the nature of the government and private sector activities, their objectives, and their modes of financing. Operating statements, as opposed to profit and loss statements, have been developed with a focus on the gross and net cost of governmental activities. The reporting statements have also been specifically designed to show the full cost of resources spent in delivery of public programmes, the costs recovered through levy of user charges, and the net cost of programme delivery.

So, the idea should be to modify the private sector reporting format to take care of the special requirements of government operations. Here again, benchmark guidance is available from the IPSASs. IPSAS 1 and 2 (presentation of financial statements) set out the overall considerations for the presentation of financial statements, guidance for the structure of those statements, and minimum requirements for their content. A complete set of financial statements, as suggested by the IPSASs, includes the following components (comparable statements in the private sector indicated in parentheses).

- cash flow statements (this title is common to both)
- statement of financial position (balance sheet)
- statement of financial performance (income statement)
- statement in changes in net assets/equity (statement in changes in equity)
- accounting policies and notes to the financial statements (Accounting Policies and Notes).

While discussing the Australian experience, we had noted that the Australian government also uses the Government Finance Statistics—a system of the International Monetary Fund that identifies statements required for statistical reporting purposes. These statistical statements, reporting on an accrual basis, consist of the following statements.

- balance sheet
- statement of government operations
- statement of sources and uses of cash
- statement of other economic flows

However, there are some key differences between the statements prescribed by the IPSASs and the GFS. While historical cost is the basis in the IPSASs—as the benchmark treatment—current cost is the basis for GFS. As a result, the reporting formats used by these two systems can be very different. For example, the IPSASs identify current/non-current assets, while the GFS identifies financial/non-financial assets with the result that inventory would be classified as a current asset under the IPSASs while inventory would be classified as a non-financial asset under GFS.

The fact is both these frameworks are useful for government reporting. While the statements under IPSASs reflect the accounting focus (it is driven by the idea that government accounting should operate just like private sector accounting), the GFS is tailor-made for government policy purposes. GFS is useful in assessing the impact of government's policy on the economy, and to that extent it is useful for macroeconomic analysis. There is also a need for aligning the Indian government's accounting framework with the revised international statistical standards that use the GFS framework. We would recommend that the Indian government should choose to report in both these frameworks. Some work is being done for harmonizing these two frameworks, but total harmonization is not possible. However, what could be done is that, with sufficient advance planning in a system development effort, a common database on an accrual basis could be developed. This can meet the needs of both the systems (for the purpose of preparation of financial statements); a subject to which we will revert while discussing accounting system development.

As we had pointed out in Chapter 2, the budget presented to the Indian Parliament is essentially an accounting document in the sense that it addresses key question regarding the affordability of programmes and operations of the Indian government. In addition, the budget is widely publicized, with a view to inform the electorate about financial plans and policies of the government, and is almost always commented upon by the media. So, formatting the budget as an accounting statement in accrual terms is of key importance. Neither the IPSASs nor the GFS prescribe any statement for the purpose; independent work needs to be done on how to format this important accounting statement.

In addition, the Indian Parliament would require a comparative report indicating whether the money voted by it has been spent as approved. This would call for a statement indicating the actual expenditure against the budgeted outlay. In the present cash-accounting system, a statement is prescribed that provides a comparison between the budgeted outlay and the actual expenditure. The preparation of such a comparative statement is not a requirement under the IPSAS or the GFS, but it needs to be generated in order to meet the legislative requirement.

On the whole, issues relating to financial reporting are important and complex, and they need to be addressed by an expert body. The countries whose experience with reforms we studied, have either set up expert bodies for the purpose or given the responsibility to existing expert bodies. In New Zealand, for example, the Institute of Chartered Accountants of New Zealand has been given this responsibility: the financial reporting standards board of the institute develops the financial reporting standards which are approved by the Accounting Standards Review Board, a statutory body. In the United Kingdom, the Financial Reporting Advisory Board—which brings together representatives from the treasury, government departments, national audit office, Audit Commission, Accounting Standards Board, industry and academia—is the expert body in charge of financial reporting.

LEGISLATIVE FRAMEWORK

The nature of legal authority, under which conversion to accrual accounting was authorized, has varied in these four countries. In the case of New Zealand and the UK, it was by way of legislative enactments. In the Swedish government, it was under an enabling provision in the budget act, supported by a number of ordinances providing detailed frameworks. In Australia, it was effected by executive fiat. The balance of advantage would seem to lie in enacting a specific legislation, for the following reasons.

- The legislation will provide the necessary explanation for proposed reforms. During the course of parliamentary debate on the draft legislation, issues can be clarified and doubts can be set at rest.
- Giving the reforms a legislative cover would enlist political support. Thereby ensuring that political parties get committed to the changes.
- The legislation would send down the important message to civil servants that the accounting reform is permanent in nature.

It is important that salient features of the reforms are incorporated in the legislative framework, particularly those features that seek to make fundamental changes. At a minimum, the legislation should provide for:

- the accounts to present a true and fair view, and to conform to GAAP—modified as necessary to reflect the requirements of government operations
- creation of an accounting standards body to develop and monitor accounting standards
- creation of a financial reporting, expert body to develop and monitor financial reporting
- the accounts to be presented in statements which, at a minimum, should consist of a statement of outturn showing actual expenditure against the budgeted outlay, a statement of financial performance (equivalent of a profit and loss statement in the private sector), a statement of financial position (equivalent of a balance sheet), a cash flow statement, and a statement relating costs to departmental objectives
- requiring the CAG to audit the accrual accounts sent to him by the departments
- placing a duty on the Indian government to prepare consolidated accounts for the government (whole-of-government accounts).

NATURE OF THE AUDIT OPINION

With adoption of accrual accounting, the nature of audit opinion needs to change to a 'true and fair' opinion, as given by auditors in a private company. This differs from the opinion 'properly presents' currently given in the appropriation accounts, thus reflecting a change from cash to accruals. However, the other part of CAG's comment that 'the accounts are correct' (the regularity assertion) needs to continue. So, the audit opinion in an accrual setting should reflect

- a true and fair view,
- that money provided by the Indian Parliament has been expended for the purpose intended,
- that resources authorized by the Indian Parliament have been used for the purpose in relation to which the use was authorized, and
- that financial transactions covered by the accounts are in accordance with the relevant authority that governs them.

In addition, there are two contingencies that need to be provided for. First, there should be a legal provision authorizing the CAG to audit the whole-of-government accounts and for them to be laid before the Indian Parliament. Second, if in the course of audit by the CAG it is discovered that there has been a material use of resources that required but did not receive the necessary authorization of the government, the CAG should inform the government which may retrospectively authorize the expenditure. Ideally, changes required in the nature of audit opinion, as a result of conversion to accruals, should be incorporated in the legislative framework itself.

A CHART OF ACCOUNTS

The structure of an accounting system is defined by the chart of accounts, in which the account heads are grouped logically under a functional hierarchy of main heads, subheads, and sub-subheads. The structure of the chart is particularly important in an accrual setting because its nature determines whether the accounting system can be computerized.

While designing the chart of accounts, private sector standards can be taken as the point of departure with suitable modifications and additions of new accounts to suit the special requirements of government operations. In addition to the normal classifications, addition of the following classifications may be necessary to reflect the special requirements of government.

- a classification to enable a comparison between the budgeted outlay and actual expenditure

- a classification to store and retrieve information in various dimensions in order to follow up and evaluate the results of government operations; this would help in
  - performance reporting
  - monitoring the cost of different activities in a department as well as the cost of products and different kinds of services
  - measuring the input of resources versus output of services
  - allocating costs between different organizational units in a department. The classification can also be used to assess the efficiency of governmental operations
- a classification to enable the government to capture financial information on a geographical basis; this will help in the analysing cost of services provided to specific constituencies for planning and control purposes.[4]
- an economic type of framework classification for stocks and flows. It should have sections to look after the reconciliation of net operating results, with cash flows from operating activities, intra departmental transfers and revaluations, and other changes in the volume of assets.

ACCOUNTING MANUAL

In Indian administration, manuals have played a significant role as reference literature in the implementation of schemes and programmes. This has been so since the colonial times. In the case of government departments implementing accounting reforms, a manual is doubly important because the external consultants may not fully comprehend how government departments function. Therefore, an accounting manual should be in a position to capture and blend the typical elements of governmental functioning with professional expertise. The accounting manual should set out, as exhaustively as possible, the statutory and regulatory environment, the procedures involved, the compliance steps, and the budgetary structure. At a minimum, the manual should contain inputs on:

- existing procedures, accounts, forms, and formats required under the cash accounting system
- the changes contemplated under the new accounting system
- statutory and regulatory stipulations to be complied with
- accounting policies and disclosure norms
- chart of accounts
- budgetary requirements to be complied with

- procedures and processes to be followed
- the various forms and formats under accrual accounting.[5]

We have seen how the comprehensive and well-crafted accounting manual in Tamil Nadu—which detailed every procedure, account and format of the new accounting system—contributed so significantly to implementation of the reforms. What is particularly instructive about the Tamil Nadu experience is the intense participative process; in which expert bodies with domain knowledge, stakeholders, and user groups were consulted while finalizing the contents of the accounting manual. Ideally, the accounting manual should be the end result of a participative process that should include consultations with user groups, stakeholders, and expert bodies with domain knowledge.

PREPARING GUIDELINES FOR THE IMPLEMENTATION OF THE REFORMS

In addition to the accounting manual, which will be in the nature of a formal document, it may be necessary to issue guidelines for effective implementation of the reforms. At a minimum, the guidelines should set out:

- the philosophy of the reforms, explaining the purpose of reforms: how accrual accounting and budgeting will bring about efficiency, transparency, and accountability, and how the accrual information will help government functionaries in their day-to-day operations and decision-making
- the framework of the proposed reforms, describing the accounting policies, standard setting process, financial reporting format, legislative framework, and nature of the proposed audit process; it should also set out the broad outlines of the accounting manual
- role definition, depicting how roles are defined for the implementation process, and how task responsibilities are allocated. This should outline the role and responsibilities set out for the lead agency, and for the ministries and departments
- implementation plan, describing the various steps proposed for implementing the accounting reforms
- milestones, trigger points, and the procedural steps for monitoring progress
- communication and coordination mechanisms describing the formal structure for implementing the reforms, rules and procedures, communication channels, coordination mechanisms, controls, and who does what

- financial outlays including a discussion on what budgetary outlays are provided, how to operate them, what limits are placed on the authorization controls, and what are the budgetary and financial rules and procedures to be followed.[6]

The guidelines should be made as comprehensive as possible. Ideally, they should be written and presented in a language and manner that can be understood by an average accounting employee.

CHANGE MANAGEMENT

The adoption of accrual accounting calls for a culture change on the part of staff essentially through an acceptance of the benefits it offers, an understanding of how to use the additional information generated by accrual accounting, and inducing an ownership of the reforms. Each department should set up change management teams by selecting staff who have proven change management skills and an understanding of the proposed accounting reforms.

It is necessary that a strategy for change management is evolved, put in place, and implemented before setting out on the actual process of conversion. The strategy should include, *inter alia*, educating the top civil servants manning the ministries and departments. They should be made aware of the new information flows from accrual accounting and the benefits these offer for effective decision-making. It is also necessary to convince the top management of the need for accountancy reforms, so that there is ownership of the reforms at the top. It will also be necessary to educate employees who are in charge of the accounting function, in the department such as, the accounting clerks and the accountants. Ideally, the change management should be a department-wide exercise.

The key point in a change management strategy should be to ensure that all the participants, involved in process of change to accrual accounting, fully understand the nature of changes to be introduced. In New Zealand, this was done through:

- a video that captured the key ideas
- a plain language booklet that described the various elements of the reforms and the nature of the legislation
- briefings for senior civil servants in the departments.

It is worth considering whether a similar strategy could be adopted in the Indian government. However, while preparing the material for dissemination for change management purposes, care has to be taken to see that the various means create the required financial awareness. This could be done by inviting attention to:

- accounting system changes and the changes in the system operations of department
- accounting policy changes in terms of understanding by the departmental staff
- changes resulting from the introduction of accrual-based reviews and resource baselines, together with an understanding of how accrual accounting will fit into the fiscal framework of the Indian government as a whole, and the impact it will have on the planning processes within the department
- wider changes such as the need for analysis and interpretation of information generated by accrual accounting for decision-making purposes.

TRAINING

For an initiative such as adoption of accrual accounting to succeed, adequate training has to be given to departmental staff. It is only training that can provide a degree of sustainability to the accounting reforms. Training modules need to be developed by a professional body that has the necessary outreach to provide venues for training. The training modules should include inputs on:

- training the trainers
- sensitization and orientation to be imparted at different levels, such as departmental staff, elected representatives, auditors, and accountants
- accounting manual and the guidelines
- how accrual system is a part of the overall fiscal framework of the government
- how accrual system enhances the planning process in the department
- how information generated by accrual accounting helps the decision-making process in the department.

While a professional body in the private sector can be asked to develop the training modules (because they have the experience of working in an accrual set-up), care has to be taken to see that these modules do actually reflect the typical requirements of government departments. This can be achieved by evaluating:

- whether the training needs reflect the special requirements of government departments, particularly their planning process
- how these needs have been quantified and stratified
- what steps have been taken to translate the quantified needs into a specification that the training provider can deliver
- how the training is linked to assessing the overall effectiveness of the individual employee of the department and the department itself

The bottom line, however, is the effectiveness with which an average accounting employee of a government department—who is used to the nuances of the cash-accounting system for long years and is unlettered in the complexities of accrual accounting—is enabled through the training process, to make the difficult transition from a single-entry accounting system to a double-entry bookkeeping system.

OPINION-BUILDING

An opinion-building exercise targeting stakeholders and user groups is crucial because it helps engender ownership and willingness to reform in this important constituency. It also makes the process broad based and ensures sustainability of reforms in the longer term. That is why a well-structured opinion-building exercise should be organized explaining various aspects of the accounting reforms. The exercise should ideally include all the stakeholders who are involved in the management of the department—legislators, oversight agencies, members of the standing and consultative committees of the Parliament for the department, top management in the ministries, external members of the management councils and boards of the department, and auditors and user groups such as administrators, bankers, investors, and economic analysts. At a minimum, such an exercise should familiarize stakeholders and user groups with the additional information that flows from the adoption of accrual accounting and how they can exploit the incremental information flows to their advantage.

As we noted in the case of Ahmedabad Municipal Corporation, the participation of stakeholders and user groups in the implementation process was conspicuous by its absence because no opinion-building exercise was ever attempted. On the other hand, there was participation of stakeholders and user groups in the case of Tamil Nadu, Bangalore, and Hyderabad where elaborate opinion-building exercises were carried out ensuring the active participation of stakeholders and user groups, thereby ensuring successful transition to the new accounting system.

ALLOCATING RESOURCES

Introduction of accrual accounting and reporting is an expensive proposition in terms of the systems to be installed and manpower to be deployed. For the conversion process to proceed without interruption and be realized in a time-bound manner, it is essential that necessary resources—both financial and non-financial—be estimated accurately and provided for. It is only after allocation of adequate resources and manpower that the process of conversion should start.

PREPARATION OF THE OPENING BALANCE SHEET

An important step in the implementation of accrual accounting is the formulation of an opening balance sheet for the departments. For this to happen, an inventory of assets owned by the departments needs to be prepared. Accounting for fixed assets under an accrual system could be a challenging task for the departments, because valuation and assessment of assets acquired in the past would require

- locating the assets,
- defining the method of valuation,
- finding out how much was paid for acquisition of the assets or otherwise placing a value on them, and
- determining their useful life.

Since a decision on the valuation principles and rules of depreciation of departmental assets would have been taken centrally, the departments have to perform rest of the tasks. In any case, it is imperative that a reliable asset register be set up before the actual process of conversion to accrual accounting starts. A necessary prerequisite for preparing the balance sheet is to identify surplus properties that can be sold off subsequently.

In a similar exercise, the liabilities need to be calculated in order to set up the opening balance sheet. In actual practice, departments in the Indian government have the liability data but it generally extends to debts. Information on unfunded pension liability and contingent liabilities has to be added.

The question arises—should external professional support be enlisted for setting up the opening balance sheet? In our considered view, this may be necessary, particularly when preparing an inventory of assets in accrual terms. Actuarial assistance may also be called for in assessing pension liabilities.

INITIAL NATIONAL ASSET REGISTER

On the basis of asset registers prepared by the departments, it would be possible to prepare an initial national asset register, listing out all the assets held by the departments and their affiliated organizations. The asset register—feeding as it does on information gathered by the departments for setting up their opening balance sheets—should be in a position to give an indication of the assets that the Indian government owns. While preparing the initial national asset register, care should be taken to see that it includes details on:

- all tangible fixed assets including heritage, emergency, and infrastructure assets
- all intangible fixed assets including intellectual property rights
- all fixed asset investments, such as share holdings owned by the departments.

The indications given by the initial national asset register would be useful, in that they would reveal the full cost of holding and using assets. Thereby, providing a clear incentive to the departments to sell off costly, non-productive assets. Although what such an initial national asset register would indicate could be very preliminary in nature, it would provide the basis that could be refined further to produce a final and updated national asset register—providing a comprehensive list of all the assets owned by departments of the Indian government and affiliated organizations.

INTRODUCTION OF A CAPITAL CHARGE

It will be necessary to levy a capital charge in order to improve asset management in government departments. This has to be done centrally by a direction from the Ministry of Finance that a charge be levied on the cost of capital tied up in all the assets that a department owns. The scheme could be as follows.

If a department has Rs 10 crore in assets, the government will levy a charge of 10 per cent (the rate ideally should be equivalent to the long-term government bond rate). This means that the department will have to pay Rs 1 crore annually to the Ministry of Finance. When it is decided to levy a capital charge, the appropriations to all the departments should be increased by the amount of their capital charge, so that there is no net impact on the departments or for the Indian government as a whole. However, the departments should be permitted to dispose off surplus assets, so that they could save themselves from the capital charge on surplus assets while retaining the original appropriation. This will provide the necessary incentive to the departments to sell off underutilised, surplus assets.

SPECIFICATION OF OUTPUTS

Outputs to be produced by the departments have to be specified. After specifying the departmental outputs, they have to be aggregated to output classes: homogeneous categories of outputs entered into the budget estimates to be presented to the Parliament. In any case, information about the outputs should specify what is being delivered rather than how much is being spent on staff, capital, and equipment.

DEVELOPMENT OF COST- ALLOCATION SYSTEM

The departments need to develop a cost-allocation system so that all the departmental costs are allocated to outputs. At a minimum, the costs to be so allocated should include overhead costs, depreciation, and capital charge.

ACCOUNTING SYSTEM DEVELOPMENT

The introduction of accrual accounting is greatly helped by a computer-based information system. Development of a computer-based accounting system should be carried out in four steps: assessment, design, procurement, and implementation.[7]

Assessment

This should consist of the development of a general design of system application. System assessment will have four dimensions.

   (i) a survey to be conducted of the present system
  (ii) the information needs of the users to be identified
 (iii) the system requirements to satisfy the information needs of the users to be identified
 (iv) a systems analysis report, documenting the user specifications of the present system and the overall conceptual design of the proposed system, to be prepared.

While drawing up the user specifications, attention has to be paid to accommodate the special requirements of government operations. For example, accountability to the legislature would require additive features. In case the GFS is adopted, it will be necessary to accommodate the coding structure that the GFS manual requires to be used in the preparation of financial statements.

Design

This step consists of preparing detailed specifications of the proposed system. The design function has three dimensions:

(i) alternative designs for the proposed system need to be evaluated
(ii) detailed design specifications to be prepared
(iii) the systems design report, describing the details that are necessary to actually implement the proposed system, to be prepared.

The design of the system should ideally be based on the chart of accounts. An accounting system provides for separate accounts to store recorded monetary information from transactions. Each account is assigned a number from the chart of accounts, which is essentially a numbering system designed to classify and organize the accounts; for such classification, a coding system is provided by the chart of accounts. That being the case, the design of the proposed system should be linked to the local structuring of the chart of accounts.

Procurement

The software requirements of the system should be based on the specifications identified while designing the system. Both the software and hardware specifications should be incorporated in an RFP (request for proposal) and bids obtained. The process of evaluation of the bids is greatly helped by the fact that cost-effective, user-friendly accounting software is freely available. Since all software solutions are more or less similar in respect of their capabilities, there may be no need to compile a large number of requirements by the systems instead, the questions that need to be asked are:

- ease of use
- costs
- how quickly the systems can be positioned and made operational.

Implementation

Implementation will depend on the system finally selected, but there are a number of key considerations that have to be kept in mind at the implementation stage.

- Staff in the departments, who will be called upon to handle the system, need to be trained in those areas where it may be necessary to accommodate, maintain, and implement the system.

- Project management techniques may have to be used in order to control implementational activities.
- Once the system is in position and operational, there should be a formal follow-up and evaluation of the new system.

INTEGRATED FINANCIAL MANAGEMENT INFORMATION SYSTEM

We had suggested earlier that both the IPSAS and GFS frameworks should be adopted for financial reporting. While work is now under progress to harmonize the two frameworks, total harmonization is not possible. What is possible, however, is the creation of a common database on which both these frameworks can feed. That is why the development of an integrated financial management information system (IFMIS)—providing a database that incorporates the facets of both these frameworks of financial reporting—is necessary.[8] Such a database would also help in the audit certification on fair presentation of data.

Ideally the IFMIS should be based on advanced Web-based technology. It needs to be implemented progressively, starting with the finance ministry or the lead agency, and then, transferred to other ministries and departments. The final objective being to enable the online processing of all transactions at source, where the transactions are generated.

It is important that the network architecture of the IFMIS is designed with the functional requirements in mind. The finance ministry could operate a Web-based architecture with central servers and unified databases installed and maintained at the finance ministry. By implementing such an architecture, it can be assured that the IFMIS is installed and managed entirely on the servers in a central location while eliminating the need for desktop software installations and upgrades; this will significantly reduce the cost and enable the transmission of the data in a faster and cost-effective mode.

It will be necessary to provide training on the usefulness and benefits of the IFMIS. It will also be necessary to provide sufficient number of computers in order to impart training on inputting data, maintaining budgetary control, and generating financial statements. A digital library of accounting-related material will have to be developed for study and reference.

ORGANIZING THE ACTIVITIES

The steps that we have outlined above do not have to be implemented in a linear manner. What is suggested below is the categorization of these steps into groups of related activities and implementing them in a parallel mode.[9]

- All the conceptual and framework design activities such as designating the lead agency, allocating roles and responsibilities, developing accounting policies, standard setting, evolving reporting framework, defining the nature of the audit opinion, preparing the accounting manual, compiling guidelines, and developing the chart of accounts could be categorized into one group.
- Activities consisting of compiling data in respect of the assets and liabilities, setting up of the opening balance sheet, developing a cost allocation system, specifying outputs, and introducing the capital charge could be categorized into one group.
- Activities relating to change management, training of personnel, and opinion building exercises could be categorized into one group.
- Activities consisting of procurement and installation of necessary hardware and software, training the prospective users, creation of the IFMIS and provision of related training, and establishment of the digital library could be categorized into one group.

These groups of activities could be taken up simultaneously. Once they are completed, the following steps could be taken up in a linear mode.

A PARALLEL RUN

It is advisable to take up a parallel run leading up to the actual implementation of accrual accounts (it is called a parallel run because both the new and the old accounting systems are run parallell for some time). The parallel run could be limited to a few important departments, with or without preparation of the opening balance sheet. However, it is necessary that the accounting manual, guidelines, and the various accrual-based books of accounts should be in place and training of the staff completed for taking up the parallel run. The duration of the parallel run should be neither too short nor too long.

REVIEW OF THE PARALLEL RUN EXPERIENCE

It is necessary to take up a review of the parallel run experience in order to ascertain whether any correctives need to be applied to the new accounting system. Such a review should provide crucial information on what revisions and refinements are necessary. It should also provide important inputs on changes to be made within the organizational structure and work/information flow linkages between the departments. On the basis of the insights gained, action should be initiated to make the necessary changes, in consultation with the technical consulting firm.

REVISION OF TRAINING AND OTHER NEEDS ASSESSMENT

Review of the parallel run experience should also provide insights into the adequacy and efficacy of the training imparted, the opinion-building exercises conducted, and the change management measures undertaken. On the basis of such an assessment, suitable changes may have to be made in the training process and, if necessary, a secondary opinion-building exercise may have to be undertaken.

UPGRADATION OF HARDWARE AND SOFTWARE

Review of the parallel run experience should also provide information on performance of the computer hardware and software already installed. On the basis of the review, information needs are to be assessed in consultation with the technical consulting firm, and necessary upgradation of software and hardware carried out, if necessary.

COMPREHENSIVE NATIONAL ASSET REGISTER

Review of the parallel run experience should also enable an assessment of the correctness and adequacy of the data on assets, liabilities, and the opening balance sheets. Such an assessment should, in particular, verify whether the inventory includes all tangible fixed assets including emergency and heritage assets, all intangible fixed assets including intellectual property rights, and all fixed asset investments such as share holdings. On the basis of the assessment, suitable corrections, if necessary, may have to be made and it should now be possible to prepare a comprehensive and reliable national asset register.

WHOLE-OF-GOVERNMENT ACCOUNTS

On the basis of the parallel run experience, it should be possible to delineate the requirements for preparing accounts for the government as a whole. While the parallel run might have been conducted for a few departments only, the experience should provide important insights on how to prepare whole-of-government, commercial-style accounts covering the entire Indian government.

THE LEGISLATIVE PROCESS

By the time the parallel run exercise is taken up, a draft of the proposed legislation to introduce accrual accounting should be ready. A review of the parallel run experience would provide guidance on whether changes are required in the proposed legislation. Changes, if any, should be incorporated, and the final draft bill should be prepared. Thereafter, it will be necessary to set the legislative process in motion, culminating in the enactment of the legislation by both houses of the Parliament. It is important that the legislation should designate an appointed date for giving effect to the new accounting system.

A MISSION MODE

It will be necessary to implement the accounting reforms in a mission mode. For the purpose, targets have to be set up, milestones prescribed, a timeline delineated, and monitoring mechanisms put in place to ensure that the mission is completed in time. We have seen how in the case of Ahmedabad Municipal Corporation, the accounting reforms took more than seven years to implement. On the other hand, in the case of New Zealand, the departments were given the responsibility of developing accrual accounting arrangements within a two-year time frame from 1 July 1989, but they were able to complete them by 1 January 1991; that is, a full six months ahead of the targeted time. This was possible because of stipulating a timeline depicting milestones and monitoring the progress made by the departments against them. We have also seen how, in the UK, a trigger-point strategy was adopted to ensure that the accounting reforms were implemented in a time-bound manner. It may be a good idea to incorporate a trigger-point strategy into the mission mode, with appropriate triggers defining the monitoring points.

FULL IMPLEMENTATION

The system of accrual accounting and budgeting should become operational from the appointed date the legislation stipulates. However, problems may arise even after the transition to the new accounting system. Corrective actions need to be taken to address these problems with a sense of urgency, otherwise the new accounting system may get into operational difficulties. In any case, finding solutions to problems, while running the new system, may also require support from the technical consulting firm.

At the time of writing this book, disturbing items of news appeared about big multinational corporations—which account on an accrual basis—

indulging in creative accounting in order to bolster their financial results. The kind of creative accounting that happened in the private sector is not likely to take place in the Indian government because there are a number of institutional safeguards available. These include a highly public form of accountability to the legislature, having the CAG as the single auditor who does not take up consultancy functions, and the absence of some of the major problem areas which have bedevilled the private sector such as the results of trading, mergers and acquisitions, and transactions across borders and companies.

The book will like to make a final caveat. During the last two decades, the forces of globalization have been ascendant as never before. The four countries whose experience with reforms we studied, did realize early on that if they were to compete in a fiercely competitive global environment, they needed to make a transition to the more disciplined and rigorous framework of accrual accounting. In doing so, these countries were only responding to the demands of the forces of globalization; it is a foregone conclusion that the same forces will goad India to adopt accruals sooner or later. So, the question is: why not make the transition now itself?

NOTES

1. Chander (2003), p. 42.
2. Ibid.
3. GASAB (2004), p. 3.
4. Hughes and Abu-Izz (2002).
5. Joshi (2004), p. 356.
6. Ibid., p. 355.
7. Based on Hughes and Abu-Izz (2002).
8. Hughes and Abu-Izz (2002), p. 46.
9. Joshi (2004), p. 359.

Bibliography

Aiyar, Swaminathan S. Anklesaria (2003), 'A neo-Hindu Budget', *The Times of India*, 9 March 2003.

Ball, Ian, Tony Dale, William D. Eggers, and John Sacco (2000), *Reforming Financial Management in the Public Sector*, Frontier Centre Policy Series No 6, http/www.fcpp.org/publications/policy- series/hpg/reforming/financial/ December 2000.

Bartos, Stephen (2000a), 'Accrual Budgeting in the Public Sector', *Address to the Centre of Excellence,* on 23 March 2000.

———(2000b), 'The 'Whole' truth: the DoFA view', *Australian CPA*, April 2000.

Blondal, J.R. (2001), *Budgeting in Sweden*, Paris: OECD.

Burman, Soma Roy (2003), 'An Examination of Certain Liabilities in the Public Account of India and their Impact on Budget and Account', Paper Presented at the *International Seminar on Accounting for Results*, New Delhi, 9–11 June.

Carlin, Tyrone M., and James Guthrie, (2000), 'A review of Australian and New Zealand Experiences with Accrual Output Based Budgeting' Paper presented at the Third Bi-annual Conference of the International Public Management Network, Sydney, Australia, 4–6 March.

Chander, Avinash (2003), 'Development of Accounting Standards in the Government Sector', Paper Presented at the *International Seminar on Accounting for Results*, New Delhi, 9–11 June.

Commonwealth of Australia (1998), *Reforms to the APS*, Canberra: Australian Government Publishing Service.

Das, S.K. (1998), *Civil Service Reform and Structural Adjustment*, New Delhi: Oxford University Press.

Department of Expenditure, Ministry of Finance, Government of India (2003), *Controller General of Accounts: Role and Functions*.

Douglas, Roger (1993), *Unfinished Business*, Auckland: Random House.

Economic Survey (2002-03), Ministry of Finance, Government of India.

ESV (2001), *Accrual Accounting in Swedish Central Government*.

Fulton Committee (1975), *The Civil Service*, vol.I, London: HMSO.

Ganguly, Bidisha (2002), 'The State of State Finances', the *Economic Times*, 14 December.

Government Accounting Standards Advisory Board (2004), *Facts about GASAB*.

Hepworth, Noel (2000), *Changing to accrual accounting in Central Government, (with particular regard to the experiences of the United Kingdom)*, Norway: Institute of Public Finance Limited (IPF), FEE.

Hillier, Diana (1997), 'From Cash to Accrual: The Canadian Experience', *Perspectives on Accrual Accounting, Occasional Paper 3*, Public Sector Committee, International Federation of Accountants.

HM Government (1994a), *Better Accounting for the Taxpayer's Money-Resource Accounting and Budgeting in Government*, HMSO.

————(1996a), *Competing for Quality Policy Review*, HMSO.

————(1997b), *Financial Statement and Budget Report*, HMSO.

————(2000), *Government Resources and Accounts Act 2000*, HMSO.

HM Treasury (2000a), *Resource Accounting and Budgeting*, London: HMSO.

————(2000b), *Relationship between Public Expenditure Control Aggregates under Resource Budgeting with those under Cash Budgeting*, HMSO.

————(2001b), *Frequently Asked Questions about Whole of Government Accounts (WGA)*, http://www.wga.gov.uk?pages/introduction.html

————(2001c), *New National Register Published*, http://www.hm-treasury.gov.uk

Holmes, John W. and Tom Wileman, (2001), *Towards Better Governance—Public Service Reforms in New Zealand* (1984-94), http://www.oag-bvg.gc.ca/domino/other. nsf/html/nzbody/html.

Hughes, Jesse W. and Eng.Issam M. Abu-Izz (2002), 'Building a Common Database for International Governmental Financial Statements' *Public Fund Digest*, vol. 2, no.1, pp. 46–53.

IFAC PSC (1991), *Financial Reporting by National Governments*, Study 1, New York: International Federation of Accountants.

Jones, George (1997), 'Resource Accounting and Budgeting: Another False Trail', *Perspectives on Accrual Accounting, Occasional Paper 3*, Public Sector Committee, International Federation of Accountants.

Joshi, Ravikanth (2003), 'Municipal Accounting Reforms in India: A Comparative Study', Paper Presented at the Workshop on *Accrual Accounting in the Public Sector*, organized by the World Bank at Colombo, 9–12 December.

————(2004), *From Accounting to Accountability: Building the Case for Municipal Accounting Reform*, Mumbai: Yuva Books.

Likierman, Andrew (1994), 'Management Accounting in UK Central Government: Some Research Issues', *Financial Accountability & Management*, May 1994.

————(1997), 'Accrual Accounting in the United Kingdom', in *Accrual Accounting in the Netherlands and the United Kingdom*, OECD Publication.

Little, Struan (1993), 'Inproving Financial Performance: Public Sector Management Reform in New Zealand', Address to National Association of State Auditors, Comptrollers and Treasurers, Washington D.C., mimeo.

Mellor, Thuy (1997), 'Why Governments Should Produce Balance Sheets', *Perspectives on Accrual Accounting, Occasional Paper 3*, Public Sector Committee, International Federation of Accountants.

Miley, Frances and Andrew Read (2000), 'Comparing government reporting: looking for accountability', *Australian CPA*, February.

Ministry of Finance, Government of India (2001), *An Assessment of Government of India's Pensionary Liability*, June 2001.

Montesinos, Vincente and Jose M. Vela Bargues (1997), 'Bases of Accounting and Reporting Foci in Spanish Governmental Accounting', *Perspectives on Accrual Accounting, Occasional Paper 3*, Public Sector Committee, International Federation of Accountants.

Moore-Wilton, Max (1999), New Performance Paradigms for the Public Service, *Paper presented at the National Public Sector Accountants Conference*, Adelaide, 7–9 April.

NAO (2001), *Measuring the Performance of Government Department*, National Audit Office, HMSO http://www.nao.gov.uk/publications/nao-reports/00-01/0001301es.pdf.

New Zealand Treasury (1987), *Government Management: Brief to the Incoming Government*, vol. I, Wellington, NZ: The Treasury.

OECD (1993), *Accounting for What? The Value of Accrual Accounting to the Public Sector*, Paris: Organisation for Economic Co-operation and Development.

——— (1999), *Strategic Review and Reform—The UK Perspective*, Paris: Organisation for Economic Co-operation and Development.

Olsen J. and B. Peters (eds) (1996), *Lessons from experience: experimental learning in administrative reform in eight democracies*, Reading Mass: Adison Wesley.

Pant, U.S. (1998), *Budgeting & Public Financial Management in India*, New Delhi: Impact Books.

——— (2003), Transparency and Accountability Issues in Public Sector Accounting, Paper Presented at the *International Seminar on Accounting for Results*, New Delhi, 9–11 June.

Proceeding of the Twenty-third Annual Meeting of OECD Senior Budget Officials, *Accrual Accounting and Budgeting: Key Issues and Recent Development*, PUMA/SBO (2002), Washington D.C., 3–4 June.

Ramanathan, R. (1999), *Government Accounting: Principles & Practices*, Faridabad: Allahabad Law Agency.

Rao, Govind M. (2003), 'Lost Chance?', the *Hindu*, 25 March.

Redburn, Stevens F. (1997), 'How Should the Government Measure Spending? The Uses of Accrual Accounting', Perspectives on Accrual Accounting, *Occasional Paper 3*, Public Sector Committee, International Federation of Accountants.

Richardson, R. (1997), 'Opening and Balancing the Books: The New Zealand Experience', *Perspectives on Accrual Accounting, Occasional Paper 3*, Public Sector Committee, International Federation of Accountants.

Robinson, M. (2001), *Accrual Accounting and the Public Sector*, mimeo.

Rose, Aidan (2003), *Results-Oriented Budget Practice in OECD Countries*, Working Paper 209, Overseas Development Institute, London.

Ross, Kevin (1999), 'Are You Ready for RAB?', *IT Insight*, Issue 2.4

Schick, Allen (1998), 'Why Most Developing Countries Should Not Try New Zealand's Reforms', *World Bank Research Observer*, vol. 13, no 1.

Shiromany, Alok (2003), 'Transparency and Accountability in Urban Local Bodies', Paper Presented at the *International Seminar on Accounting for Results*, New Delhi, 9–11 June.

Simpkins, Kevin (1998), *Budgeting and Accounting Issues—New Zealand*, Presentation to the International Federation of Accountants (Public Sector Committee), Washington D.C., 30 April.

State Services Commission (1994), *New Zealand's Reformed State Sector*.

Strom, Sten (1997), 'Full Accrual Accounting in Sweden', *Perspectives on Accrual Accounting, Occasional Paper 3*, Public Sector Committee, International Federation of Accountants.

Tanner, Lindsay (2000), *Restoring Openness in Government*, Australian Labour Party Home Page, http:// www.alp.org.au/policy/pdpog/ November 2000.

Thaplliyal, B.S. and S.N. Pattanayak (2003), 'Form and Contents of Accounts', Paper Presented at the International Seminar on Accounting for Results, New Delhi, 9–11 June.

Thimmaiah, G. (1984), 'Budget Innovation in India: An evaluation', *Public Budgeting and Finance* (4), pp. 40–54.

Treasury (1999b), *Fiscal Policy under Accrual Budgeting: Information Paper*, Canberra: Commonwealth Treasury.

Vertigan, M. (1999), *Review of Budget Estimates Production Arrangements*, http:// www.dofa,gov.au/pubs/vertiganreport/July 1999.

World Bank (1995), *Bureaucrats in Business: The Economics and Politics of Government Ownership*, New York: Oxford University Press.

Further Reading

AARF (1995), *Financial Reporting by Government*, Exposure Draft 62, Melbourne: Australian Accounting Research Foundation.

ABS (1996), *Introduction of an Accruals basis in Government Finance Statistics*, Canberra: Australian Bureau of Statistics.

———(1997), *Information Paper: Developments in Government Finance Statistics*, Canberra: Australian Bureau of Statistics.

———(2000), *Information Paper: Accrual-based Government Finance Statistics*, Canberra: Australian Bureau of Statistics.

———(2001), *Government Finance: Accrual-based Government Finance Statistics*, Canberra: Australian Bureau of Statistics.

Anthony, Robert N., and David W. Young (1994), *Management Control in Nonprofit Organizations*, 5th edn, Homewood, IL: Richard D. Irwin.

Arwidi, Olof, and Lars A. Samuelson (1993), 'The Development of Budgetary Control in Sweden: A Research Note' *Management Accounting Research*, 4/2 (June).

Auberbach, A., J. Gokhale and L. Kotlikoff (1994), 'Generational Accounting: A Meaningful Way to Evaluate Fiscal Policy', *Journal of Economic Perspectives*, 8(1).

Auditor General of Canada (2001), *Toward Better Governance—Public Service Reform in New Zealand (1984-89) and its Relevance to Canada*, http://www.oag-bvg.gc.ca/domino/others.html/nzbody.html

Bale, M. and T. Dale (1998), 'Public Sector Reform in New Zealand and Its Relevance to Developing Countries' *The World Bank Research Observer*, Vol 13 (1), pp. 103–21.

Ball, Ian (1994), 'Reinventing Government: Lessons Learned from the New Zealand Treasury', *The Government Accountants Journal*, Fall 1994.

Barzelay, Michael (2001), *The New Public Management: Improving Research and Policy Dialogue*, Berkeley: University of California Press.

Blondal, J. R. (1998), *Accrual Accounting and Budgeting in OECD Member Countries*, Paris: OECD.

Boston, Jonathan, John Martin, June Pallot, and Pat Walsh, (1996), *Public Management: The New Zealand Model*, Auckland: Oxford University Press.

Bowsher, Charles A. (1993), 'Budgeting and Accountability in Large Countries: Problems and Opportunities', *Government Accountants Journal*, Spring 1993.

Brash, Donald T. (1996), *New Zealand's Remarkable Reforms*, Fifth Annual Hayek Memorial Lecture, Institute of Economic Affairs, London, 4 June, http://www.rbnz.govt.nz/speeches.

Budget Department, Swedish Ministry of Finance (1993), *Management of Government Administration and Financial Conditions for State Agencies*.

———(1994), *In search of Results and Financial Incentives—Recent Advancements in the Swedish Central Government Budget Process*.

———(1995), *Annual Performance Accounting and Auditing in Sweden*.

———(1996), *Productivity in the Public Sector in Sweden*.

Buiter, W. (1985), 'A Guide to Public Sector Debt and Deficits', *Economic Policy*, November 1995.

———(1990), *Principles of Budgetary and Finance Policy*, Cambridge, Mass: MIT Press.

———(1995), 'What do Generational Accounts Tell Us about the Effects of the Budget upon Intergenerational Distribution and Saving Behaviour?', *Conference Paper*, s.111, Centre for Performance Seminar, Cambridge.

Campbell, Paul (1989), 'Accounting Standards for the Public Sector in Australia', *Financial Accountability & Management*, Spring 1989.

Central Government Receipt and Payment Rules, Government of India.

Chakraborty, D.K. (1989), 'Public Sector Enterprises and Corporate Accounting in India', *Indian Journal of Accounting*, June.

Chan, James L. and Rowan H. Jones (eds)(1988), *Governmental Accounting and Auditing*, London: Routledge.

Civil Accounts Manual, Government of India, Ministry of Finance.

Codori, Carol A. (1987), 'International Perspectives on Federal Government Reporting: A Seminar Summary', *International Journal of Government Auditing*, January.

Commonwealth of Australia (1995), *Accrual Accounting—A Cultural Change*, The Parliament of the Commonwealth of Australia Joint Committee of the Public Accounts Report 338.

Council of Europe (1994), *Structure and Operation of Local and Regional Democracy: Sweden*, Strasbourg: Council of Europe Publishing.

Craig, Russell (1986), 'Government Involvement in the Setting of Accounting Standards', *International Accountant*, September.

Das, S.K. (1995), 'Disempowerment of Indian Bureaucracy' *Economic and Political Weekly*, 14 January.

———(2001), *Public Office and Private Interest*, New Delhi: Oxford University Press.

Dean, Peter. N., with Pugh, C. (1989), *Government Budgeting in Developing Countries*, London: Routledge.

Dean, Peter N., and Salvatore Favazza (1994), 'Assessing the Quality of Government Accounts of 135 Countries', *Journal of International Accounting Auditing & Taxation*, 3/1, 1994.

Delegation of Financial Powers Rules, Government of India.

DOFA (2001), *Financial Reporting Guidelines (FMOs) 2001-2002*, Canberra: Department of Finance and Administration.

Dye, Kenneth M. (1989), 'Public Sector Committee of the International Federation of Accountants', *Singapore Accountant*, May .

Evans, Lewis, Arthur Grimes, and Bryce Wilkinson, (1996) 'Economic Reform in New Zealand 1984-95: The Pursuit of Efficiency,' *Journal of Economic Literature*, 34, December.

Expert Group on Public Finances, Government of Sweden (1996), *Productivity Trends in the Public Sector in Sweden*.

Federal Accounting Standards Advisory Board (1993), *Objectives of Federal Financial Reporting—Statement of Federal Financial Accounting Concepts*, No. 1 (SFFAC 1).

Federal Accounting Standards Advisory Board (1996), *Accounting for Revenue and Other Financing Sources-Statement of Federal Financial Accounting Standards* (SFFAS 7).

Financial Accounting Standards Board (1985), *Statement of Financial Accounting Concepts No. 6* (SFAC 6).

Fowles, A. J. (1993), 'Changing Notions of Accountability: A Social Policy View', *Accounting Auditing & Accountability*, 6/3, 1993.

Fundamental Rules & Supplementary Rules, Government of India.

Government Accounting Standards Advisory Board (2003), *Exposure Draft on Guarantees given by Governments*.

Gavens, Hohn (1988), 'Accounting Standards and the Public Sector', *Australian Accountant*, May.

General Financial Rules, Ministry of Finance, Government of India.

Gray, Andrew and Bill Jenkins, (1993), 'Codes of Accountability in the New Public Sector', *Accounting, Auditing & Accountability*, 6/3.

Guthrie, James (1993), 'Australian Public Business Enterprises: Analysis of Changing Accounting, Auditing and Accountability Regimes', *Financial Accountability & Management*, May.

———(1998), 'Accrual Accounting in the Public Sector?' *Financial Accountability and Management*, January.

Harr, David J. and James T. Godfrey, (1992), 'The Total Unit Cost Approach to Government Financial Management,' *Government Accountants Journal*, Winter.

Haveman, R. (1994), 'Should Generational Accounts Replace Public Budgets and Deficits?' *Journal of Economic Perspectives*, vol. 8(1).

Hay, David (1992), 'Public Sector Accounting in New Zealand: An Update and Clarification', *Financial Accountability & Management*, Spring 1992.

Henry, David (1994), *Reform of a Major Service Delivery Agency: Not Platitudes but Action*, Service for the Citizen's Charter Conference: London, December.

HM Government (1982), *Efficiency and Effectiveness of the Civil Service*, HMSO.

———(1984), *Government Purchasing: Review of Government Contract and Procurement Procedures*, HMSO.

————(1985), *Lifting the Burden*, HMSO.

————(1986), *Building Business...Not Barriers*, HMSO.

————(1988), *Releasing Enterprise*, HMSO.

————(1991a), *Making the Most of Next Steps*, HMSO.

————(1991b), *Competing for Quality*, HMSO.

————(1991c), *The Citizen's Charter*, HMSO.

————(1994b), *The Civil Service: Continuity and Change*, HMSO.

————(1995a), *Better Accounting for the Taxpayer's Money- The Government's Proposals*, HMSO.

————(1995b), *The Civil Service: Taking Forward Continuity and Change*, HMSO.

————(1995c), *Treasury Minute on the 15th and 18th to 25th Reports of the Committee of Public Accounts*, Session 1994-95, HMSO.

————(1996b), *Development and Training for Civil Servants*, HMSO.

————(1997a), *Treasury Minute on the 9th Report of the Committee of Public Accounts, Session 1996-97*, HMSO.

HM Treasury (1985), *Accounting for Economic Costs and Changing Prices: A Report to the HM Treasury by an Advisory Group*, London: HMSO.

————(1993), *Financial Statement and Budget Report 1994-95*, London:HMSO.

————(1994), *Fundamental Expenditure Review of the Treasury*, London: HMSO.

————(1997), *Equipping Britain for Our Long-Term Future: Financial Statement and Budget Report*, London: HMSO.

————(1999), *Economic and Financial Strategy Report and Financial Statement and Budget Report 1999*, London: HMSO.

————(2001a), *Introduction to Whole of Government Accounts*, http://www.wga.gov.uk/pages/introduction.html

Hood, Christopher (1990), 'De-Sir Humphreyfying the Westminister Model of Bureaucracy: A New Style of Governance?' *Governance: An International Journal of Policy and Administration*, vol 3(2).

————(1991), 'A Public Management for All Seasons?' in R.A.W. Rhodes, (ed.), *The New Public Management*, Oxford: Basil Blackwell.

Hughes, Colin (1990), 'Whitehall Learns to Take a Business-like Approach', *The Independent*, 31 October.

Humphrey, Christopher, Peter Miller and Robert W. Scapens, (1993), 'Accountability and Accountable Management in the UK Public Sector', *Accounting Auditing & Accountability*, 6/3.

IASC (1999), *Framework for the Preparation and Presentation of Financial Statements in International Accounting Standards*. International Accounting Standards Committee.

IFAC PSC (1995), *Definition and Recognition of Assets*, Study 5, New York: International Federation of Accountants.

————(1998a), *Guideline for Governmental Finance Reporting-Exposure Draft*, New York: International Federation of Accountants.

————(1998b), *Presentation of Financial Statements*—Exposure Draft, IPSAS 1.

————(1998c), *Cash Flow Statements*—Exposure Draft, IPSAS 2.

————(1998d), *Net Surplus or Deficit for the Period, Fundamental Errors and Changes in Accounting Policies*—Exposure Draft, IPSAS 3.

————(1998e), *The Effect of Changes in Foreign Exchange Rates*—Exposure Draft, IPSAS 4.

————(1998f), *Borrowing Costs*—Exposure Draft, IPSAS 5

————(1998g), *Consolidated Financial Statements and Accounting for Controlled Entities*—Exposure Draft, IPSAS 6

————(1998h), *Accounting for Investments in Associates*—Exposure Draft, IPSAS 7.

————(1998i), *Financial Reporting of Interest in Joint Ventures*—Exposure Draft, IPSAS 8.

————(1999a), *Revenue from Exchange Transactions*—Exposure Draft, IPSAS 9.

————(1999b), *Financial Reporting in Hyperinflationary Economies*—Exposure Draft, IPSAS 10.

————(2000a), *Construction Contracts*—Exposure Draft, IPSAS 11.

————(2000b), *Inventories*—Exposure Draft, IPSAS 12.

————(2000c), *Leases*—Exposure Draft, IPSAS 13.

————(2001a), *Events After the Reporting Date*—Exposure Draft, IPSAS 14.

————(2001b), *Financial Instruments: Disclosure and Presentation*—Exposure Draft, IPSAS 15.

————(2001c), *Segment Reporting*—Exposure Draft.

————(2001d), *Investment Property*—Exposure Draft.

Jones, L.R. and Fred Thompson (2001), *Responsibility Budgeting and Accounting*, http://www.willamette.edu/-fthompso/publicfin/Responsibility-Budgeting.html.

Joseph, M. J. and Raju Sharan (2003), 'Accounting for Results', Paper Presented at the *International Seminar on Accounting for Results*, New Delhi, 9–11 June.

Kam, V. (1990), *Accounting Theory*, Singapore: John Wiley and Sons.

Kemp, Peter (1990), 'Next Steps for the British Civil Service', *Governance: An International Journal of Policy and Administration*, vol. 3, no. 2.

Krueger, Anne O. (1974), 'The Political Economy of the Rent-Seeking Society', *American Economic Review* vol. 64, no. 3.

Lapsley, Irvine (1993), 'The Accounting and Organisational Consequences of Privatisation and Regulation', *Financial Accountability & Management*, May.

Likierman, Andrew (1994), 'Management Accounting in UK Central Government: Some Research Issues', *Financial Accountability & Management*, May.

Lindauer, David L. and Ann D. Velenchik (1992), 'Government Spending in Developing Countries: Trends, Causes and Consequences', *World Bank Research Observer*, vol. 7(1).

List of Major and Minor Heads, Government of India.

Maitra, U.K. (2003), 'Accrual Accounting in the Public Sector', Paper Presented at the *International Seminar on Accounting for Results*, New Delhi, 9–11 June.

Mascarenhas, R.C. (1996), 'Searching for Efficiency in the Public Sector: Interim Evaluation of Performance Budgeting in New Zealand,' *Public Budgeting & Finance*, 16/3, Fall 1996.

Mayston, David (1993), 'Principals, Agents and the Economics of Accountability in the New Public Sector', *Accounting Auditing & Accountability*, 6/3.

McCulloch, Brian W. (1993), 'New Zealand leads in Government Management Reform', *Government Accountants Journal*, Spring 1993.

Miah, Nuruz Zaman (1991), 'Attempts at Developing a Conceptual Framework for Public Sector Accounting in New Zealand', *Financial Accountability and Management*, Summer 1991.

Micallef, Frank (1994), 'A New Era in Reporting by Government Departments', *Australian Accountant*, March.

Mody, Ashoka and Christopher M. Lewis (1997), 'The Management of Contingent Liabilities: A Risk Management Framework for National Governments', in Timothy Irwin and others, eds., *Dealing with Public Risk in Private Infrastructure*, World Bank Latin American and Caribbean Studies, Washington D.C.: World Bank.

Mody, Ashoka and Dilip K. Patro, (1996), 'Valuing and Accounting for Loan Guarantees', *The World Bank Research Observer*, 11(1), February 1996.

NAO (1995), *Resource Accounting and Budgeting in Government*, Report by the Comptroller and Auditor General, National Audit Office, HC 123. HMSO.

———(1996), *Resource Accounting and Budgeting in Government: The White Paper Proposals*, Report by the Comptroller and Auditor General, National Audit Office, HC 3034, HMSO.

New South Wales Treasury (1995), *Guidelines for the Valuation of Land and Heritage Assets in the NSW Public Sector*.

Nunberg, Barbara N. (1990), 'Civil Service Reform and the World Bank', *Policy Research Working Paper Number 422*, Washington D.C.: World Bank.

——— (1992), 'Managing the Civil Service: What LDCs Can Learn from Developed Country Reforms', *Policy Research Working Paper 945*, Washington D.C.: World Bank.

OECD (1995), *Budgeting for Results: Perspectives on Public Expenditure Management*, Paris: Organisation for Economic Co-operation and Development.

——— (1997a), *Issues and Developments in Public Management: Survey 1996-1997 on Sweden*, Paris: Organisation for Economic Co-operation and Development.

——— (1997b), *Issues and Developments in Public Management: Survey 1996-1997 on the United Kingdom*, Paris: Organisation for Economic Co-operation and Development.

——— (1997c), *Accrual Accounting in the Netherlands and the United Kingdom*, Paris: Organisation for Economic Co-operation and Development.

——— (1997d), *Examples of initiatives in public sector budgeting in Australia*, Paris: Organisation for Economic Co-operation and Development.

——— (2003), *Budget Reform in OECD Member Countries: Common Trends*, Paris: Organisation for Economic Co-operation and Development.

Olsen J. and B. Peters (eds) (1996), *Lessons from experience: experimental learning in administrative reform in eight democracies*, Reading Mass: Adison Wesley.

PAC (1995), *Resource Accounting and Proposals for a Resource-based System of Supply*, Committee of the Public Accounts, 9th Report Session 1996-97, HC 167, HMSO.

———(1997), *Resource Accounting and Budgeting in Government*, Committee of Public Accounts, 15th Report Session 1994-95 HC 407, HMSO.

Pallot, June (1994), 'The Development of Accrual-Based Accounts for the Government of New Zealand', *Advances in International Accounting*, vol. 7.

Pandey, I. M. (1990), 'Development of Finance Management in LDCs: The Indian Experience', *Research in Third World Accounting*, vol. 1.

Parker, Lee D. and James Guthrie, (1993), 'The Australian Public Sector in the 1990s: New Accountability Regimes in Motion', *Journal of International Accounting, Auditing & Taxation* 2/1.

Pendelbury, M., R. Jones and Y. Karbhari, (1992), 'Accounting for Executive Agencies in the UK Government', *Financial Accountability and Management*, 8(1), Spring 1992.

Planning Commission (1991), *Guidelines for Classification of Expenditure (Plan and Non-Plan) for the Tenth Five Year Plan (2002-07)*.

Pollitt, Christopher (1993), *Managerialism and Public Services: Cuts or Cultural Change in the 1990s?* Cambridge MA: Basil Blackwell.

Quiggin, John (1998), 'Social Democracy and Market Reform in Australia and New Zealand,' *Oxford Review of Economic Policy*, 14/1, Spring.

Reid, Gary. J. and Graham Scott (1994), 'Public Sector Human Resource Management in Latin America and the Caribbean', *Civil Service Reform in Latin America and the Caribbean*, World Bank Technical Paper Number 259, Washington D.C.: World Bank.

Reserve Bank of India, *Study on State Finances*, 2002–03.

Rhodes, R.A.W. (1997), *Understanding Governance: Policy Networks, Governance, Reflexivity and Accountability*, Buckingham: Open University Press.

Robinson, M. (1996), 'The Case Against Balanced Budgets', *Australian Journal of Public Administration*, vol. 55(1).

——— (1998a), 'Accrual accounting and Public Sector Efficiency', *Financial Accountability & Management*, vol. 14(1).

——— (1998b), 'Measuring Compliance with the Golden Rule'. *Fiscal Studies*, 19(4).

———(2001), *Accrual Accounting and the Public Sector*, mimeo.

Sarkar, Jyoti Bikash (1991), 'Management Accounting in Government Finance: Problems and Prospects in the Indian Context', in Bhabtosh Banerjee (ed.) *Contemporary Issues in Accounting Research*, Calcutta: Indian Accounting Association Research Foundation.

Saxena, Sandeep (2003), 'Classification of Government Transactions', Paper Presented at the *International Seminar on Accounting for Results*, New Delhi, 9–11 June.

Schick, Allen (1996), *The Spirit of Reform: Managing the New Zealand State Sector in a Time of Change*, State Services Commission: Wellington http://www.ssc.govt.nz/Documents/Schick-report.pdf

Scott, G. (1994), 'Strengthening Government Capacity to Manage Human Resources: The New Zealand Experience', in Civil Service Reform in Latin America and the Caribbean, *World Bank Technical Paper* (259).

Scott, G. and Ian Ball (1993), 'Financial Management Reform in the New Zealand Government', mimeo, April.

Scott, G., P. Bushnell, and N. Sallee (1990), 'Reform of the Core Public Sector: The New Zealand Experience', *Governance*, 13/3.

Scottish Parliament (2001), Finance Committee, *7th Report*, Resource Accounting and Budgeting.

Swedish Agency for Administrative Development (1995), *Governing Sweden*.

Swedish Ministry of Finance (1994), *Top Managers' Forum, Joint Action to Modernise Public Administration with Assistance of IT.*

————(1995), *Leadership in Government Administration.*

————(1996), *The Public Sector Labour Market in Sweden.*

Swedish National Audit Office (1993), *Accounting Model for Swedish Government Agencies.*

————(1994), *Internal Accounting-Some Ideas.*

TCSC (1995a), *Simplified Estimates and Resource Accounting*, Treasury and Civil Service Select Committee 4th Report, Session 1994-95, HC 212, HMSO.

————(1995b), *Simplified Estimates and Resource Accounting*, Treasury and Civil Service Select Committee, 4th Special Report, Session 1994-95 RC 483, HMSO.

The *Economic Times* (2003a), 27 February.

————(2003b), 28 February.

Thompson, Fred (1994), 'Mission-Driven, Results-Oriented Budgeting: Financial Administration and the New Public Management,' *Public Budgeting & Finance*, 14/3 (Fall).

Treasury (1995), *Reference: Inquiry into Fiscal Responsibility Legislation and Whole of Government Reporting for the Commonwealth, Submissions*, vol. 1, Canberra: Commonwealth Treasury.

————(1999a), *Budget Paper No 1, 1999-2000*, Canberra: Commonwealth Treasury.

————(2000), *Final Budget Outcome, 1999-2000*, Canberra: Commonwealth Treasury.

————(2001), *The Uniform Presentation Framework*, Canberra: Commonwealth Treasury.

TSC (1996a), *Resource Accounting and Budgeting in Government: The Financial Reporting Advisory Board*, Treasury Select Committee 5th Report 1996-97, HC 309, HMSO.

————(1996b), *Resource Accounting and Budgeting*, Treasury Select Committee 2nd Report 1996-97 HC 186, HMSO.

————(1997), *Public Expenditure Survey and Spending Objectives*, Minutes of Evidence, 5th March 1997, Treasury Select Committee 1996-97 HC 355, HMSO.

United Nations (1965), *A Manual for Programme and Performance Budgeting*, New York: United Nations.

Wright, M. (1995), Resource Budgeting and the PES System, *Public Administration*, Vol. 73, No 4, Winter 1995.

Zimmerman, Jerold L. (1995), *Accounting for Decision Making and Control*, Chicago: Irwin.

Index